D1548273

A PAUL ROTHA READER

Exeter Studies in Film History
General Editors: Richard Maltby and Duncan Petrie

Exeter Studies in Film History is devoted to publishing the best new scholarship on the cultural, technical and aesthetic history of cinema. The aims of the series are to reconsider established orthodoxies and to revise our understanding of cinema's past by shedding light on neglected areas in film history.

Published in association with the Bill Douglas Centre for the History of Cinema and Popular Culture, the series will include monographs and essay collections, translations of major works written in other languages, and reprinted editions of important texts in cinema history. The series editors are Richard Maltby, Associate Professor of Screen Studies, Flinders University, Australia, and Duncan Petrie, Director of the Bill Douglas Centre for the History of Cinema and Popular Culture, University of Exeter.

Parallel Tracks: The Railroad and Silent Cinema
Lynne Kirby (1997)

The World According to Hollywood, 1918–1939
Ruth Vasey (1997)

'Film Europe' and 'Film America': Cinema, Commerce and Cultural Exchange 1920–1939
edited by Andrew Higson and Richard Maltby (1999)

A Chorus of Raspberries: British Film Comedy 1929–1939
David Sutton (2000)

Left to right: Michael Orrom, Edgar Austey, Stanley Hawes, John Taylor, Basil Wright and Paul Rotha, May 1983.
(*Photographed by Wolf Suschitzky*)

A PAUL ROTHA READER

edited by Duncan Petrie
and Robert Kruger

UNIVERSITY
of
EXETER
PRESS

First published in 1999 by
University of Exeter Press
Reed Hall, Streatham Drive
Exeter, Devon EX4 4QR
UK
www.ex.ac.uk/uep/

British Library Cataloguing in Publication Data
A catalogue record for this book is available from the British Library

ISBN 0 85989 626 9

Typeset in 11/13pt Adobe Caslon by Kestrel Data, Exeter

Printed and bound in Great Britain by
Short Run Press Ltd, Exeter

Contents

Acknowledgements   vii

Preface   ix

CONTEXTS

The Early Years—*Robert Kruger*   3

Paul Rotha and the Documentary Film—*Robert Kruger*   16

Paul Rotha and Film Theory—*Duncan Petrie*   45

ROTHA'S WRITING

I The Art of the Film: Theory and Criticism—*The Editors*   87

The Development of the Film as a Means of Expression (1930)   91

Production—Off the Studio Floor (1929)   110

Rhythm—and its Creation (1929)   113

The Magnificence of Fairbanks (1930)   117

City Lights (1931)   120

Earth (1931)   132

Pabst (1967)   144

Some Principles of Documentary (1935)   148

Films of Fact and Fiction (1938)   161

Neo-realism: *Bicycle Thieves* (1950)   169

Umberto D (1955)   173

II   Cinema and Britain: Culture and Industry—*The Editors*   179

The 'Unusual' Film Movement (1940)   183

Repertory Film Movement (1931)   187

A Museum for the Cinema (1930)   191

The British Film (1930)   195

Korda

   1933 Interview   203

   1956 Interview   204

   The Private Life of Henry VIII (1933)   205

The Government and the Film Industry (1945)   208

A Plan for British Films (1949)   221

The Problem of the Short Film (1966)   226

III   Film Practice—*The Editors*   233

The Technique of the Art-Director (1928)   235

The Art-Director and the Film Script (1930)   239

Making *Contact* 1932–33 (1973)   244

Presenting the World to the World (1956)   273

Select Filmography   277

Select Bibliography   283

Index   287

Acknowledgements

The editors would like to jointly acknowledge the support and assistance of the following individuals in the preparation of this book: James Patterson, Bryony Dixon and Kathleen Dickson of the National Film and Television Archive, Janet Moat of the British Film Institute Special Collections Department, and David Sharp of the BFI Library. We would also like to thank Wolfgang Suschitzky for sharing his memories of working with Paul Rotha with us.

Robert Kruger would personally like to thank Peter Ward for his encouragement and support in writing on Paul Rotha and for making it physically possible through the gift of a word processor. I would also like to remember the contributions of Rotha's 'associates': Donald Alexander, Michael Orrom, John Taylor and Francis Gysin. And finally I would like to thank my wife Joan, who was in the film industry herself and still loves film, and my sons Stephen and Richard, both working in other branches of the media.

Duncan Petrie would personally like to thank Lee Grieveson, Regenia Gagnier, Susan Hayward, Nick Groom, Leo Enticknap, and the numerous other colleagues and students at the University of Exeter who contributed to discussions of drafts of the essay 'Rotha and Film Theory'; Richard Crangle and Peter Jewell of the Bill Douglas Centre, for their assistance and advice; and the IT staff of the Faculty of Arts at the University of Exeter, for technical help in preparing this manuscript. I would also like to express my gratitude to Rebecca Russell for her constant patience, love and support.

The editors would also like to acknowledge the various original publishers of Roth's ideas, particularly Secker and Warburg as the publisher of *Documentary Diary* and Faber and Faber who published Rotha's own selection of his writings, *Rotha on the Film* in 1958.

Preface

The need to reassess the contribution of Paul Rotha to film culture may at first appear a rather odd proposition. He was, after all, widely acknowledged as one of the key figures—second perhaps only to John Grierson—of the British documentary movement in his capacity as both film-maker and critic. His many films, including *Contact*, *Shipyard*, *The Face of Britain*, *World of Plenty*, *Land of Promise*, *The World is Rich* and *The Life of Adolf Hitler*, stand as landmarks in the history of the British documentary. His books were, for many years, standard texts in film history and theory, and continue to grace the shelves of most libraries and second-hand bookshops.[1] But reputations are not carved in stone. Some are subject to revision and rediscovery while others quietly drop from sight. In Rotha's case, it is fair to say that since his death in 1984, appreciation of his contribution to film-making and particularly to the development of film theory and criticism has gradually drifted into obscurity. The documentary has been relegated to the sidelines by revisionist approaches to British cinema history, and Rotha's work (films and writings) rarely appears on the rapidly growing number of film studies programmes on offer in British universities and colleges.

This is an unfortunate state of affairs for several reasons. While it was clearly necessary to challenge the former critical over-emphasis on the documentary realist tradition as the only major achievement of British cinema, it is equally important not to lose sight of the significance of this tradition altogether. The commitment of Rotha and others to a politically and socially progressive cinema is still echoed loud and clear in the work of an important and influential British film-maker like Ken Loach, while the impulse of the documentary to inform and educate can still be discerned in some of the better factual programming on British television. But even more importantly, Paul Rotha's writings embrace a wide range of issues which remain fundamental to the historical study and understanding of the cinema as an art form, as an educative medium and as a means of communication. In addition to propagandizing for the British documentary, Rotha's numerous published works address some of the major historical shifts in film theory and criticism, offer polemical arguments for the importance of both a vibrant film culture and a viable film industry in Britain, and, drawing on his first-hand experience as a practitioner, consider the development of numerous aspects of film-making. These writings are illuminative and inspirational and offer a great deal to anyone seriously interested in the history and development of the cinema as the popular medium most able to confront the complexities, the problems and the needs of the modern world.

This telegram, sent on 27 September 1979 to Mr Susama Moto in Japan, when Rotha was just over 70 years of age, helps to sum up his attitude:

To all Young Documentary Film-makers in Japan! Greetings from an Old Man!

Democracy in a Bottle is Good—but *only* if you know *who* fills the Bottle. It must be a liquid of Human Understanding and Comradeship, and against all Greed, Hatred, Violence and Jealousy for the Love of Money and Self-Profit. I have been to 85 countries and found Men and Women of all skin colours (not important), of many so-called Gods and faiths. Some have been good and happy: others have been evil and full of Devils.

It is the sacred duty of *all* documentary film-makers in *all* countries to devote their minds, skills and techniques to spread Understanding among *all* Peoples, the so-called 'High' and 'Low'. (I like the 'low' the best but for me, there are only *People*). We must use documentary film to develop Mankind, through Real Peace—not War. Nuclear Power is the World Force today, so be careful who holds its control. We—the documentary people—must see that it is used only for Peace, not for Greed, Profit and Violence.

So, drink a bottle of Democracy with Me!

One day, perhaps, *if* I am still alive, I shall come to visit you in the lands of Hokusai and Ozu and Kurasawa. My Love to Them and You all!

Remember, *all* Children are *born* good!

Something of this spirit inspired this new collection of Paul Rotha's writing, a collection which we hope will help to restore his reputation by shedding new light on his considerable achievements and, even more importantly, bring him to the attention of a new generation of students and film-makers alike.

The Editors

Note

1. Indeed, the demand for Rotha's writings remained constant for many years. *The Film Till Now*, the book which made his name when it first appeared in 1930, was enlarged and revised in 1949, reprinted in 1951, revised again in 1960, reprinted in 1963 and revised for a final time in 1967. His other major work, *Documentary Film*, similarly appeared in a number of different editions in 1935, 1939 and 1952, with the third, substantially enlarged version reprinted in 1963, 1966, 1968 and 1970.

Contexts

The Early Years

Robert Kruger

Recording the realities of life in cinematic terms has been the chief
occupation of Paul Rotha. . . . [His] films mirror his outlook on life
. . . a common understanding of mankind and a belief in the basic
goodness of the individual. . . . He sees the medium as a powerful
instrument for social progress.

(Herbert G. Luft, quoted in Current Biography,
New York: H.W. Wilson, 1997)

Few would disagree with this assessment, written shortly after World
War II, of Rotha's life and work. But how did this outlook, these
opinions, the beliefs which lay at the root of his work and were
its source, come about? How important were his early experiences in
shaping the subsequent intellectual and moral formation which would
inform his activities as a film-maker and a writer? There can only be few,
if any, of Paul Rotha's contemporaries still alive. As far as I know, there
are none who knew him when he was young, no close friend privy to his
early thoughts, dreams and hopes. Those who are alive and who knew
and worked for or with him are all of a younger generation. Most of
them, including myself, held and still hold deep feelings of respect,
of admiration and of friendship for him. But we knew little, if anything,
of Paul's childhood, youth and family. He was a very private man, one
who rarely, if ever, spoke about himself—as opposed to his work. For
most of us it was difficult, if not impossible, to imagine in the successful,
well-known and highly influential film-maker we knew, the younger
Paul Rotha starting out on his career. Even his last completed book , the
autobiographical *Documentary Diary*, has little to say about his childhood; his parents are just about mentioned, his brother and two sisters
not at all.

I consider myself to have been extremely fortunate in joining Paul Rotha's Films of Fact in 1944 as a seventeen-year-old, just out of school. I started as a trainee and general run-about and was one of the last to have been able to benefit from Rotha's teaching, advice and vast experience. He was for me then a stern, almost god-like figure, but one who at the same time could be extremely kind and helpful. Later, in the early 1960s I was able to edit his final two films: the documentary *The Life of Adolf Hitler* (1961) and the feature film *De Overval* (*The Silent Raid*) produced in 1962. Both of these films were produced abroad, in West Germany and Holland respectively, and the former was two years in the making. We worked together closely, spent a great deal of time in each other's company, and, I am proud to say, became friends—a friendship that lasted until he died.

Rotha's ideas, beliefs and achievements arose, just as they do for everyone, out of his past. In this biographical sketch I have attempted to 'reconstruct' something of this past from the very few 'personal' notes he left. But scanty though they are, it is possible to see and recognize a great deal, in embryo as it were, of the man he became. The basic facts are quickly told. The son of Dr Charles John Samuel Thompson and Ethel May (née Tindall) Thompson, Paul Treeve Fawcett Thompson (as he then was) was born in Wealdstone, near London, on 3 June 1907. He had one elder brother who became a journalist and two elder sisters, one in the antique book trade, the other a librarian. His father, who was curator of the Wellcome Historical Medical Museum in London and, later, conservator at the Historical Collection Museum of the Royal College of Surgeons, was also the author of many medical books. Rotha married three times: to Margaret Louise Lee from 1930 to 1939; to Margot Rose Perkins, his secretary at Films of Fact and responsible for much of the day-to-day running of the unit, from 1944 to 1960; and from 1961 to 1982 to Constance Rose Smith, the film actress who in the late 1940s and 1950s made a considerable name for herself in the UK, in Italy and in Hollywood. Paul Rotha died on 7 March 1984.

The origins of his adoptive name are explained in unpublished notes which he wrote in 1952:

> 'If you aim to take up theatre design, change your name to some-thing sounding foreign', said Professor Tonks, head of the Slade School of Art. He peered at my costume designs through his steel-rimmed glasses with undisguised disdain. His curved nose looked more than vulture like. The next day I awoke at sunrise.

4

Across from the bed stood a mahogany bookcase that had belonged to my grandfather. The sun lit up the book-titles. My eyes ranged along a row of a red-backed collected edition of an Edwardian historical novelist now out of fashion. One title included the name of Rotha. I turned it over in my mind. It was short. It was unusual, it sounded European. So Rotha it became in 1926—at first only for signing work, later for everything, finally to be legalised after my father's death. But perhaps there was more to it than haphazard choice.

In the notes he left[1] Rotha clearly shows how his love for drawing, painting, art and literature was encouraged and supported by his family. The beginnings of his interest in history and the society in which he lived, the love for his country and people, its traditions and values (he was to become, in many ways, a very English film-maker), are all there. Above all, we can trace the beginnings of his passion for film and for the cinema.

Rotha wrote more of his father than of anyone. They were obviously very close, and enjoyed a relationship which was of immense importance to Paul in his childhood and youth, equalled only perhaps by his close attachment to John Grierson later in his life. Above all it was Rotha's father, described as a 'tolerant and liberal man', who nurtured and encouraged his interest in the arts and in 'craftsmanship':

> He bound copies of his own books in leather and tooled good designs on them. He played the piano by ear and often in later years played the organ in the village church. Although he never drew well, he painted in oils a great deal in his youth and was very proud that the 19th Century landscape painter Thomas Creswick, R.A., was a relative. My father's reverence for old things, his absorption in the past, (he was very proud of his family tree; tracing back his family to the 16th Century) his instinctive good taste, his ability to tell at a glance an original from a fake, all these assets gave us as children a similar understanding of and respect for tradition.[2]

Art, drawing and painting were always of immense importance to Paul and came to inform his subsequent vocational passion for 'the art of film'. So was the value of craftsmanship: every one of his films was a 'quality' product; from the titles to the camera work, sound quality and music, there was never, whatever the circumstance, anything slipshod about them. I believe (and I am not alone in this) that it was this insistence on the highest technical and craft quality that helped to give his films their weight, their authority. Anything but politically conservative, Rotha nonetheless respected 'tradition', holding the values which his father had taught him—tolerance, a suspicion of authority and a hatred of bullying and brutality. He did not always succeed in curbing his own 'authoritarian' urge to have his own way, to insist on his own opinions and values, but he always tried. And he was always independent, very much his 'own man'.

In 1916, at the age of nine, Rotha's parents felt that he was ready for boarding school. His formal education was a rather complicated affair. He attended more than thirteen private educational establishments during his childhood, some for only a few weeks, but none of which he particularly enjoyed. Boarding schools were the worst. The memories which left the most lasting impression on him were not of schooling and learning but rather the sadistic beatings and the bullying which were endemic and seemed to be condoned by the masters. Many of the films he was later to make deal overtly, or more often covertly, with the subject of brutality, with the persecution of the weak and helpless by the strong. There was nothing that he abhorred and hated more.

During the school holidays much of Rotha's time was spent in his father's museum in Wigmore Street. His father worked for the drug company Burroughs Wellcome which led to his establishing and running the Wellcome Historical Medical Museum based around a collection of 'Rare and Curious Objects relating to Medicine, Chemistry and Pharmacy and the Allied Sciences' which was opened to the public in 1913. One of Rotha's father's major tasks was the collection of material for the museum. This led him to travel widely in Europe, Africa and Asia, and sometimes he would allow his children to accompany him on his trips abroad. The children would assist by taking photographs or drawing the articles which he was able to procure. Rotha recalled one of these trips:

> In 1924, I was the lucky one and went on a two months journey that took in Paris, most of Switzerland, North Italy and the South of France. In a chain-library in St Gallen, several days were spent in making detailed copies of illuminated manuscripts. In Lugano, I pointed out to him (after the deal had been made) that among the two dozen Roman surgical instruments he had bought in the back-room of a filthy antiquaries was a bulls-head type of tin-opener, admittedly rusty, of recent manufacture. Being a man of great calm

and stoic philosophy, he took such things in his stride and called, as ever, for 'encore café'.[3]

Rotha's father was also a prolific writer. In his youth he had written a number of unpublished novels, and from the early 1920s until his death in 1942 produced a book on average every two years. Rotha recalled that:

> Into them, in pleasing general terms for the ordinary reader, he poured all the knowledge and information he had gleaned on his special subject and its many allied fields. The titles of his books gave some idea of his tremendous wealth of experience: *Poison Mysteries in History, Romance and Crime, The Mysteries and Secrets of Magic, The Lure and Romance of Alchemy, The Mystic Mandrake, The Quacks of Old London* . . . and many others. Monsters, apparitions, mandrakes, astrologers, quacks, impersonators—they all fascinated him. Fiction, or rather biography in fictional form, still attracted him when he wrote *The Witchery of Jane Shore*, but his two biographies *Lord Lister, the Discoverer of Antiseptic Surgery* and *Edward Jenner, the Discoverer of Vaccination* were serious, considered works. In collaboration with the late Sir D'Arcy Power, his *Chronologia Medica* (1923) was, and still is a standard book of reference.[4]

None of these books sold widely, but the modest royalties were an important contribution to the Rotha family income. Rotha's mother was also an important figure in his childhood and he remembers her as:

> thrifty, immensely hard-working and, as befitted a minister's daughter from a long line of Yorkshire Wesleyans, tolerant beyond description. She had great energy and seldom relaxed. And she was very beautiful; a beauty which she preserves with dignity to this day. As a girl she painted and played the piano well, but she could not continue these luxuries and at the same time bring up a family of three.[5]

Rotha himself was rarely well off in his adult life. Documentary film-making, especially before the late 1940s, was very badly paid and for long and repeated periods of his life Paul was quite poor. Indeed, the final twenty years of his life were spent in real poverty. It is often overlooked that for artists and film-makers—however glamorous, exciting and worthwhile their job might be—their work is *also* a way to making a living, a way to pay the rent. Frequently difficult compromises are necessary; somehow the need to make a living has to be reconciled with the artist's aspiration. Rotha never was very good at compromise. I don't believe he ever made a film purely for cash.

Among other things, Rotha was to inherit his father's love of writing. At the age of ten he had his first written work published:

> A boy's paper offered a half-guinea prize for the best 500-word description of something seen on a walk. One Sunday afternoon I sat overlooking a pool in the pine-forest and wrote down a description of all I saw and felt. Not only did I proudly see my piece in print, but as part of the prize I was also made the hero of next week's short story.[6]

The virtues of Rotha's writing are clear not only in his published works but also in his many notes, letters and diaries. Here is just one example, recalling the end of the war in the following way:

> During the morning of that day, factory hooters began sounding and excited knots of people gathered in the streets. At first we thought it was a monster daylight raid. Mounting my cycle, I set off to find out the cause of the commotion which an errand-boy soon told me. To celebrate the occasion, I returned home, informed my mother of the good news, decorated my bicycle with the Allied flags and cycled off around the town. Two days later my . . . father took me in to Charing Cross. The excitement of the London crowds had by no means died down. Trafalgar Square was a seething mass of people. It took several hours, so it seemed, to weave our way through the cheering crowds. Buses, taxis, private cars—mostly at a standstill —were overflowing with people waving flags and singing. We fought our way into the Corner House.[7] The staircase down was packed with men and girls in uniform, most of whom had exchanged hats. . . .[8]

We can see here, I believe, some of the basic elements that fed his visual imagination, so necessary to a film-maker. The swirling crowds, the emphasis on movement, interrupted now and again by more quiet and personal vignettes like the boy on his decorated bicycle celebrating the event and the young service-men and women exchanging their hats. This is very noticeable too in his description of the work he did in London's East End during the blitz of 1940.

October 11th, 1940

Spent last night and early this evening with Father Groser's mobile canteen. He is a much-beloved Stepney priest, Anglican, who did so much good work in the rent strikes two years ago. Today he is doing equally great work in the bombed and devastated parts of Stepney. Work consists of shifts with a mobile canteen: from 5.30 to 7.30 at night and from 5.30 to 7.30 in the morning: to which add an hour on either end for preparations, sandwich-cutting, lamp filling, cleaning up, etc. The canteen was given by Marks & Spencer. Location for the canteen is under a railway arch half a mile from the Vicarage in Watney Street, off Commercial Road. The other arches are used as shelters and it is the occupants of these, many of whom have no gas or other heating in their homes, that we supply. The Vicarage is a sort of open house, dealing out clothes to those who are bombed out . . . Sensible practical work with a purpose.

October 23rd 1940

Days and nights have been going fast: the work with Father Groser is long and hard, but wholly satisfying. It does give you the sense of doing something with an honest purpose—a relief after the figging around at the MOI. It brings you into close contact with real people; the people who are taking the real brunt of this air attack. It will be harder work still when the black-out begins at 4.30 and it will be cruelly cold in the early morning. But these people of the arches and the street shelters depend on this canteen for so much of their sustenance. You cannot give it up. So one adapts oneself to this new kind of life: sleeping along with Father Groser and the other helpers in the brick surface shelter in the yard of the church; writing like *The Times* nineteenth century foreign correspondent on a small collapsible table with the people snoring in the bunks around. The corner pub is gay and noisy. They sing, these people, so that the noise drowns the crack of gun fire and the drone of planes. They sing until the pub closes at 10.30 and they sing on the way home—home being a shelter . . . The shelters smell, the rain comes in, they are breeding grounds for disease. But they offer some kind of protection against the night-raider. Up in the early hours: no airplanes or gunfire if it's wet and overcast: but things happen right up till dawn if it is fine. But the canteen goes out just the same. And up at the arch, the same group of invisible figures in the darkness wait for the cups of tea. Then the shelter sleepers get up in two's and three's and come, with coughs and cold faces, for something hot to drink.[9]

It isn't just the visuals so vividly described in these diary entries that reveal the film-maker, it is the sound too—above all the sound of singing. Singing in the pubs, the streets, even in the cinemas where in most of the big film-theatres in the blitzed cities community-singing was part of the programme. The sound of the community at war. He tried very hard at this time to interest producers in a feature film using the Stepney railway arches as a background, but failed.

It is clear that from a very early age film was to be Rotha's first love. His passion for the cinema was first nurtured during the years of the Great War of 1914 to 1918. During this period Rotha's father was commandant of an auxiliary military hospital in Harrow which came to hold up to forty men at any one time. One of the many social amenities offered to the patients was free admittance to a local cinema, presenting an opportunity which the young Rotha could not resist:

> Somehow or other I contrived to be with a party of the men at least twice a week and in this way became a motion picture addict. A close friend of mine was Mr Tipping, who was the doorman in pale-blue uniform, although to me he was owner-manager- and projectionist combined. Mr Tipping, with the butt-end of a cigarette singeing his yellow fringe of a moustache, became my hero. I fancy he let me past that red velvet curtain many times unaccompanied by soldiers in blue and red. There it was, anyway, that I heard coconuts beating out horses hooves in the orchestra pit as Beau Brocade rode by in the moonlight. There I was scared stiff by the flames that destroyed the hunting lodge in *Rupert of Hentzau* because the red-tinted film stock made it so real. There, also, were seen the early Fairbanks pictures, of which I recall *He Comes Up Smiling*, *Say Young Fellow* and *The Man from Painted Post*. The title of every film was carefully recorded in a notebook. This regular film-going to Mr Tipping's during the war was not, however, my first introduction to the cinema. My father took me to the Scala Theatre in Charlotte Street (where the New London Film Society has its shows today[10]) in 1912 to see the *Delhi Durbar* in Kinemacolor (of which I can remember nothing) but I fancy that in the same programme was a short John Bunny comedy in which the fat comedian was kept from sleep by mice nibbling his toes.[11]

Whenever he could, Rotha visited his local cinema. His early habit of making notes about the films he saw must have been extremely useful when he came to write his first published book, *The Film Till Now*. His interest in reading moved beyond books to cinema magazines. He recalls buying his first copy of *Picture Show* which had Chaplin on the cover in blue and green. Later he also began writing to film distributors for stills:

> Some were responsive, some were not. But the first stills in my collection (which later became one of the best in the world and is now part of the National Film Library) were naturally enough from Douglas Fairbanks films. The local flea-pit, conveniently placed just down the road, was smaller than Mr Tipping's in Harrow but you could suffocate in the smoke-laden atmosphere behind the red plush curtain just as well. There I saw dozens of pictures, including Elsie Ferguson in *Barbary Sheep*, Fairbanks in *Mr Fix-It* and a serial called *The Mystery of the Double Cross* of which every instalment was seen. There were also serials with Pearl White and Houdini.[12]

As time went on, his interest in cinema gradually became more 'serious', reflecting changes in his perception about the possibilities of the medium. This was encouraged by his older brother:

> He bought every kind of film magazine, including Trade papers, which was my first introduction to *The Bioscope*, the fore-runner of today's *Kinematograph Weekly*. The cinema was at that time beginning to acquire a kind of snob-respectability by its big new films being given a first-run in a London West End Theatre equipped for projection. The Palace, The Hippodrome, The Scala, Covent Garden Opera House and Theatre Royal, Drury Lane, were those mainly used. There I saw the spectacular Fairbanks pictures *The Three Musketeers* and *Robin Hood*. I began to collect the illustrated souvenir programmes which were issued for these premier runs. My bedroom at home was covered with stills and art-plates from the movie-magazines. It was my brother who took me to see *The Cabinet of Dr Caligari* at the Marble Arch Pavilion in 1922, and to other Continental films.[13]

As is evident from *The Film Till Now*, *Caligari* made a deep and lasting impression on Rotha, as did Carl Mayer, one of the two writers of the film, who later, while in exile in Britain, became one of his closest friends.

It was around this time that the young Paul was faced with the necessity of choosing a career. He had rarely been happy at school. Nor had he been particularly successful at any subject other than English.

And so, in 1923, when Paul was just 16 years old, he and his father decided it was time for him to leave.

> At the end of term, it was the school's custom for those boys who were leaving to pass in single file before the Head Master in the big School Hall, while the rest of the school looked on. As he shook hands with each boy, the Head murmured words of farewell mixed with wisdom into his ear. Of the two boys in front of me, one said he was going to be a chartered accountant and the other was going into law. Each received a wink and a blessing. Confronted by me, obviously younger than most of the boys of school-leaving age, he cocked his head on one side not knowing me from Adam. In fact, although I had been at his school for three years, we had scarcely met before and certainly not face to face. 'Well?' he asked expectantly. 'An artist, sir' I replied. 'A what, my boy?' he said, with a slight twitching of his ginger whiskers and a gleam in his eye. 'A painter, sir, a . . .' Words failed both of us. I was brusquely passed on and a would-be banker restored the equilibrium.[14]

These then are just some of the young Paul Rotha's memories of his childhood and school days, noted down in 1952. In many ways his experiences seem very typical of middle-class boys in the England of the time: boarding school from an extremely young age, a degree of loneliness, and of course the war. Air raids, shelters, bomb damage and rationing, and above all the many war wounded he met and got to know at his father's hospital. Many of them he remembered by name for the rest of his life. But they also vividly convey much of what, later, concerned him as a film-maker. His close relationship with his father stands out; a man who encouraged his imagination and creativity, his interests in drawing and painting, reading and writing, his love of English literature and history. For those who knew him later there is more than a hint of what the boy became when he grew to be a man—the independence, the integrity, the feeling that as a boy he was already very much 'his own man'. Strong-willed, perhaps even a bit truculent—an 'odd man out.'

When Paul Rotha went to the Slade in 1924, the greater part of his time was still spent seeing films. As he wrote in his *Documentary Diary* some fifty years later:

> It is pointless to record the hundreds of films I saw in the habitual way. My only wish is to stress how I grew up, like many others of

my generation, with the movies. Their continuous flow over me must have made a deep subconscious impact . . . the fact that I can still remember in great detail the rescue over the ice-floes in *Way Down East* and Fairbanks swinging from the draperies across the baronial hall in *Robin Hood* is of significance to me. It was the movement itself that has remained in my mind, not the episode involved. In the same way later, it is the movement in *Song of Ceylon* that remains so significant but now I remember the reason for this movement and not just the movement itself. The Fairbanks films were fulfilling a desire for pleasurable emotion; Basil Wright's film was conveying a sociological meaning through its movement.[15]

Rotha felt in later years that his work at the Slade was not especially distinguished. He did, however, win a prize for theatre costume design at the International Theatre Exhibition in Paris in 1925. Moreover, art school did provide him with a training in design and visual composition within a frame, which he subsequently found both an advantage and a disadvantage in his film career:

The rigid edges of a canvas or a sheet of paper induce a static concept as opposed to the dynamic of the cinema screen. Most of my first film was observed in static terms, except for the editing . . . It was at the Slade that there arose my first and everlasting interest in typography. I find as much aesthetic as well as functional delight in Eric Gill's Perpetua as I do in a (Augustus) John drawing. I suppose it is called graphics. It has a lot to do with the cinema.[16]

Rotha paid for his fees at the Slade with earnings from commercial work, including book illustrations, posters, menu cards and so on, but eventually the time came when he had to seek more regular employment. He quickly found that the theatre design world proved to be a closed shop and consequently attempted to find work in the film industry, which was as difficult to enter then as it is today. It was during this period that he began writing regular criticism. He was working on the production of *The Connoisseur*, an expensive monthly magazine devoted to antiques and old masters, when the editor gave him the opportunity to review exhibitions of 'modern' painters like Van Gogh, Modigliani, Toulouse-Lautrec and Marie Laurencin.

But by now he *knew* that it was in cinema that his future lay, and so one day he strapped a portfolio of drawings and designs on the back of his bicycle and rode from his small room in Hampstead to the British

International Pictures studios at Elstree. His initial attempts to gain admittance were blocked at the gate. But fate was to be on his side that day:

> It so happened that the studio's Supervising Art Director was passing through on his way from the canteen. His name was Norman Arnold and he was a watercolourist 'manqué'. He overheard my enquiries and took me up to his department. My work was liked but there was no vacancy. He would get in touch with me but meantime advised a study of architecture and interior design and furniture. During the next month or two, I undertook this study in spite of the fact that my commercial hackwork brought in less than £1 per week. My instruction was mainly gained in the Victoria and Albert Museum.[17]
>
> Unlike most people in the film business, Norman Arnold fulfilled his promise. Three months after my visit to the studios, a telephone message told me that a job was available. It was what was called an 'outside man'. Each evening I was supplied with a list of furniture, ornaments, properties of all kinds (including animals), required by the art-director for a set to be built the next day and 'dressed' the day after. With a Ford van and a driver, armed with the list, it was my duty to go to London, visit the suppliers of the articles needed, drive a bargain for the hire of same, and then return with my load to the studio usually around 8 pm. Often it was found that, in my absence, the director had changed his shooting-schedule and left orders that the set which had been built that day should be ready 'dressed' by 8 am the next morning. As in most cases the set-dressers had gone home at 6 pm, the 'outside man' (who had clocked in at 8 am that morning) had to turn set-dresser overnight . . . all this was for 25 shillings a week and, of course, no overtime. *But I had begun in the Film Industry*.[18]

This first job in film-making was to last only a few months; he was fired for writing a critical article on production design in British studios. But so began a career which was to preoccupy Paul Rotha for the next thirty-five years and make his name as one of the leading documentarists and critics of his generation.

Notes

1. These were mainly notes contained in a draft chapter for a possible autobiography which Rotha compiled in 1952. These notes, as well as his

diaries and scripts, are housed in the Paul Rotha Special Collection in the library of the University of California, Los Angeles.

2. Paul Rotha, notes from an unpublished draft chapter of autobiography.
3. Ibid.
4. Ibid.
5. Ibid.
6. Ibid.
7. Lyon's Corner Houses were then, and remained until after the Second World War, large buildings (often of four floors) containing a number of restaurants, each different in style and decor. Relatively modest in price, they were extremely popular. This is where one learned to 'eat out'.
8. Paul Rotha, notes from an unpublished draft chapter of autobiography.
9. Paul Rotha, 'wartime diary,' housed in the Special Collections Department at the University of California, Los Angeles.
10. That is, in 1952.
11. Paul Rotha, notes from an unpublished draft chapter of autobiography.
12. Ibid.
13. Ibid.
14. Ibid.
15. Paul Rotha, *Documentary Diary: An Informal History of the Documentary Film, 1928–1939* (London: Secker & Warburg, 1973), p. 3.
16. Ibid. p. 4.
17. Ibid. p. 8.
18. Ibid. p. 8.

Paul Rotha and the Documentary Film

Robert Kruger

Forget all about Rotha's writing when you consider him as a film-maker. He is, as every student of film appreciates, our film historian; and he is the keeper of our conscience as much as the keeper of our records. On questions of film movements and film influences of the past he is an analyst of quality.

As a creator of film he happens to be none of these things. The history of his subject-matter does not concern him nearly so deeply as its good looks in still and tempo. Analysis of his subject-matter—of the influences which affect it and the perspectives of social and other importance which attend it—is not so important to him as the general impression it gives. For lack of a better title I should call him an impressionist.

(John Grierson, review of *Shipyard*, *Cinema Quarterly*, vol. 3, no. 3, 1935).

Rotha and the Craft of Film-Making

Paul Rotha is remembered, above all, as a documentary film-maker. His many published writings were clearly important and influential, but it was the actual *making of films* which he considered to be his primary and most important activity. Rotha was a practical, hands-on film-maker; meticulous in planning his work, schedule and budget, he left little to chance. His notes, constantly taken during the day, were checked each evening, amended if necessary and, if not dealt with, transferred onto a new list. He was always extremely well-prepared when shooting a film, appearing on location or at the studio every day with a complete shot-list and story-board—his ideas on particular set-ups, angles, lenses carefully thought out and recorded. At the same time he was always open to new ideas and suggestions, and even, if the need or possibility arose, improvisation.

There were few elements of the craft of film-making Rotha could not turn his hand to. But it was film editing that was his real love and he became a very fine editor indeed. He was a 'moviola' man (there weren't many editing tables available in Britain during his working life-time; indeed, the first time he came across one was during the making of *The Life of Adolf Hitler* in Hamburg in 1960). He loved the feel of celluloid, the physical work of cutting and joining strips of film, to be the first to see what would happen when one shot was juxtaposed to the next. He was used to the time-consuming and laborious job of making alterations to the picture (always near the end of a reel, or so it seemed) after all the tracks had been laid, and would never stop until he was completely satisfied. His perfectionism made him a disciplinarian as far as cutting-room 'housekeeping' and organization was concerned; no excuses were acceptable if a shot (or even a couple of frames) could not be found instantly. There was no splicing tape then; pieces of film were joined by cement and woe betide the assistant if or when a join fell apart.

For Rotha, editing was the most important element of the film-making process, raising it from a craft into an art. This is clear in both his theoretical writings and in his acute appreciation of the achievements of the Soviet masters Eisenstein and Pudovkin and the way in which editing was fundamental to the documentary film. This belief in the central importance of editing also informed his working methods. It was in the cutting-room that he balanced *art*—in terms of feeling, emotion, the quality necessary to move an audience by the selection of the 'right' shot, by movement, and above all by rhythm—with what he wanted the film to say, to express. These two separate ideas of film as art and purpose[1] necessarily went hand-in-hand, each aspect depending on and affecting the other, unified by a 'classical' structure of exposition, tension, climax, and release.

It is important to realize too that despite his reputation in certain quarters as a dry, intellectual documentary film-maker he had a great love of show business. From childhood onwards he was excited by Fairbanks' swashbuckling adventure films. He also knew a great deal about music, especially jazz, and had a fine collection of records which accompanied him when he was away on lengthy location shoots. Music played an important part in many of his films. In the cutting-room he would usually have a possible, not-yet-written score in mind: a steady rhythm perhaps, an acceleration, a mood, the climax. He spent a great deal of time during the editing process just listening to music, and this fed into the creative process:

> After hours of preliminary discussion, the time arrives for the music score of a film to be recorded. You can sit and just listen to music being played and recorded which has been specially created for your work. It has been my good fortune to have collaborated with some very talented and co-operative composers—among them William Alwyn, Walter Leigh, Britten, Clifton Parker, Elisabeth Lutyens and Siegfried Franz. Whenever possible they have entered the film at an early stage. Alwyn would often take part during scripting. I have never been disappointed by the music written for any of my films, largely because of collaboration and flexibility.[2]

The influence of music can be discerned in all of his films. In the Hitler film, for example, an underlying rhythm drives the action, and the deliberate 'pastiche' musical passages—of Wagner in particular, but also of popular songs—were planned at the editing stage to make particular points. But the most memorable musical sequence edited by Rotha was probably that of the Halle Orchestra in *A City Speaks*.

A number of his films featured interesting dance sequences, including a cancan sequence in *New Worlds for Old* which Rotha made in 1938 for the gas industry. Thinking over its subject—the fierce competition between gas and electricity—and how it could be treated in film terms, he recalled the 'Living Newspaper'[3] which had so much impressed him during his recent stay in New York and which provided an idea to which he would return in future:

> I decided to try and use some of its techniques but translate them into filmic terms. I thought up two protagonists to put the pros and cons of gas versus electricity in the sound track (they were not seen of course). This was the first time I tried the idea of recording each speaker separately without their meeting, and knitting their sentences together into a continuous coherent dialogue in the cutting room. It worked, and I was to use the method extensively in later years.[4]

Over and above the importance of the editing in relation to particular shots and sequences, the overall structure of the film played a vital role in grabbing the attention of his audience, while at the same time conveying a sense of *purpose* and underlying *meaning*. When Rotha was preparing his very first documentary film, *Contact*, in 1932, he produced an outline around which the film would be constructed. The film was to engage with 'Man's new "Conquest of Space and Time" with an emphasis on the close communication between peoples being made possible by air travel, and by airmail'.[5] The film's 'outline'—at this stage little more than a list—encapsulates much of Rotha's way of working and of thinking about film. It provided a guide to what had to be shot, and how, remembering that it was in the cutting-room that it would be realized, that its *meaning* would be revealed. As such, it demonstrates the documentary idea in action. But Rotha states his themes as well, which is typical of his need to express what *he* feels about the subject, in this case the future of air transport and the poetry of flight. It was always the purpose, the meaning, which overrode everything. Rotha made films because he wanted to express himself and his feelings and/or opinions about a certain issue; *he always had something to say*, and he chose the most 'popular' medium—film, the medium more accessible than any other during his life-time—with which to do so.

Although he never considered himself a teacher, Rotha instructed and inspired a great number of film technicians, directors and producers imparting not only what he felt a documentary film ought to be and say, but also how to create the desired result. More importantly perhaps (at least to this writer) he conveyed and implanted an attitude towards film which stressed its importance as an art form and as a means of expression, as well as the necessity of at least trying to put all of oneself, however modest the film might be, into the task of helping to make the film as good as circumstances allowed. Whether a shot was intended for a feature-length documentary or a one-minute trailer was irrelevant—it deserved the same care in lighting and composition, as did the individual cut or the film's structure. The opportunities he provided for many—the chance to make mistakes, to solve problems, to practise and practise and practise again, and, with time, to gain experience—as well as the expert supervision and creative criticism he offered, has never been forgotten by many of his former colleagues and friends. Above all, he taught many to hear and recognize the 'song' a well-cut sequence 'sings' when it conveys what is intended. Watching, listening and constant practise was, of course, the way he had learned himself, as had most of the film-makers of that time:

one learned by watching those more experienced . . . studying Flaherty at work while making *Industrial Britain* . . . Flaherty would watch a process, such as glass-blowing or pottery-making, for a long time and with deep concentration. He would observe every movement of the workers on the job so that when he came to use his camera, he could anticipate their every action . . . The film was notable for its continual use of big close-ups with very simple lighting; for its sensitive camera movements anticipating action; and for its industrial landscapes. The wonderful faces, caught in all their concentration on the job in hand, linger in one's memory for many years. If *Industrial Britain* was significant for no other reason, it put the real faces of British work people onto the screen in a manner not seen before, except for *Drifters*. They were given their natural dignity.[6]

To be given the opportunity to work independently and for the first time on a Rotha film was an experience never forgotten. While never interfering directly, his support and interest was manifest. He was always on hand to offer advice and to discuss ideas and to solve problems.

The British Documentary Movement

As producer and director, Rotha was to make more than 250 films, ranging from shorts just a few minutes in length to features for the cinema. Many of them are considered 'classics' today, winning awards both in the UK and abroad. His career in documentary began in 1931. Using the recent publication of his *The Film Till Now* as a pretext he contrived to introduce himself to John Grierson, the founder and self-styled leader of the emerging British documentary 'movement' and head of the Empire Marketing Board film unit. Rotha told Grierson how impressed he had been by his film *Drifters*, but apparently Grierson made no reciprocal comments about his book. Moreover, there were no immediate vacancies at the unit. But a couple of months later Rotha was called back:

I went to see Grierson, in a sparsely furnished basement room he then occupied in the EMB offices in Queen Anne's Gate Building, near Parliament Square. He talked a great deal, of which I understood little. Then he fired, 'What do you find in cinema?' I replied, 'Drama'. 'What is drama?' he demanded. 'Beauty', I said. That stopped him. I was told to report to the Wardour Street cutting room the next week.[7]

This meeting turned out to be perhaps the most important in Rotha's life. Not only did it result in his joining the EMB unit, it also had major consequences for his subsequent writing about film. And it started a relationship between Rotha and Grierson that proved to be the most important and influential in the former's life as a film-maker. Rotha felt deeply that the documentary was Britain's major contribution to world cinema and his second major book, *Documentary Film*, remains one of his most important works on the subject, tracing the history of documentary, examining its purpose, defining what he believed it should be. And by and large he remained committed to what he wrote in 1935 for the rest of his life, and remained faithful to Grierson's beliefs and values:

> The documentary film was . . . an essentially British development. Its characteristic was the idea of social use, and there, I believe, is the only reason why our British documentary persisted when other aesthetic or aestheticky movements in the same direction were either fitful or failed. The key to our persistence is that the documentary film was created to fill a need, and it has prospered because that need was not only real but wide. If it came to develop in England there were three good reasons for it. It permitted the national talent for emotional understatement to operate in a medium not given to understatement. It allowed an adventure in the arts to assume the respectability of a public service. The third reason was the Empire Marketing Board and a man called (Stephen) Tallents.[8]
>
> The film with its documentary possibilities was, indeed, just one among the magic pointers against the blackboard. But I liked the idea of simple dramatic art based on authentic information. I liked the idea of an art where the dramatic factor depended exactly on the depth with which information was interpreted. I liked the notion that, in making films of man in his modern environment, one would be articulating the corporate character of that environment again, after a long period of sloppy romanticism and the person in private, an aesthetic of the person in public. But the initiative lay with Tallents. Without him, we would have been driven exhausted by this time into the arms of Hollywood or into the practice of a less expensive art. Tallents marked out the habitation and the place for our new teaching of citizenship and gave it a chance to expand. In relating it to the art so variously called 'cultural relations, public relations and propaganda', he joined it with one of the driving forces of the time and guaranteed it patronage . . . His need, and our purpose, coincided so precisely that an alliance between public relations and the documentary film was struck which was capable of

withstanding all later temptations to commercialise our skill. It was
a strange alliance for Whitehall.[9]

The documentary film did not, of course, stand on its own in the
cultural and political thinking of the period. It was influenced by certain
political, economic and cultural changes in the late 1920s and the 1930s
and their consequences: the stagnation of much of industrial Britain at
the time, the high rates of unemployment and poverty, and the rise of
extreme right-wing political ideas and parties. At the same time however,
the 1930s also witnessed a rapid development of new and modern
industries around London and the South East, the construction of new
housing and the modernization of the country's infrastructure, including
the establishment of new roads, the national grid and so on. And cultural
changes, such as the continued development of the cinema as the major
leisure activity, were also having their effect.

One major response to these developments was the perceived need for
an educated and 'informed' citizenry, equipped with the skills to enable
them to understand and overcome the social and economic problems
they increasingly faced in their daily lives and to make the most of new
opportunities. The need for social and political reforms was felt by many,
and public discussion of the key issues was ensured by organizations such
as the BBC, the Workers Education Association, the trade unions and
many others, supported by the development of, for example, cheap
paperback books. It is important to recognize just how difficult it was
then, before television and the development of mass communications, for
the public at large to be informed about the world. That world was
inevitably more complex than most representations would suggest. Social
scientists, artists, and politicians of all political persuasions were laying
the intellectual foundations for many of the major social and political
reforms of the post-World War II period. This was the context against
which the documentary movement was established and to which it would
make a significant contribution.

When Rotha joined the EMB film unit it was still very small. Apart
from Grierson, there were just three or four permanent members of
staff; six months later there were ten. In addition to Rotha, the group
included Basil Wright, John Taylor, Arthur Elton, Edgar Anstey, Stuart
Legg and Donald Taylor—all to become significant film-makers in the
future. Rotha recalls that 'the majority of them had a public school
and university (Oxbridge) education and stemmed from what are
called middle-class families'.[10] While coming himself from a liberal

middle-class family, Rotha's own education had been very poor. He had left school at the age of sixteen and the relatively short period he had spent at art college was frequently interrupted by his need to make money to support himself. It is possible that this lack of a formal, academic education worried and affected him in later life. In the company of highly educated men and women he often had the air of a slightly uncomfortable 'outsider' about him. This had repercussions for the development of his career in documentary. He had a reputation of being difficult to work with, he could be pompous and was always conscious of his own position as a leading member of the documentary movement, of his books and of his films—he had to be the boss. This might well have been the result of insecurities stemming from his background.

It is interesting to note that even in the reputedly left-wing documentary movement something of the period's class-system remained, though in a very liberal manner. Writers, directors and producers tended to be solidly middle-class, social-democratic reformers by temperament who cared deeply about issues such as inequality, poverty, and health. They were the 'officers', promoting political and social reform from the top as it were. While the 'other ranks'—the editors, cameramen and members of the many crafts involved in film-making—tended to be highly professional with long experience in the film industry, and rarely middle-class. Interestingly, Rotha respected and possibly felt more at ease with them.

Despite the great number of films he was to make over more than thirty years, Rotha remembered the EMB unit with great affection. When he joined, the unit was still very young and of the group only three had had any previous film experience, including Rotha's own brief period at Elstree studios in the art department. Always short of equipment and resources, Rotha recalled that in the early months of its existence the unit had no proper editing machine or film-splicer. Editors were expected to read the film by eye and cut and join it by hand. The camera equipment was not much better, comprising an old silent Debrie and two small hand-held cameras that had an unfortunate tendency to scratch the negative. Basic equipment, meagre budgets and low wages were always the conditions under which the documentary film-makers of the 1930s and 1940s had to work. Frequently they had to devise their own methods of telling stories and producing films.

As long as he lived, the memory of his first assignment remained vividly with Rotha:

The first chance given me to go out and actually shoot some film was in May. On fine mornings, Sir Stephen Tallents was in the habit of walking from his office in Queen Anne's Gate Building across St James's Park and so to the Film Unit in Oxford Street. He suggested to Grierson that the magnificent display of British tulips in the Park might make a nice very short film. For some reason known only to himself, Grierson thought I was right for the job. So Jimmie Davidson, as cameraman, John Taylor as humper and I as director were ordered the next fine day to go film the tulips. We got to the Park by bus, the conductor swearing at our bulky equipment. Perhaps influenced by early German films, I saw at once that the tulips must be shot with their swaying heads against the sky. After an argument with a park-keeper, a small pit was dug in the grass beside a tulip bed and the camera—the one and only hand-turned Debrie—was placed in the hole . . . and we took the required shots. Those few shots of tulips (only 400ft of film, just over 4 minutes long) were the only footage made by me, other than some Poster films[11] while at the EMB Film Unit.[12]

But Rotha's period at the EMB was to be a rather short one. Grierson liked to switch production personnel around even when a film was in the making, to bring what he thought might be a fresh approach. Even then, Rotha was not in sympathy with this method and before long this brought him into conflict with Grierson who asked him to leave the unit. This was to be the first of a number of disagreements, every one of them, we can be sure, painful for Rotha. For the rest of his life Grierson was to remain the man he respected most, thinking of him almost, it seems, like a surrogate father whom he always wanted to please. But Rotha was also a man of principle. Compromise was an anathema to him, and all of his documentary films, from *Contact* onwards, were to be made independently. He had to be in charge. It was *his* film expressing *his* point of view. He never found it easy to work for anyone, or within an organization or institution. That is not to say that he did not value advice, discussion, help; indeed, most of his films are notable by his collaboration with the leading experts in their fields—scientists, writers, academics, and economists. And despite the differences between the two men, Grierson's influence remained important. His opinions, his reviews and criticisms Rotha valued above all others.

The Social Purpose of Documentary

And so, in September 1931, Rotha found himself without a job. However, those few months at the EMB had been, of immense importance. What he had learned imbued everything he did for the rest of his life. In short, his major principles included a belief in the film as a medium of creative potential that could be used in the public service in a field other than entertainment. The costs of production, distribution and exhibition met by the government as an alternative to any commercial interests. The medium could be a powerful instrument of communication between peoples. Its creative opportunities could attract to it talent for good film-making that otherwise would have had no outlet. And the achievements of the documentary movement were dependent on a unity of purpose above all. It was this more than any other factor that distinguished the British documentary from the more or less sporadic efforts being made elsewhere.

After a few months of semi-employment, writing feature film scripts with Miles Mander,[13] Rotha met Ralph Keene, then assistant manager at Tooth's Art Gallery in London, which led to an introduction to J.L. Beddington, head of publicity and advertising for Shell-Mex and the BP oil companies. Beddington was one of a number of public relations officers[14] responsible for developing new approaches to the field of publicity and public relations. Although a company employee for a major private corporation, Beddington had a strong social-democratic perspective and sense of public duty and he believed that providing 'information' rather than just publicity material was of vital importance. After a number of productive meetings, discussing ideas and possibilities, Beddington suggested to Rotha that he make a film with Imperial Airways about their overseas air routes. The result was *Contact*. The subsequent success of the production ensured that for the remainder of the 1930s work for Rotha was never in short supply. At the age of 25 he found himself at the beginning of one of the most productive periods of his career.

The essence of documentary film production involves filming on location. One of the great rewards of location work is the opportunity it provides to see new places, to get involved in situations and processes and to meet people with whom one would not normally have come into contact. In isolated mining villages, health centres, shipyards, schools, slum streets and run-down housing estates, at work, at play, the documentarians came productively into contact with ordinary men and women living their lives. We can follow a little of how this affected Rotha, and what it meant to him, through the letters he wrote to his friend Eric Knight:

23rd January, 1934. Sheffield
The smoke and dirt of these industrial towns of England are unbelievable. Drabness and squalor everywhere. The centre of the town is invariably Victorian, big official buildings, but in the worst possible style. Otherwise the city centre is filled with cheap smart tailors' shops and cut-price food stores and gaudy picture palaces and dance halls. The slum areas are appalling. The main streets are choked with clanging trams and swerving trolley-buses. Above all is a permanent pall of smoke. The noise everywhere is deafening. . . .

18th July, 1934. Scotland
The journey by car through the industrial Midlands, the North and Scotland during 1934 showed me at first hand the grim poverty of the British people, so many of whom were existing on what was then called the dole. The appalling legacy of the rape of so much of the natural wealth which had made Britain famous as the workshop of the world sharpened my social conscience, a sharpening that was permanent.

On the way here everything was marked by tragedy. All through the industrial Midlands and Lancashire, the terrible slums of Glasgow and the Clyde Valley, you could see the scarred mess that greedy men have made of this handsome country. So much of it is now derelict and polluted. Great slabs of countryside are mutilated by rusting factories and smokeless chimneys . . . today two-thirds of chimneys no longer smoke. The gaunt bones of factories reflect their drab images in filthy motionless canals. Men sit around on the grass verges of the new by-pass roads and play cards. Now and then the police in fast cars pay them a visit and arrest them for gambling and their dole money is forfeited.[15]

These very depressed and poverty-stricken areas of Britain could not fail to have an effect on Rotha, as they did on most of those working on documentary films then. For many it was a shocking revelation. And as his own experience of filming in the depressed areas of Britain grew, Rotha became more and more outraged at what he saw. For the rest of his working life he was to be concerned with the causes and effects of poverty, malnutrition, poor health, inequality and the lack of opportunity. Most of the films he was to make dealt with these issues, and the search for answers to these problems and the ways in which they might be solved. He became politically engaged. His family had been Liberal, but Rotha remembered no political discussions or talk at home. He, on the other hand, was always something of a radical, ploughing an independent and often isolated furrow. As a result of his experiences, he moved to the 'left', though it is doubtful that he ever committed himself totally to any political party. He was too independent a man to do so. He was, first and foremost, a critic of society as it then was: the quintessential English radical in the mould of Orwell or William Cobbett—a true non-conformist, enemy of all Establishments, Left, Right or Centre, and of compromise. It was the struggle against unemployment, poverty and inequality, and later fascism, that was, and remained, important to him. This provided the 'main-spring', the force, the purpose and meaning to his films.

The war against fascism, the post-war reconstruction, the foundation of the welfare state and the National Health Service all meant much to him. And as time went on, his belief in the progressive force of social democracy came to dominate his thinking. That was the central meaning of his final documentary film—*The Life of Adolf Hitler*. At the same time he resisted labels. He held differing, sometimes contradictory opinions, and his belief in and love of humanity was ultimately more important to him than an overtly political creed. In notes he left for a proposed second volume of *Documentary Diary*, he wrote that he had 'learned more from reading and re-reading Vincent's [Van Gogh] letters to his brother, Theo, than from any analysis of the works of Marx or Lenin'.[16] The idea of a socialist guild of artists, working independently but with a common purpose appealed to him greatly and it is very likely that he saw the documentary movement in this light.

After *Contact* his next significant film was *Shipyard*. It was filmed in the Barrow-in-Furness yard of the Vickers Armstrong Company with funding from Vickers and the Orient Shipping Line. Rotha's account again demonstrates the way he brings his political and social interests to bear on the subject-matter:

> Very soon I was in Barrow to make the all-important first-hand survey of the subject. I had already made up my mind that a film merely showing the building of a liner stage by stage would be dull. In Barrow the theme became immediately obvious. There was a great deal of unemployment there. There was only one ship on the stocks, where there should have been six or seven. This was a sister

ship, for the P & O line, to the one I was to use. (Happily the building of this other P & O ship was three months in advance of 'Orion', my ship. To all intents and purposes, they were identical. Therefore when I came to shoot, I could use the two ships alternately and match them together into one in the film.) The two ships meant some employment for the town, until they came to be launched at the end of a year's work. My theme was thus not just the building of 'Orion' but its effect on the social life of the town.

I spent a good deal of time in people's homes, in their kitchens mostly, at their favourite sport of whippet racing, in pubs and clubs, at the Employment Exchange, and at the Labour Party committee room, as well, of course, as in the yard itself. There, side by side were the two ships. No. 696 rising three months ahead of No. 697, the about-to-be-born 'Orion'. So for nearly a year, in 1934 and 35, I paid monthly visits to Barrow for a few days each time. I lodged at a fly-blown commercial hotel which had no hot water and poor food. The ship grew and the film grew with it . . . Each visit to Barrow built up to the final day, the day of the launch. When 'Orion' went sliding down the slipway it would be a day of triumph for the shipbuilders who had created her, from draughtboard designer to plater and riveter, but at the same time a tragedy, because again there would be unemployment in Barrow. That is something I tried hard to bring across in the final sequence of the film; the despair of those men watching her slide away, hands in their pockets, and then turning off to the Employment Exchange.[17]

The critical impact of *Shipyard* is effectively conveyed in John Grierson's remarks at the beginning of this essay.

Promoting the Documentary Movement

By now recognized as a leading figure in the British documentary movement, Rotha became busier than ever. In addition to making films—including *The Face of Britain* which arose directly from what he saw on his journeys to Barrow—he continued writing and lecturing, and was involved, with Grierson and other leading directors, in the setting up of the 'Associated Realist Film Producers' (ARFP) organization—a kind of guild, an independent body to guide and preserve the unity of the 'movement'. The documentary movement, of course, was still very small at this time and the 'politics' of establishing it as a major force within both the British film industry and in British culture more generally was very important. There were reports to be written, plans to be made, and there was the issue of the distribution of its films, on getting them seen by as many people as possible. And so it was the 'movement' which developed non-theatrical distribution and established film libraries from which films could be borrowed for shows in clubs, film societies and so on. The experience gained in this field was of immense value during the war when mobile projector vans covered the country.

Once the prestige documentary idea was accepted, two routes lay open to an organization interested in sponsoring a film. It could set up its own film unit, as Shell did, or it could hire an existing film company of proved reputation. The first of these independent documentary companies to be formed was Strand Films in 1935.[18] Rotha became Strand's director of production and all the major films that subsequently came to Strand in those years (up to 1937) were through Rotha's contacts.

> To turn from being a director to become a producer of films means to some extent giving up the excitement of filming oneself and assuming the role of catalyst. It is both a pleasurable and a thankless task. Pleasurable when a film emerges bright and fine; thankless when one has to take the whole blame if the film has emerged only a part success. Knowing that the full responsibility both financial and artistic rests on the producer's shoulders, he is ever tempted to interfere with his director during production. He must share his skills and experience with his director but not restrain that director's own personal style and development as a film-maker. The medium demands a lot of co-operation and collaboration, patience and persistence, above all on the part of a producer with a plethora of talents on which to call.[19]

It was at Strand that Rotha could really start to train new people. It also provided him with the opportunity to exercise more control over the titles and credits of a film (he had always been interested in typography and the graphic arts) and to work more closely with composers on the music for his productions.

Rotha proved himself to be a very good producer. He had the gift of making everyone working on his films—even those working in the most junior position—feel important, make them feel that whatever he or she was doing was vital to the success of the film and to what it had to say. But he could be a hard taskmaster, demanding a total commitment to the job in hand, however many hours it took. A run of 18-hour-long working days was not unusual. Sequences were cut and re-cut, the film's structure recast a number of ways as he struggled to find the most effective way of telling the story. Work in his cutting-room was tough, but all who worked for him knew that it was worth it.

Rotha remained torn between his two roles as director and producer for the whole of his career. His own feelings are conveyed in a letter he wrote in December 1937 to an old friend then living in South Africa:

> I feel that now I am 30, I should make some big move in my life but I do not know what. I'm not at all sure but that British documentary is not entering its old age. The new sociological urge which has gone into the latest Grierson films has killed all the cinematic quality to them . . . I feel that under Grierson's new outlook (much influenced by the slip-shod snap-shot methods of 'March of Time') we are all losing our hold on the movies as movies. I am not being at all arty about this but I do believe that a film, no matter whether sociological or political in purpose and content, should be a film. This means that cinematically we are not going forward . . . Maybe in all this there is perhaps a solution to my problems. Maybe I should not go back to being a producer and organiser. I did my term of 18 months at Strand and produced for them some 20 or so films. Maybe I should now take up direction again and create myself.[20]

Soon afterwards the desire to return to directing became a reality. 'I needed to have strips of film in my fingers once more, and it was not long before I had'.[21] After making *New Worlds for Old* and a number of other films, he began work on what was to be his last film before the war, *The Fourth Estate*, made for *The Times* newspaper. The script was written during the winter, and in May 1939 Rotha set out with his cameraman, Harry Rignold, on one of the happiest location trips he could remember. The script called for a great number of shots, to be obtained at many locations. A few days in the studio followed, but the majority of the film was shot at the *Times* itself in Printing House Square, where it had been produced almost from its very beginnings. By the end of August, just a few days before war broke out, filming had been completed. The film itself was ready to be shown by the end of January 1940, but then the news came through that it was not considered suitable for wartime propaganda. In the event, it was not shown for many years and is still relatively unknown.

An International Agenda

After the war broke out in September 1939, it took a while for film policy within the relatively new Ministry of Information to be formulated. Plans were prepared and then discarded, policy reviewed and re-reviewed. Documentary film-makers were amongst the many others within the industry to bombard the Ministry with ideas. For the independent companies and film-makers 'times were hard', frustrating because they knew that there was a job to be done, and they wanted to get on with it. In January 1941 Rotha finally set up his own company, Paul Rotha Productions Ltd, or PRP. There was just a little money in the bank, but a few contracts (from the MOI) had been obtained. It was an extremely difficult time to start a film unit. There were a great number of films to be made but budgets had to be fought for; they were always cut to the bone by the financial officers at the Ministry, and overheads were paid at a minimum. There was a great shortage of technicians; most of them had been called up. Young trainees had to take their place and be trained at the same time. Film stock and equipment was in very short supply. The producers at all of the units were overworked and under pressure, but they felt a moral duty and responsibility for the vital contribution they had to make to the war effort in terms of propaganda, instruction, education and morale. Levels of productivity were extraordinary. For example, at Paul Rotha Productions around one hundred films were made during the war, ranging from major documentaries to instructional shorts and magazine programmes.

In addition to his duties as a producer running his own unit, Rotha found the energy to direct a number of films during the 1940s which are considered, by many critics and academics, to be his best work. All of his cumulative experience went into their production, as did his beliefs about society and what it should be like in the post-war world. With these films he had arguably reached the climax, the pinnacle of his achievements in documentary. The films were *World of Plenty*, released in 1943, *Land of Promise* (1945) and *The World is Rich* (1948). They were originally conceived as a trilogy, discussing the post-war problems to be faced on a global scale and the social and political changes necessary to solve them. This had been, of course, Rotha's concern throughout his life as a film-maker; it had always been the *purpose*, the reason why they were made:

In the early days of the making of *World of Plenty* it had been envisaged by those of us concerned with its script that it could be the first of a trilogy dealing with the problems arising from man's basic rights of living. Food, a home and a job. This conception was much in the minds of John Boyd-Orr, Ritchie Calder, Eric Knight and myself. In fact it was the basis of Boyd-Orr's small but all-important book *What We Are Fighting For* . . . Although *World of Plenty* achieved an international success after much launching controversy and battling, the MOI were far too nervous to embark on the second of our trilogy—the film about homes and housing. Added to which it must be remembered that *World of Plenty* was born out of an Anglo-American theme inspired by the lend-lease policy. The housing film on the other hand, although it had basically an international reference, was more a domestic issue of how the British Government and the people it represented could meet this vast problem of overcoming the legacy of the past left over from the 19th & early 20th Centuries, the then contemporary housing issues created by the demolition of property by the Nazi blitz and how the future might be faced in the post-war years by sensible and intelligent planning.

Before attempting to find a non-government sponsor for *Land of Promise* (as the projected housing film became known) Rotha invested his own company's money for research and scripting by Ara Calder-Marshall and Wolfgang Wilhelm. By 1944 he felt able to approach the Gas Council, who were themselves then planning for post-war reconstruction in general and housing in particular, and who then sponsored the writing of a full script for a film to be made immediately after the war was over. Foreseeing an immediate general election after the war, Rotha could only guess at its outcome, but realized and prepared for what he saw as inevitable problems whoever won the election by obtaining an RIBA seal of approval to give the proposal a 'respectable background'.

So far as can be seen ahead, some but certainly not by any means all documentary films can be scripted in advance of actual production. It depends on theme and subject. *Land of Promise* went through three stages of scripting. First, the synopsis or general outline of the theme, a short but visionary document not necessarily filmic in form. Second, a treatment developing the synopsis indicating the filmic shape . . . Lastly, a shooting-script; a far more detailed work, involving visual description of sequences and shots to be taken (or found from stock sources) and the draft of narration (or dialogue) to be spoken. For *Land of Promise* all three stages of scripting were successfully negotiated. It will be remembered that in previous social films, we had hit on the notion of bringing in subject-experts by way of camera-interviews (later to be much used and abused by TV) . . . Lord Boyd-Orr, Lord Woolton, Sir John Russell et al on *World of Plenty*. For *Land of Promise* Sir Ernest (later Lord) Simon of Wythenshaw was our choice. An expert on housing and author of several books on the subject, he was an important and influential MP, at first Liberal and then a Labour convert.[22]

World of Plenty also gave Rotha the opportunity to develop a particular approach to the editing of voices which had initially been inspired by the techniques of 'The Living Newspaper' in America and which he had attempted to translate into filmic terms on the production of *New Worlds for Old* which he had made in 1938 for the gas industry. The method had worked and became a major feature of his later work, most notably in *World of Plenty* and *Land of Promise*

> The 'speech track' of *World of Plenty* was based on dialogue of two or more persons (written jointly by Eric Knight and myself with a few additions by Miles Malleson). *World of Plenty* was made only for English speaking audiences. So was *Land of Promise*, an advance on *World of Plenty*. (*The World is Rich* did not pursue this dialogue technique because one of the requirements laid down in its commission was that its speech could be easily translated into foreign languages.) [In these films several separately recorded voices were used, each representing a specific opinion or point of view as well as factual information.] Thus, although several voices (seven) were used; nevertheless in juxtaposition they carried forward the overall argument when the words were joined together in the cutting room. Eric Knight recorded his part of *World of Plenty* in Washington DC: the persons with whom he agreed or asked questions were recorded in London. It was fun assembling a continuous dialogue from fragmentary sentences.[23]

The third film in the trilogy was concerned with the subject of international food. It was premiered in Geneva at a United Nations Food and Agriculture conference. But like so many documentaries, it achieved only a very half-hearted showing in cinemas. Like *World of Plenty* and *Land of Promise* the film was well received critically. In a contemporary review of *The World is Rich*, Richard Winnington wrote:

In April 1946, the Government commissioned Paul Rotha to make a film on the subject of international food. He completed it by August 1947. Since then its fate has balanced delicately between trade opposition and CoI (Central Office of Information) tardiness. Tomorrow it will be shown at the New Gallery and Tivoli cinemas. Its chances in the matter of distribution are uncertain. Men in Wardour Street may decide that you are too light-minded to endure for 35 minutes an able and sincere document on a vital theme that you yourself have paid for.

Rotha in *World of Plenty* and *Land of Promise* developed a platform technique that some found overbearing, some irresistible and none could ignore. *World of Plenty* was disconcertingly box-office. In *The World is Rich* Rotha has cut down on the Isotypes[24] with their abstract and, to me, chilling authoritarianism. And equally happily he has lost the gormless man-and-woman-in-the-street and their smart Aleck interlocutor.

Seven voices toss the argument about as scenes of starvation and plenty from the world's archives, some familiar, others new, pound at our propaganda-drunk consciences. And it is an argument. A bit diffused in tense and geography, a bit specious in the fictitious black market gorgings, a bit jejune, it is in the main exposition irrefutable, impassioned and timely. *The World is Rich* closes the didactic phase of documentary on themes of contemporary life. The individual, contrary to the Grierson tenet, becomes more and more important. He will be the core of the new documentary, whose aim will be to reach your mind not by giving a lecture but by telling a story.[25]

Rotha himself was proud of the 'important fact that we were the *only country* in the world that were making films about what *could* happen when the war was over'.[26] With this group of films Rotha had reached the pinnacle of his career as a director. Other documentary films were to come, including *The Life of Adolf Hitler*, but none were to reach the lasting importance achieved by this trilogy.

By the end of the 1940s, both Rotha and the British documentary movement, as established by John Grierson nearly twenty years before, were approaching the end of their special and unique importance and influence. Since its establishment there had been vast social and cultural changes, culminating in a war that had totally engaged the people of Britain, individually and collectively as a community. Many of the problems that had interested the documentary film-makers were on the way to being solved. Moreover, new concerns and realities were arising that demanded new methods and new forms than those evolved

and practised by Rotha and Grierson. Whereas the documentary movement had projected a sense of collective experience—the community,
the factory, the nation—the post-war world saw a growing interest in the
individual and subjective experience. This was not only confined to
documentary film-making but was embraced by the arts as a whole.
Rotha's attempt to meet this challenge took the form of a growing
interest in fictional narrative film-making.

Paradoxically, the documentary found a new home on the rapidly
expanding medium of television and in doing so reached a considerably
larger audience than ever before. The arrival of television also changed
the nature of patterns of sponsorship/patronage for documentary production. This meant that the kind of independence Rotha had enjoyed
became very rare. Large documentary units continued to exist—the
British Transport Film Unit and the National Coal Board Unit, as well
as a number of smaller units. Important films were made, but the era of
the socially-conscious sponsored documentary was largely finished.

Rotha continued working even though projects were getting very
difficult to realize. After making a number of further documentary films
and projects—the most important of which was *World Without End*
(co-directed by Rotha and Basil Wright, who filmed the lives of peasants
in Mexico and Thailand respectively)—Rotha joined the BBC's television service in May 1953 as Head of Documentary Film, a post he held
until 1955. But he was never happy working within an organization,
describing the period as 'the most unhappy years in my life. Not my loyal
department but the duplicity and devious dealing of the bureaucratic,
mandarin structure'.[27] Nevertheless, during that period he produced more
than 75 films on British life and on international subjects. But he
remained a film man seeking a communal audience, be it in the cinema
or in the classroom.

New Directions

After the closure of his own unit, Films of Fact, in 1948, his thoughts
turned more and more to feature films. There were projects that, after a
great deal of thought and work, did not get made: a film based on Leo
Walmsley's novel *Phantom Lobster*, for example, as well as an involvement with John Grierson's NFFC-sponsored Group 3. Rotha recalled:

> The next I knew of Group 3 first-hand was when he called me to
> see him. He had a script, he said, right made for me. It was about an

American army deserter in the East End. I read it later that day and was mildly interested. That night, I happened to meet John Garfield, that admirable US actor, and told him the story. He said it was good but he himself had to get back to New York. Grierson called me to say that he'd now dropped the idea but had a new one. The new subject was the Great North Road, its truck-drivers, cafes and girls. Montague (Monty) Slater was to script with me. After reconnaissance, we did. Obviously it was for 95% exterior filming. Grierson liked the script but said that because he had Southall Studio to fill, the whole film must be shot in the Studio. 'Remember the great old UFA pictures? We'll build the bloody Great North Road in the studio'. That was the end of that project and the last I had to do with Group 3.[28]

But finally, in 1951, he was able to direct his first feature, *No Resting Place*, to be followed in 1958 by *Cat and Mouse*. *No Resting Place*, though quite modest, was a considerable success. A contemporary review by Richard Winnington is interesting not only as a discussion of Rotha's film as such but of its context:

With *No Resting Place* Rotha has proved that it is possible to make a film drama, employing professional and non-professional actors and using real locations (interior and exterior) throughout while grappling with the worst weather conditions in Irish memory—at under £60,000 and well within schedule. The film shows no signs of stringency or makeshift. Shot in Ireland and based on Ian Niall's highly readable novel, it is a realistic story of Nemesis. The illiterate, itinerant tinker (Michael Gough) who accidentally kills the game-keeper is defeated in the end as much by his own divided nature as by the relentless shadowing of the obsessed police guard (Noel Purcell). His plight is that of all outcasts who defy Society and are broken by it. The lush Irish backgrounds are an unfailingly lovely setting for this slow, somewhat aloofly presented tragedy. It is good to look at and listen to—the natural Irish voices free of whimsy and blarney, the natural sounds punctuated with identifiable bird song and the sparse pastoral music of William Alwyn. And there are fascinating glimpses of the tinker's strange wayward life and flashes of real insight in the direction. If Rotha, through his own austerity, has failed to generate the passion that would have made *No Resting Place* a landmark, it is none the less a milestone (it has incidentally given Michael Gough the best acting part of his film career and discovered to the British a fine actress in Eithne Dunne). Producer

Colin Leslie's act of courage in backing this fresh and unusual film with every penny he possessed has been fully justified. He has made his point and put us all in his debt.[29]

No Resting Place was made in a documentary manner, shot on location and telling a story with a social and political dimension rooted in fact. The same can be said of his final feature film, the Dutch production *De Overval/The Silent Raid* (1962), which was based on a daring raid on a German prison in occupied Holland by members of the Dutch resistance in 1944. Shot on the actual locations where the incident took place, the film was greeted by almost unanimous approval by the country's press and was a huge success at the domestic box office. Seeing the film today, in a dubbed and slightly shortened English language version, one is struck by its similarity to the then current television drama. Even its location sequences have the feel of studio shooting; it is relatively static and somewhat slow. At the same time though, it does possess a real and convincing atmosphere of what was an actual and important event. One cannot help but feel that it was that quality that made the film such a success in the Netherlands. For the Dutch people, who had lived through the events, it was a first—a Dutch film made in Dutch, with Dutch actors and a Dutch script.

In 1960, now in his early 50s, Rotha embarked on what turned out to be his last, 'pure' documentary film. A feature-length compilation intended for theatrical release in the cinema, *The Life of Adolf Hitler*, was produced by the West German company Real Films at Studio Hamburg. Thirty years after shooting his tulips in St James's Park, Rotha now faced the greatest challenge of his career as a director and as film-technician, leading a small Anglo-German team, each member of which was deeply and emotionally involved in the film's subject. The war and its effects were still very close, as was the horror of Nazism and, above all, the Holocaust. He met, as did all of the team's members, former Nazis, including members of Hitler's personal staff, as well as survivors of the concentration camps. Rotha faced a major difficulty in the production not only of the Hitler film, but also of his Dutch feature a couple of years later. In both contexts he was a foreigner, an Englishman, and it was difficult for him, if not impossible, to ignore his own experiences of the war and imagine what it felt like to live in Germany during the 1930s or in the Netherlands under the occupation. Moreover he spoke neither German nor Dutch and found it difficult to make friends, especially in Germany. It proved to be an immense challenge to him as a man—to his imagination, his understanding and above all, to his humanity.

The Life of Adolf Hitler is an attempt to show and to explain, especially to young people in Germany, *how* and *why* it could all have happened —Nazism, racism, the war, murder, the concentration camps. The film succeeded in showing the horror, but probably failed in finding an explanation.[30] But it remains a pioneering attempt.

Film libraries were few then and, by today's standards, relatively disorganized. In 1960 the film-maker had to undertake his own film research, then even more difficult as much of the necessary material could only be obtained from sources behind the Iron Curtain. Moreover, there was still something of a secretive and conspiratorial atmosphere, especially in Berlin and in the 'private' libraries and collections, and not even a rough script could be written until it was known what material might be available. It was a long and difficult search. Hundreds of thousands feet of material arrived in the cutting-room (usually in the form of a scratched print) which involved a colossal 'house-keeping' process. But, eventually, editing and scripting could begin. To balance these two quite separate processes, to bring them into accord and then to 'structure' the material, filmically and historically, was perhaps Paul Rotha's greatest achievement.

The making of *The Life of Adolf Hitler* greatly affected all who worked on it. For Rotha it was at times an overwhelming experience:

> This afternoon a three hours walk through the Tiergarten to the ruined Reichstag. Soviet war memorial. Grim. Peered through Brandenburg Gate into East Berlin. The really extraordinary thing is our unique experience of seeing ruins like the Reichstag now when only a day or so ago and for four weeks we have been seeing it as it was in the 20s, 30s and 40s with the figures of history mounting its steps. No one could equal this unique situation that we are in. We are steeped in celluloid history and then come to see its remains today. This needs writing about more fully. A most moving experience.[31]

Nineteen months after starting, the film was complete. Rotha recorded the moment in his diary with a certain anxiety:

> Aug. 28th 1961—Hamburg.
> In two hours time I see for the first time the final completed copy of my film, in German of course. It is always for me the worst moment

of a whole production and this one has been very long—19 months! You can imagine how I feel! But it is too late to change anything now. Hamburg is plastered with posters announcing the premiere next Friday. And then the film will be released simultaneously in 22 cities in Germany—so for once I cannot complain that no one sees my work . . . No, there will be no clove carnation on Friday night, I am glad to say, just ordinary clothes. This is good for this kind of film, which calls for no glamour. They expect demonstrations, I am told, because there are still a good many ex-Nazis around who will not like the film. But this does not worry me.[32]

But there were no demonstrations. The film was well received and ran for months in German cinemas, as well as in Britain and in many other countries. It has been shown a number of times on German, and British television, and was used for educational purposes (in schools and colleges) for many years.

Concluding Remarks

And so ended Paul Rotha's career as a documentary film-maker. His final documentary encapsulated a great deal of what had concerned him during the previous thirty years, as an artist and as a citizen. This last documentary film, (*De Overval* was still to come) reveals almost as much of Rotha's own feelings as it does of Hitler's. Above all, perhaps, his commitment to democracy and social justice. During his working life the world had changed a great deal and with it the role of the documentary as a communicative and educative medium. Rotha himself recalls some of the contrasts and changes between the heyday of the British documentary and the post-war period:

> That great man John Boyd Orr once said about the growing of food 'You must put more into the earth than you take out'. The same is true of the documentary film-maker. Technical skill by itself is not enough to contribute. That is what characterised British documentary in the 50s and 60s. It is the aim of the film, what it is trying to say about social progress, which matters and to which the creative film-maker must give of his attitude towards living, towards his fellow human beings. Hundreds of films have been made of 'nuts and bolts' operations and their variants, all beautifully photographed and sound-recorded, all pleasing their sponsors in the long hope of selling products, but they have added nothing to the documentary

story. In the 30s, it must be remembered, it was the documentary film-maker who found the human aspect of his subject, not the sponsor. When the Orient Line commissioned *Shipyard* they had in mind a film descriptive of building a ship from keel to launch. It was the film's director who added the social reference that made the film of wider concern than shipbuilding as an industrial process. Occasionally there was a sponsor like the Gas Council, thanks to S.G. Leslie, which permitted a social approach from scratch. Most often it was the documentary man who sought out the social aspect of the subject and 'educated' his sponsor to it. It is that process of 'educating the sponsor' which, in my opinion, disappeared firstly during the war years (due to the dominance of the MOI) and then to a much bigger extent during the 50s. It is a particularly hard problem for film units which are a part of the nationalised industries. One vital aspect of Grierson's approach was that he 'sold' the concept of imagination to the British Post Office. Is the same true of films made by the British Transport and National Coal Board Units?

For Rotha, the achievements of the 1930s had been dependent on intensive activity on three interrelated fronts: in finding and educating potential sponsors, in propagating the documentary idea via journalism and lecturing, and in making films as good as circumstances and abilities permitted.

To these three must be added a fourth front as the decade went on, that which grew to be of increasing importance—the field of distribution for our films when made.

The British documentary film movement had been very successful. Many films of lasting value were made, films that speak to us even today, not only as a record of what life was like for many in the Britain of the 1930s and 1940s but also in what they have to say about the people who made them. The individuals concerned developed the non-fiction film from a programme-filler into an important genre of its own. Its respectability, and its quality, attracted academics and intellectuals who beforehand had thought of film as a form of entertainment hardly worth their attention. The influence that the documentary film enjoys today owes much to the pioneering work of the original documentary film-makers. The key, perhaps, to the success of the 'movement' was *independence*. All of its leading members fought for it—and gained it;

none more so than Paul Rotha. He was tough and pugnacious; he had to be, to enable him to use the film medium as a means of personal expression. And as an art. As Grierson once wrote:

> In any case it is of the greatest value that Rotha should reach out separately in this way, and of the greatest importance that his growing point should prosper. It may be that two separate arts are involved (in documentary) and that we must look for the development of both. The one is cold and, with power, may yet be classical; the other is rhetorical and may yet, with power, be romantic. But this is certain: in our realistic cinema, all roads lead by one hill or another to poetry. Poets they must be—or stay for ever journalists.[33]

And a poet Rotha remained. The struggle to resolve and 'bring together' the opposing poles of 'purpose' and 'the art of film' was at the heart of his creativity, it was the engine of his films' rhythm: the tension, the excitement. To achieve his purpose, Rotha could be uncompromising, demanding, ruthless even; he could be pompous and (some said) 'difficult to work with'. He was also, on a personal level, immensely kind, sensitive and understanding. To have known him, to have worked for and with him, to have shared just a little of his thoughts, ideas and knowledge, and to have learned from him not only a love of film but also an appreciation of its importance and value as a medium to be *enjoyed*, has been, for this writer, an experience for which he will continue to be grateful. Paul Rotha was always wonderful company.

The British film industry, now more than a hundred years old, has played a considerable part in the development of British popular culture. Faced with great difficulties—a relatively small market and, above all, the overwhelming competition of the American cinema—there is much to be proud of. There have been a great number of films and many film-makers of distinction. But it can be argued that 'up until 1940, there was only one real coherent movement in the young art of the cinema which was destined to have an influence on Western film-making, and to attract world attention among critics and audiences; that was the movement of documentary film-making in Britain in the 1930s'.[34] Among those who made it happen, Paul Rotha was one of the most eminent, exerting an influence still noticeable today. He was a man totally dedicated to the documentary film, its ideals and purposes. He loved film of all kinds and from all countries; it was *the* art form of the twentieth century and he was one of its greatest practitioners.

Notes

1. Making films with social/political purpose, that is films dealing with subjects such as unemployment, housing, planning, poverty, food and the like, was what distinguished 'the documentary' from travelogues, general interest films, instructional and educational films and so on. John Grierson, the 'father' of the British documentary film movement defined them as films employing 'The creative treatment of actuality'. Rotha later expanded this into 'The use of the film medium to interpret creatively and in social terms the life of the people as it exists in reality'.

2. Paul Rotha, *Documentary Diary: An Informal History of the British Documentary Film, 1928–1939* (London: Secker & Warberg, 1973, p. 153.

3. The Living Newspaper was a technique developed to present dramatically and on a stage, news events or issues of current interest, the war in Abyssinia, for example, or the building of a dam to generate electricity. Characters representing not individuals generally but types or groups or classes acting in simple and often expressionistic settings discuss the subject at issue, rapidly and usually contrapunctionally. Rotha came across this technique while in the US in the late 1930s where it was developed extensively by the Federal Theatre Project as part of the government's work relief programme. This technique had in fact been used in Britain during the late 1920s, in Salford for instance.

4. Paul Rotha, *Documentary Diary*, p. 226.

5. Ibid. p. 71. The chapter on the making of *Contact* is reprinted in this volume.

6. Ibid. pp. 55–7.

7. Ibid. pp. 38–9.

8. During the late 1920s and early 1930s Sir Stephen Tallents was Secretary of the Empire Marketing Board which had been set up in 1925/26 to further 'the marketing in this country of Empire products'. He became interested in using the film-medium to assist the work of the Board—the first, *One Family*, was made by Walter Creighton. In February 1927 he met John Grierson, whose ideas much impressed him, and engaged him to join Creighton as films officer. It was not long before *Drifters* was made and the first documentary film unit established. It was Tallents who, as the senior civil servant in charge, made the documentary movement possible. His vision and skill, and his relationship with John Grierson, proved to be decisive.

9. John Grierson, 'The story of the documentary film', *Fortnightly Review*, August 1938. Quoted in Rotha, *Documentary Diary*, pp. 43–4.

10. Rotha, *Documentary Diary*, p. 45.

11. The so-called 'poster films' made at the EMB unit during its early years

were, in Rotha's words, 'endless loops of film (about 30ft long) intended for use on continuous daylight projectors at exhibitions and in shops. They were made out of trick tiles, abstract effects, models and whatever ingenious devices could be thought up. A new one had to be made from a drawn script to a completed film in one week at a cost of no more than £25. Basil Wright and I took turns to make them. Typical subjects were Scottish Tomatoes, Empire Timber, Australian Wine, Wool and Butter . . . They demanded imagination and a strict economy over costs . . . It was a wonderful discipline for beginners.' *Documentary Diary*, p. 49.

12. Ibid. pp. 40–1.
13. Mander was a writer, director and actor. Some of the scripts they collaborated on were made into films including *Fascination* (Miles Mander, 1931), a remake of Hitchcock's silent classic *The Lodger* (Maurice Elvey, 1932) and *Don Quixote* (G.W. Pabst, 1933).
14. During the 1930s the role of public relations officer became very important and influential. Many of them were men of ideas interested in the part that the documentary film might be able to play. J.L. Beddington has already been mentioned, but there were others who were to contribute a great deal to the 'documentary movement'. Frank Pick of London Transport, Snowden Gamble of Imperial Airways, S.C. Leslie of the gas industry were just some of them.
15. Rotha, *Documentary Diary*, pp. 99–103.
16. Rotha, notes written during the 1970s and 1980s towards an unrealised second volume of 'Documentary Diary'. These are lodged in the Special Collections Department of the library of the University of California, Los Angeles (UCLA).
17. Rotha, *Documentary Diary*, pp. 100–1.
18. Strand Films was to be the first independent documentary production company. It was set up by Donald Taylor, Ralph Keene and C.L. Heseltine in 1935. Rotha became Director of Productions.
19. Rotha, *Documentary Diary*, p. 145.
20. Copies of a number of letters to David Schrire are currently lodged in the Special Collections Department of the BFI.
21. Rotha, *Documentary Diary*, p. 213.
22. Notes towards unrealized second volume of 'Documentary Diary'.
23. Ibid.
24. Isotypes were a system of signs and symbols very useful to explain statistics and provide information (rather like those now used universally to denote toilets for instance) and incorporated into a number of Rotha's films. He wrote, 'I had for some years been an admirer of the work of Dr Otto and Mrs Marie Neurath and their work at the Isotype Institute in Vienna. When they became refugees and visited England, I had the pleasure of

meeting them. I was anxious to see if their work could be adapted for use in films. It could . . .' (notes for unrealized second volume of 'Documentary Diary'). The Isotype archive is at the University of Reading.

25. From the *News Chronicle*, 15 February 1948. Republished in Richard Winnington, *Film Criticism and Caricatures, 1943–53* (London: Paul Elek, 1975). Edited and introduced by Paul Rotha.

26. From a letter to Robert Kruger, 7 March 1984.

27. From notes towards an unrealized second volume of 'Documentary Diary'.

28. Ibid.

29. From the *News Chronicle*, 13 July 1951.

30. The purpose of the film was to inform the German public, above all young people, what happened, how it happened, and why. Most adults, of course knew most of this intellectually; but many buried it naturally enough. And, we had to remember that people in Germany too suffered from the bombing; had a tough war and so on. It would have been difficult for them to think of themselves, always, as wicked, or evil, or mad etc. We could not ignore this. While in a sense a 'history lesson', this was not an educational film in the 'school or college' sense. It was to be seen without back-up material, without a teacher. It was used as such later on, but it was primarily to be shown in a public cinema. People had to be enticed to visit the cinema, to pay for their seats.

31. Paul Rotha, 'Hamburg diary,' lodged in the Special Collections Department, UCLA.

32. From a letter to his sister Ki, 28 August 1961.

33. John Grierson, 'Two paths to poetry', *Cinema Quarterly*, vol. 3, no. 3, 1935.

34. Rotha, *Documentary Diary*, Preface, p. xiii.

Paul Rotha and Film Theory

Duncan Petrie

Introduction: Why Rotha?

Paul Rotha's reputation as a film-maker, theoretician and critic tends to be associated with the discourse of documentary-realism and a particular version of cinema history and criticism, one which has been progressively eclipsed by subsequent developments in cinema scholarship. The last fifteen years have witnessed a major process of critical reassessment, revaluation and transformation in our knowledge of British films and film-makers, genres and aesthetic traditions, prompting Alan Lovell to revise significantly his 1960 description of British cinema as 'an unknown cinema'.[1] But in displacing the hegemony of the realist discourse, revisionist history has tended to relegate the documentary to the margins of British cinema and to consequently overlook or underplay the broader importance of some of the key figures synonymous with it. It is in this context that I wish to reconsider the significance of Rotha. However, my primary interest here is not to recuperate the documentary movement, but to demonstrate that Rotha's contribution is much broader and embraces formative issues and debates in the developments of film theory and criticism over three decades.

In his writings, Rotha made a major contribution to the development of an expressly intellectual film culture in Britain, a culture which took film seriously as an art form in its own right and as an important and effective medium for the communication of ideas. It was the emergence of such a climate in the late 1920s and early 1930s which helped to ensure that a broader range of films, particularly those from Continental Europe, were distributed, exhibited, written about and discussed in Britain. The explicitly cosmopolitan and modernist inclinations of the minority film culture (a term distinguishing it from the commercial

Hollywood-dominated mainstream) also exerted an influence that can be subsequently traced through the development of the documentary movement and the British feature film. It can be equally discerned in the films of ambitious and innovative story-tellers like Alfred Hitchcock and Anthony Asquith, producer Michael Balcon and the leading documentarians John Grierson, Alberto Cavalcanti and, of course, Paul Rotha. In this way the reconsideration of the intellectual appreciation of cinema is not only an important moment in understanding the development of British film culture, it also provides a way beyond the ultimately sterile oppositions documentary/fiction, realism/fantasy which are still all too prevalent in cinema scholarship.

Rotha's value also lies in his major contribution to the development of film theory, particularly during the 1930s. As I will subsequently demonstrate, his work embodies a fundamental transformation from a broadly formalist conception of cinema art to a realist position. These theoretical moments are usually associated with distinct thinkers: Eisenstein and Arnheim on the one hand, Kracauer and Bazin on the other. But Rotha's own intellectual development—influenced by a combination of the emergence of the British documentary and his subsequent involvement in this field as a practitioner, and the social, political and economic climate of the early 1930s—provides a unique insight into the major issues, debates, problems and contradictions of early film theory. As the influence of more recent theoretical activity inspired by semiotic and psychoanalytic concepts has begun to wane, then the time is ripe for a reconsideration of the historical development of film theory. The writings of Paul Rotha provide a major contribution to just such a project.

Rotha and the Minority Film Culture

Several commentators have described the emergence in the 1920s of an intellectual film culture in Britain.[2] One of the major reasons for the rise in the status of cinema in Britain during the 1920s was a response to the emergence of certain 'art' cinema movements on the Continent. As Tom Ryall notes:

> The 1920s was a crucial decade in the development of specialised minority film cultures in the major European film-producing countries as well as in Britain. It was a period of self-conscious artistic experiment in the cinema in which the key artistic

revolutions of the early twentieth century—Expressionism, Cubism, Futurism, Dadism and so on—found an outlet in the cinematic experiments of film makers in Germany, France and the Soviet Union. Whereas the development of the cinema previously had been dominated by the concerns of a popular narrative art, the 1920s see the emergence of cinemas which bear the imprint of 'art' and 'high culture' attracting the attention of the educated classes who had previously scorned the medium.[3]

Such developments also critically informed attempts by intellectuals during this period to elaborate a systematic theory of film. What united this first wave of theorizing was an attempt to establish the cultural credentials or prestige of the medium by positing the cinema as a distinct medium or art form with its own intrinsic aesthetic properties. Paul Rotha's own emergence as an intellectual figure is bound up with this formative phase in film theory and will be explored in some detail below.

One of the reasons why the art cinema of the 1920s could be accurately described as a 'minority' cinema lay in the extremely restricted ways in which such films could be distributed and exhibited in Britain. Hollywood's stranglehold on the British market was extreme, and 90% of films exhibited in the mid-1920s in British cinemas were American. This situation was exacerbated by the extreme conservatism of distributors and exhibitors unprepared to take a risk on anything as commercially doubtful as a 'highbrow' film from Europe, on the one hand, and the stringent fanaticism of the British Board of Film Censors deeply suspicious of anything with overt experimental or political aspirations, on the other. But there were ways of circumventing such constraints and the most successful initiative came in the guise of the Film Society.

The first council of the Film Society was founded in 1925 by a group of professionals and enthusiasts including Ivor Montagu, the actor Hugh Miller, critics Iris Barry and Walter Mycroft, film director Adrian Brunel, exhibitor Sidney Bernstein and sculptor Frank Dobson. Founder members included such notable artistic and intellectual figures as George Bernard Shaw, H.G. Wells, J. Maynard Keynes, Dame Ellen Terry, Roger Fry, Augustus John and E. McKnight Kauffer.[4] They were subsequently joined by various individuals who were to become important figures in British cinema, including Alfred Hitchcock, Anthony Asquith, Michael Balcon, John Grierson, Basil Wright and the 18-year-old Paul Rotha. Some of them contributed to the programming of the Society while others worked in the cutting-rooms of Adrian Brunel and Ivor Montagu's editing company which, among other activities, was involved in the technical preparation of films screened.

The new body was modelled on the Stage Society which existed to promote plays that could not otherwise be performed either for censorship reasons or because they were considered uncommercial. Included among the playwrights whose work was championed by the Society were Shaw, Ibsen, Strindberg, Cocteau, Gorki, Odets, Wedekind and Pirandello. Performances were organized on Sundays for a private audience and so circumvented the jurisdiction of the Lord Chamberlain's office, which censored theatrical works. The kind of work supported also demonstrated a commitment to experimental and committed drama, which was to be a similar driving force behind the Film Society.

The Society secured the use of the New Gallery Kinema in Regent Street for screenings and some 1,400 people attended the first programme, on Sunday 24 October 1925. Top of the bill was the German feature *Waxworks* (1924), directed by Paul Leni. This was accompanied by a programme of supporting shorts including Walther Ruttmann's experimental *Absolute Films, Opera 2, 3 and 4* (1923–25), an American Western, *How Broncho Billy Left Bear Country* (1912), Adrian Brunel's short burlesque, *Typical Budget* (1925) and the Chaplin film *Champion Charlie* (1916). This form of mixed programming proved to be a great success and over the next fourteen years the Society screened around 500 films, of which more than 300 were being shown for the first time in Britain.[5] It was responsible for introducing to Britain the work of such key figures in European art cinema as Leni, Ruttmann, G.W. Pabst, V.I. Pudovkin, Dziga Vertov, René Clair, Carl Dreyer, Jean Renoir, John Grierson, Jean Vigo, and Alexander Dovzhenko. In addition to screenings, the Society also organized public exhibitions, discussions and lectures relating to both aesthetic and technical issues. Distinguished film-makers were also invited to address the Society and in 1929 both Sergei Eisenstein and Hans Richter were in London and ran 'study groups' for Film Society members. Eisenstein's comprised a series of six lectures on aspects of montage, while Richter's culminated in the group production of an 'abstract film' entitled *Everyday*.[6] Such pioneering cultural initiatives reinforced and augmented the central role of the Society in cultivating a sophisticated and informed understanding of the cutting edge of film art.

Membership grew steadily and in 1929 the Society was forced to move screenings from the New Gallery to the larger Tivoli Palace cinema in the Strand. It also influenced the development of similar bodies in other cities which began to appear from 1929, and paved the way for the emergence of a number of specialized cinemas open to the general public rather than members only. This began with the Shaftesbury Avenue Pavilion which started screening foreign 'art' films in 1927 and was soon followed by the Curzon in Mayfair, the Everyman in Hampstead and the Academy in Oxford Street. Such developments also ultimately paved the way for the realization of a National Film Theatre and the establishment of a national network of Regional Film Theatres specializing in repertory programming.

The generation and sustenance of a vibrant intellectual film culture required more than the exhibition of films however. Equally important was a vehicle for discussion, analysis and the formation of critical perspectives on the cinema. This was provided by the journal Close Up, marking in Tom Ryall's words, 'the first attempt to provide a theoretical forum for the cinema in the English language.'[7] Close Up ran for six years from 1927 to 1933 and despite a small circulation was extremely influential. It was published out of an editorial base in Switzerland by the Pool company presided over by editor Kenneth Macpherson and a close group of associates including Oswell Blakeston, Bryher (Winifred Ellerman) and the poet H.D. (Hilda Doolittle). Other regular contributors included Robert Herring, the American critic Harry Alan Potamkin, Hugh Castle, Ernest Betts and the writers Gertrude Stein and Dorothy Richardson. In addition to publishing some very early articles relating questions of psychoanalysis and race to the cinema, Close Up championed the 'art' film in a manner which was resolutely internationalist. The contributors chronicled and analysed not only developments in Germany, France, the Soviet Union and other European countries but occasionally those from such far flung shores as Argentina, India and Japan. The journal had correspondents in London, New York, Los Angeles, Paris, Vienna, Berlin and Geneva. It also provided one of the first outlets for the theoretical writings of the Soviet film-makers, including English translations of Eisenstein, Pudovkin and Alexandrov's seminal 'statement' on the sound film, and Eisenstein's essay 'The Principles of Film Form'.

On the negative side, Close Up was extremely hostile towards Hollywood films, with only the odd exception, which somehow transcended the constraints of commercial film-making, such as Erich von Stroheim's Greed, being considered. The British cinema was subject to even greater vilification. Macpherson's editorial in the first issue (July 1927) described the current effort to revive the English cinema in terms suggesting that the national character was somewhat inimical to the art of the film:

> The truth is that the average attitude of England and the English to art is so wholly nonchalant and clownish that it is quite useless to expect any art to indigenously flower there. Isolated instances may here and there crop up, but REALLY the Englishman can only be roused to enthusiasm on the football field. A cup final will evoke tens of thousands of whooping maniacs. One doesn't mind that but in the face of it one does ask WHY attempt art? The preference between the two is so indisputable. One can see that the English revival will be exactly along old lines.[8]

For Macpherson any revival would inevitably be driven by the dictates of industry and commerce rather than art. Nineteen twenty-seven was also the year in which the protectionist quota legislation, inspired by the Hollywood dominance over British distribution and exhibition, became law. In forcing distributors and exhibitors to accept a minimum percentage of British films, the quota significantly improved British production in terms of the number of films being made and, in the case of bigger studios such as British International Films at Elstree, in terms of production values. However, the judgement of the *Close Up* critics was no less harsh. British cinema was castigated for attempting to compete with Hollywood in the world market, and the importation of Continental talent and film-making techniques (so beloved of *Close Up*) into British studios was ridiculed. Even the occasional attempt by a cine-literate British film-maker like Hitchcock or Asquith to apply Continental touches to their own films rarely found support from *Close Up*. A vibrant, successful cinema could not be merely constructed on borrowed touches, it had to discover its own intrinsic components which reflected British experience in the same way in which the Soviets have so masterfully achieved a cinematic expression of their own social and political experience in films like *Battleship Potemkin*, *October* and *The End of St Petersburg*.

It is within this cultural context that we must view the emergence of the young Paul Rotha, first as a critic and theorist and subsequently as a film-maker. By the time he enrolled at the Slade School of Art to study design, Rotha was a serious cineaste. He joined the Film Society during its first season and in 1929 was involved in the formation of The Film Group which campaigned for a repertory cinema for 'unusual' films in

London. More significantly, Rotha also began to write about film from 1927 onwards, beginning with contributions to *The Connoisseur, Film Weekly* and then *Close Up*. He also joined the first editorial advisory board of the new educational magazine *Sight and Sound* in 1932.

But prior to establishing himself as a critic of some importance, Rotha had his first brief but eventful experience of the British film industry. In 1928 he secured a job in the Art Department of British International Pictures, Elstree, where he only lasted a few months before being fired for writing an article in *Film Weekly* perceived as critical of British production design.[9] But during that brief period Rotha made the acquaintance of some of the most interesting film-makers active in the British industry at that time. In the attempt to compete with Hollywood production values and popular appeal, BIP had instigated an overtly internationalist policy which involved importing directors, technicians and actors from overseas, many of them from the German industry. These were very important people to a film enthusiast like Rotha and he found himself working on productions for such major Continental directors as Henrik Galeen (who had written the screenplay for *Nosferatu*) and E.A. Dupont. After leaving BIP, Rotha travelled to Paris to design sets for a small independent production. The assignment turned sour and Rotha returned to Britain, but not before he had taken the opportunity to meet with some of the key figures of the French *avant-garde* cinema, including René Clair, Jean Epstein, Georges Lacombe and Alberto Cavalcanti.

Unable to secure proper work in film-making, Rotha decided to channel his energies in another direction. Around this time the novelist Norah C. James suggested that he write a book about the cinema. James was also in charge of book design at Jonathan Cape, and this connection led to a contract with the publishers; Rotha thus began to work in earnest on what was to become *The Film Till Now*. Despite being given a rather meagre advance which was barely enough to live on, Rotha received a great deal of assistance and co-operation from overseas, allowing him to travel to Berlin and Paris to view films which were unavailable in Britain. Erich Pommer, head of Ufa studios, allowed him to see numerous German films and to consult the studio's files of stills, and in Paris Rotha was able to see many Russian films screened by the Soviet Trade Agency. While writing his book, Rotha was also fortunate enough to meet Eisenstein who was visiting London as a guest of Ivor Montagu.

Published in 1930, *The Film Till Now* ranks alongside *Close Up* as one of the major landmarks of the new serious appreciation of the art of the film in Britain. Rachael Low notes that the book was 'to prove one of the greatest single factors in the growth of a new attitude'[10] towards the serious appreciation of the cinema. While Tom Ryall describes *The Film Till Now* as 'the most comprehensive and influential summary of the state of film art from the British point of view . . .'[11] Even *Close Up* seemed to be impressed, with the editorial of the October 1930 issue taking the form of a review. While noting several instances of disagreement with Rotha's judgements, Kenneth Macpherson nevertheless considered the book 'a praiseworthy and conscientious work.'[12] But despite its undoubted historical importance, how does the reputation of *The Film Till Now* fare today and how can its significance or otherwise be accommodated within the revisionist histories of British cinema?

The Film Till Now and Film Theory

Rotha's first book is a formidable achievement by any standards. It combines both an extensive survey of the international cinema with a theoretical exposition of the medium, its properties and potentialities. This theoretical orientation was to be extensively revised in the light of Rotha's own subsequent thinking and experience as a director of documentaries; but in 1930 his approach embraced a conception of the film which owed a great deal to other attempts to construct a coherent theory of film in the first decades of this century. As J. Dudley Andrew suggests, these formative efforts to construct a theory of film had similar goals and drew similar conclusions which were broadly concerned with questions of form.[13] Theorists were concerned to establish the artistic credentials of the cinema. As the American poet Vachel Lindsay wrote as early as 1915: 'The motion picture art is a great high art, not a process of commercial manufacture.'[14] Lindsay identified three distinct categories of the 'photoplay'—pictures of Action, Intimacy and Splendour—which he proceeded to relate to existing established art forms, discussing them as variously as sculpture-in-motion, painting-in-motion and architecture-in-motion, or as the equivalent of the poetic categories of the dramatic, the lyric and the epic. Three years earlier, the Paris-based Italian scholar Riccioto Canudo had published an article entitled 'The Birth of a Sixth Art' in which he described the cinema as 'a superb conciliation of the Rhythms of Space (the Plastic Arts) and the Rhythms of Time (Music and Poetry)'.[15]

But early film theory also wished to establish the cinema as a unique form distinct from the other arts, in particular the theatre to which it was most frequently compared. This view regarded the 'photoplay' (the fiction film) as essentially a recording of a theatrical event staged for the camera. The opposition to such a conception necessarily invokes a much more fundamental question, that of the relationship between film and reality. The popular assumption of film as a transparent medium which mechanically reproduced whatever was placed before it undermined any claims it might have to being an art in its own right. Consequently, the primary aim of formative film theory was to separate film from reality in order to focus on those formal aspects which constituted the medium as a creative art in its own right. This project underpins the writings of practically all the important early film theorists, including Hugo Münsterberg, V.I. Pudovkin, Sergei Eisenstein, Louis Delluc, Jean Epstein, Béla Balázs and Rudolph Arnheim, and constitutes the tradition from which much of Rotha's theoretical orientation in *The Film Till Now* can be understood.

Münsterberg's pioneering work, *The Photoplay: A Psychological Study*, first appeared in 1916, and is an attempt to construct an understanding of the cinema as an art fundamentally related to certain psychic processes on the part of the spectator—anticipating the more recent interest in spectatorship which has exercised film theorists since the early 1970s. Münsterberg's theory of film combines psychology and aesthetics to demonstrate the unique properties of a medium distinct from reality and the theatre:

> the photoplay tells us the human story by overcoming the forms of the outside world, namely space, time, and causality, and by adjusting the events to the forms of the inner world, namely attention, memory, imagination, and emotion.[16]

At the same time there was considerable intellectual engagement with 'the art of the film' in France. Some critics such as Emile Vuillermoz developed a concept of the cinema as a high art which on a formal level had much in common with the musical symphony,[17] while Louis Delluc regarded the medium as a popular democratic art and consequently was more favourable towards American films than many of his contemporaries. It was Delluc (and later Epstein) who became associated with the emergence of the concept of *photogénie* as a means of identifying what was purely cinematic about the cinema—in Paul Willemen's words 'that mysterious indefinable something present in the image which differentiated cinema from all the other arts and therefore constituted the very foundation of cinematic art.'[18] This concept was rooted in the way in which the cinematic image effected a fundamental transformation of pro-filmic reality by way of the constitutive elements of mise-en-scène into something unique. As Richard Abel puts it, 'the effect of *photogénie* was singular: to make us see ordinary things as they had never been seen before.'[19]

Photogénie remained at the level of the image or the individual shot and had nothing to say about the way in which shots were combined in the process of editing. Consequently the French theorists introduced a new concept—*cinégraphie*—to encompass what Abel calls the rhythmical or structural ordering of photogénie throughout a film. Léon Moussinac, a close friend of Delluc, made the following pronouncement on 'cinégraphic rhythm' in 1923:

> Few have understood that giving rhythm to a film is as important as giving rhythm to the image, that the decoupage and montage . . . are as essential as the mise-en-scène.[20]

But as film theory advanced in the 1920s, it was the Soviet film-makers and theorists who became associated with the argument that the art of the film was rooted in *montage*. Vsevolod Pudovkin introduced his book *Film Technique* with the statement, 'The foundation of film art is *editing*.'[21] He regarded individual shots as 'dead objects' or 'soulless photographs' which were subsequently animated via the editing process. Nature provided the raw material in the form of individual shots but the creative process of film lay in how these were constructed into a whole. At the same time, his colleague Sergei Eisenstein was busy developing a more sophisticated theory of the basis of film form by way of his concept of 'the montage of attractions'. Eisenstein had a rather different concept of the raw material of film-making to Pudovkin, regarding the shot not as bits of reality to be creatively assembled to direct particular meanings, but rather as constituted by formal elements in and of itself. However, even for Eisenstein individual shots remained at the level of building blocks or 'cells' which had to be brought to life by way of montage. Rather than being merely the assemblage or linkage of shots, montage for Eisenstein was a dialectical process of collision or conflict: from the collision of two shots arises a third element, or concept.[22] Moreover, taken as an approach to film-making, dialectical montage created a cinema which directly engaged both the emotions and the intellect, a revolutionary art appropriate to the modern world.

Rotha's own theoretical approach owes a great deal to such understandings of the basis of cinema. Early fragments of his perspective form the basis of a series of articles written for *The Film Weekly* in 1929 and subsequently elaborated in *The Film Till Now*.[23] In the latter, Rotha asserts that the film is 'an independent form of expression, drawing inspiration with reservation from the other arts'. Moreover, 'the attributes of the film are derived from the nature of the medium itself, and not from other matters of subject, story-interest or propaganda'. This commitment to the film as art also predisposed Rotha more favourably towards certain kinds of cinema. Part One of *The Film Till Now* comprises a detailed account of the development of the cinema in America, Germany, the Soviet Union, France and Britain—with very brief considerations of Sweden, Italy, Spain, Japan and India. His general approach and preferences bear many similarities to the collective articles published in *Close Up*, the cinemas of the Soviet Union, Weimar Germany and to a lesser extent France receiving a generally favourable evaluation, while those of the USA and Britain are subjected to rather harsh criticism. Indeed, much of Rotha's extensive examination of the American film displays little more than contempt and scorn for what he regards as 'the lowest form of public entertainment',[24] the product of a factory system governed by the profit motive.[25] Such virulently anti-Hollywood bias was a common feature of the intellectual film culture in Britain during the period when *The Film Till Now* first appeared.

In common with other formative film theorists, Rotha first of all had to reject convincingly the view of cinema as a transparent medium engaged in the mechanical reproduction of reality—the transparent rendering of certain pro-filmic events. He begins with the (rather clumsy) proposition that 'the greatest handicap imposed on aesthetic progress was the camera's misleading faculty for being able to record the actual', before proceeding to explain how the development of story-telling in early cinema was hampered by this false relationship to reality. Rotha argues that early film-makers were content simply to photograph what was in front of the camera rather than developing any abilities to express story *through* the camera, which would involve experimentation with aesthetic and formal possibilities:

The power of the camera to record the actual on the screen fooled the audience into believing that its sole pleasure lay in the recognition of familiar things. Thus, at the outset of the story-picture, the film began its career on a false basis and it hardly need be stated, has continued along these lines (with a few notable exceptions) to the present day.[26]

The fallacy of this inherent realism lay behind Adolph Zukor's spectacularly successful entrepreneurial idea of presenting 'Famous Players in Famous Plays', which laid the foundations of a company which eventually became Paramount Studios, the first major vertically-integrated film combine in Hollywood. In a similar vein, Rotha dismisses the emergence of movie acting as 'living photography', pictures of essentially pre-existing theatrical performance, rather than a vital and dynamic element of a new mode of creative expression.

It is the substance of this critique of early cinema which leads Rotha to lavish praise on Robert Wiene's German expressionist classic *The Cabinet of Doctor Caligari* (1919). He regarded the film as a landmark in the development of film art on the grounds that it was the first time in cinema history that the director had broken with the realist veneer and worked through the camera. For Rotha it was also the first time:

> that a film, instead of being realistic, might be a possible reality, both imaginative and creative; that a film could be effective dramatically when not photographic; and finally, of the greatest possible importance, that the mind of the audience could be brought into the play psychologically.[27]

The next major breakthrough was also a product of the German cinema of the Weimar period. F.W. Murnau's *The Last Laugh* (1924) established the independence of film as a medium of expression through its exemplary use of cinematic technique, including an unprecedented camera mobility and a purely visual approach to narrative which precluded the need for explanatory intertitles. The film was, Rotha argued, 'cine-fiction in its purest form; exemplary of the rhythmic composition proper to film'.[28]

Rotha's obsession with form unfortunately led him up some blind alleys. He constructs a rather curious hierarchy of thirteen forms of cinema, at the pinnacle of which stands the abstract or absolute film, epitomized by the work of Walther Ruttmann and Hans Richter, which represents the ultimate expression of the medium as a medium. At the other end of the scale we find the categories of 'the cine-fiction film' (including various genres such as comedy, satire, farce, costume and historical drama and spectacle) and 'the music, singing and dancing film'. In other words, the kind of films associated with the Hollywood entertainment film and its imitators, which presumably constituted the least creative and inventive uses of the medium. One of the immediate oddities of such a schema is that the types of work Rotha most admires —Soviet cinema, the work of John Grierson, the German cinema—end up being ranked quite lowly in the hierarchy of forms.[29] The overtly prescriptive nature of this approach opens Rotha up to justifiable criticism, V.F. Perkins for one using it as evidence of the kind of ridiculous hierarchy which for him is the logical conclusion of all film theory rooted in formalism.[30]

More interesting are Rotha's attempts to elaborate ideas concerning the essence of the medium. He shares with other theorists of the period an obsession with the unity of purpose of the work and the unified whole of separate incidents with a film. Elements of a particular film may be hailed as major artistic achievements, but these elements have to combine to produce an integrated work if the film is to be ultimately judged a success. For example, Rotha regarded Carl Dreyer's *La Passion de Jeanne d'Arc* as 'the most supreme example of the pictorial mind', but yet it ultimately failed as a film:

> Every shot in this extraordinary film was so beautifully composed, so balanced in linear design and distribution of masses, so simplified in detail that the spectator's primary desire was to tear down each shot as it appeared on the screen and to hang it on his bedroom wall. This was in direct opposition to the central aim of the cinema, in which each individual is inconsequential in itself, being part of the whole vibrating pattern.[31]

Fritz Lang is subject to a similar critique. While praising the technical brilliance of his image-making, Rotha ultimately suggests that 'Lang . . . does not appreciate the supreme importance of the assemblage of shots on the screen'.[32] Such a failing ultimately renders his work uncinematic.

For Rotha, the unity of a film was ultimately achieved by way of the combination of three acts of montage. Montage is defined here as 'the inclusive, creative and constructive unity that is present from the first gleam of the ideas in the mind of the scenarist, to the final act of assembling the film strips by constructive editing and cutting'.[33] The first act of montage concerned the assembling of thematic narrative, a process culminating in the construction of the shooting script. The second act encompassed the assembling of material in the process of shooting, as dictated by the script. This was in part based on the director's skills of observation and understanding of human nature and the expression of this by way of the full use of the resources of the medium. The third and final act of montage embraced the editing process, the assembling of the pieces of film, calculated to produce the greatest effect on the audience. For Rotha, these three acts of montage 'are the means by which a story or theme is translated into a succession of visual images on the screen; which is capable of producing considerable emotional effect on any given audience of people in any part of the world'.[34] While Rotha acknowledges the importance of the degree of collaboration involved in this process, ultimately behind it all stands the director, 'the sole controlling mind that organises the forms of montage'.[35]

This formulation is practically identical to Pudovkin's construction of film form in *Film Technique*, which first appeared in an English translation by Ivor Montagu in 1929. After stating the central importance of editing as 'the creative force of filmic reality',[36] Pudovkin proceeds to analyse the construction of the scenario and the production process, both of which he regards as profoundly shaped by the concept of editing. The role of the scenarist is to construct a shooting script which approximates as closely as possible to the final shooting form, and the editing is central to the pre-filmic construction of shots, sequences and the entire scenario. During the actual shooting, editing—the breaking up of actions into separate shots or elements which will be subsequently reassembled in the editing stage proper—facilitates the necessary transcendence of the actors and the action (and hence the film) from the constraints of the laws of real space and time. As Pudovkin puts it, 'between the natural event and its appearance upon the screen there is a marked difference. It is exactly this difference that makes the film an art.'[37]

Rotha's own explanation of the distanciation of film from reality is augmented by a distinction drawn between filmic and real time, a distinction, he argues, which constitutes the whole basis of cinematic representation:

> When it is grasped that the formation of a scene or situation in a
> film is purely a matter of the constructive editing of visual images,

then it will be seen that the film director creates his own 'time', as well as his own 'space . . . The material with which the film director works is not 'real' in the sense that it is actually recorded time or space, but is a number of pieces of celluloid on which real actions have been recorded.[38]

Rotha also concurs with Pudovkin's concept of the relationship between individual shots and edited sequences of film, a landscape being 'a mere photograph until it assumes its place in the organisation of visual images'.[39] Similarly, an actor is described by Rotha as 'only the clay with which a director works', as raw material to be used in the composition and construction of cinematic images. As he stresses, the true aim of the film-maker is not some reflection of pre-filmic reality but rather in the construction of a new reality, a reality grounded in the properties of the cinematic medium.

The Soviet influence on Rotha's theorizing is unsurprising given his enthusiasm for the achievements of film-makers like Eisenstein, Pudovkin and Dovzhenko. Indeed, he considered the technique of such directors to have 'developed to a state of efficiency equalled by no other film-producing country in the world'.[40] This inspirational quality was proving effective in other quarters. Eisenstein's *Battleship Potemkin* was screened by the Film Society in 1929 in a bill which also included John Grierson's documentary *Drifters*. And Rotha was only one of several critics who noted the influence of the Soviet master on this little film which was to prove such an important landmark in the emergence of the British documentary movement and the future direction of Rotha's own thinking and practice. In *The Film Till Now*, Rotha called *Drifters* 'the only film produced in this country that reveals any real evidence of construction, montage of material, or sense of cinema as understood in these pages'.[41] It offered an alternative way forward for a British industry crippled by aesthetic conservatism and a slavish adherence to the values of the Hollywood entertainment film.

But it is interesting to bear in mind that Rotha's enthusiasm for documentary at this stage is framed more in terms of film art than in the relation of the film to the real. Indeed, the stress which formative film theory places on distancing the film from reality, in order to conceptualize it as an art in its own right, necessarily works against the development of any technical properties or techniques which might be regarded as reducing that fundamental distance. It should come as no surprise then to learn that another logical outcome of this approach led theorists like Rotha to be at best indifferent and at worst hostile towards such technological breakthroughs as synchronized sound, colour and three-dimensional cinematography—all key stages in the complex teleology which André Bazin has dubbed 'The Myth of Total Cinema'.[42] But whereas Bazin saw the idealist desire 'to recreate the world in its own image' as inspiring the invention of cinema and its subsequent technical development, this ran contrary to the basic tenets of Rotha's concepts in 1930.

It was the arrival of the dialogue film in America and Europe at around the same time as some of the key works of formalist film theory were being published which concentrated much of this reactive nega-tivity. Along with most of his contemporaries, Rotha regarded the silent film as 'the original and highest form of cinema' and, consequently that the addition of dialogue would necessarily constitute a regressive step away from such purity:

> a film in which the speech and sound effects are perfectly syn-chronised and coincide with their visual images on the screen is absolutely contrary to the aim of cinema. It is a degenerate and misguided attempt to destroy the real use of the film and cannot be accepted within the true boundaries of the cinema.[43]

The problem, as I have suggested, lay in the perception that sound brought the cinema a step closer to the appropriation and representation of reality. The addition of synchronised speech therefore ran contrary to the proper development of the medium as dictated by its intrinsic properties. This was a position shared by many theorists of the period. As Rudolph Arnheim put it in 1932:

> The introduction of the sound film smashed many of the forms that film artists were using in favour of the inartistic demand for the greatest possible 'naturalness' (in the most superficial sense of the word).[44]

Synchronized dialogue also reduced the distance between film and theatre. Writing some twelve years before *The Jazz Singer*, Hugo Münsterberg was already sounding a caution about the desirability of the talking film:

> A photoplay cannot gain but only lose if its visual purity is
> destroyed. If we see and hear at the same time, we do indeed come
> nearer to the real theatre, but this is desirable only if it is our goal to
> imitate the stage.[45]

The problems with this mode of thinking are clearly apparent and
constitute one of the most serious charges against formative film theory
today. However, it is worth noting that not all theorists took quite such
an uncompromising stance against the coming of sound. Eisenstein,
Pudovkin and Grigori Alexandrov co-authored a statement on the use of
sound which was first published in English by *Close Up* in 1928. While
cautioning that the naturalistic use of sound to produce synchronised
dialogue threatened to destroy the culture of montage, the 'statement'
nevertheless conceded that the *contrapuntal* use of sound in relation to
the visual montage afforded new possibilities with regard to potential
combinations of sound and image.[46] Indeed, as Richard Taylor notes,[47]
by this time Eisenstein had begun to suggest that the language of the
silent film had reached its limits and that sound, if used properly, actually
offered a way out of this impasse:

> Sound, treated as a new element of montage (as an independent
> entity combined with the visual image) cannot fail to provide new
> and enormously powerful means of expressing and resolving the
> most complex problems, which have been depressing us with their
> insurmountability using the imperfect methods of a cinema
> operating only in visual images.[48]

The influence of the 'statement' by Eisenstein and his colleagues may
account for Rotha's enthusiasm for certain forms of sound, including
synchronized musical accompaniment, such as the famous Meisel scores
for *Battleship Potemkin* and *October*. Consistent with the Soviets' position,
Rotha acknowledges that sound, as opposed to synchronized dialogue,
had the potential to emphasize and enhance visual meaning.

Formative film theory's case against colour and stereoscopic films is
often constructed on similar grounds to the opposition to the dialogue
film. For Rotha, colour would only serve to submerge the photographic
qualities of the image on the screen. Indeed, in his foreword to the
first English translation of Arnheim's *The Film*, he praises the latter's
argument that colour restricted the formative virtues of the camera by
placing greater emphasis on what is constructed and enacted before the

camera.[49] Rotha's case against stereoscopic films, on the other hand, was based on the assertion that this would encourage a return to theatrical techniques, including the use of longer and longer takes, which were already a noted characteristic of the dialogue film:

> Gradually the powerful resources of cutting and editing will be forgotten and instead there will be long scenes lasting for minutes. There will be movement of players but there will be no movement of film.[50]

This judgement, echoed by Arnheim, is almost exactly the inverse of Bazin's enthusiasm for the long take or 'the sequence shot', which, in combination with deep focus, he so admired in the films of Orson Welles and William Wyler precisely because of the technique's greater fidelity to the real.[51]

From the vantage point of the present, these objections to technological progress seem ludicrous. Sound quickly established itself as standard, and while early sound production did entail significant constraints in terms of other aspects of production such as camera mobility, these were quickly overcome. Colour took some thirty years to become the norm due to a combination of economic and ideological factors, while stereoscopic film failed to amount to much more than a short-lived gimmick. Formative theory's failure to embrace technological development proved to be its downfall. The fetishization of the silent film made it blind to the idea that the cinematic medium could transform itself, could extend its technical and aesthetic potentiality. Such inherent conservatism imposed strict limitations on film theory's ability to explain, imprisoning it instead in a rigid prescriptiveness which was becoming increasingly remote from actual film practice.

The Turn Towards the Real

The appearance in 1935 of *Documentary Film* marked the beginnings of a self-conscious shift in Rotha's thinking, unequivocally announcing in the first sentence of the foreword that the purpose of the book was 'to replace the theoretical discussions in *The Film Till Now*'. Rotha was by now closely associated with the emergent British documentary movement as both practitioner and critic, and his first-hand experience of film-making had clearly impacted on an already shifting intellectual agenda. The intention of this new book was to 'convey something of the social and economic basis on which a certain method of film-making—that which we have called documentary—is now being built to fulfil certain purposes at this moment of political apprehension and social disintegration'.[52] The central importance of the political and social context cannot be overestimated. Indeed it is the direct engagement with material and historical circumstances—in particular the social consequences of economic depression, the rise of fascism in Europe and the threat of war—which distances *Documentary Film* from Rotha's earlier aestheticism.

While radically revising his opinions on the 'art' cinemas of Germany and France—now regarded as being concerned with solely aesthetic values—Rotha continued to praise the Soviet cinema for its active social commitment. A film like *Battleship Potemkin* served a social purpose; it was not merely art for art's sake and could be counted as a form of documentary. Grierson made a similar claim for Eisenstein as a realist, in relation particularly to works such as *Potemkin* and *October* which recreated important Revolutionary moments from recent Soviet history.[53] From now on the social aspect of cinema had to be prioritized if the medium were to stand any chance of fulfilling its potential as a means for informing and educating people, and in doing so, help to reverse the tide of economic and political deterioration. The commercial cinema could not possibly achieve this, therefore an alternative basis for production other than commercial profit must be found. The answer for Rotha was to lie in the sponsored documentary, which would be later elaborated upon his other major work, *The Documentary Film*, first published in 1935.

But the roots of this shift in perspective are already identifiable in Rotha's second book, *Celluloid: The Film Today*, a collection of observations updating the project of *The Film Till Now*, which appeared in 1931. *Celluloid* marks the beginnings of a rethinking of the relationship between the medium of cinema and the real. At one point Rotha identifies a story shortage crisis in film-making, constituted by a serious lack of fresh subjects for the screen. A possible solution lay in the greater use of real locations outside the studio: 'producers have only just begun to realise the enormous wealth of natural material that exists beyond the studio floors.'[54] Some advance had already been made in this direction by the Western which frequently used real backdrops, and Rotha also praises the German mountain film, *The White Hell of Pitz Palu* (1929), directed by Arnold Fanck and G.W. Pabst, which had the virtue of presenting scenery in its proper surroundings. Rotha had expressed his enthusiasm for Pabst in *The Film Till Now*, considering him 'perhaps the one genius of the film outside Soviet Russia'.[55] At the basis of Pabst's technique was an ability to use the camera to explore character psychology within a realistic social context. His second film, *The Joyless Street* (1925), examined the effects of war on the inhabitants of a dark street in Vienna:

> It tore away the American glamour, destroyed the romanticism, and exposed the stark reality of hunger and passion under distorted conditions. No film or novel has so truthfully recorded the despair of defeat, and the false values of social life that arise after war. . . .[56]

This engagement with reality clearly interested Rotha and was to mark the direction in which his thinking would increasingly turn.

Celluloid also contains an essay exploring various connections between the contemporary cinema and the naturalistic novels of Emile Zola. This analysis foregrounds categories such as 'scientific method', 'truth' and the relationship between characters and their environment which Rotha uses to link Zola's nineteenth-century project with those of film-makers like Pudovkin and Pabst. At one point he quotes Zola's defence against accusations of pornography and obscenity made against his work:

> 'For me there are no obscene works: there are only poorly conceived and poorly executed ones. Our analyses can no longer be obscene from the moment that they become scientific and contribute a document. . . .'

A Document? Is that not the nature of a film?[57]

The idea of film as a document reveals a rather different conception of the medium to that which constitutes it as an art.

In *Documentary Film*, Rotha continues this line of thinking with the 'real' coming to occupy a much more significant role in the film-making process:

> The documentarist goes to nature, or actuality, for his visual and aural imagery in the same way that a writer goes to the dictionary for the proper sense and spelling of a word. But just as a dictionary is not a great work of literature, neither is a series of photographic views, nor a chain of recorded sounds of natural objects and persons projected on a screen and through a loudspeaker, a documentary

film. It is the reason underlying the choice of natural material, and the purpose which is in mind for bringing it to life to the screen—that really constitutes film creation.[58]

It is clear that the major influence on Rotha by this stage had shifted from Pudovkin to John Grierson. Many of the ideas in *Documentary Film* owe a great deal to Grierson's own key statement on the form, 'First Principles of Documentary'. The subtitle of Rotha's book, 'The use of the film medium to interpret creatively and in social terms the life of the people as it exists in reality' is an extended, if somewhat clumsy, version of Grierson's famous definition of documentary as 'the creative treatment of actuality'. Their respective categories of the major traditions in documentary are almost identical. Both draw the same distinction between lesser forms of 'actuality' film including newsreels, magazine items and lecture films, and the documentary proper which involves a crucial shift from mere descriptions of reality to this idea of 'creative treatment'. Rotha regards the former as little more than 'recorded facts' which 'make no effort to approach their subjects from a creative or even dramatic point of view, no attempt to govern the selection of images by methods other than plain description, no endeavour to express an argument or fulfil a special purpose'.[59]

In his recent polemical attack on the entire basis of what he terms 'the Griersonian documentary', Brian Winston seizes upon the inherent contradiction in Grierson's formulation and proceeds to systematically critique the foundations, and many of the subsequent achievements, of the tradition of documentary film-making emerging out of the work of the EMB and GPO film units. Winston suggests that 'the supposition that any "actuality" is left after "creative treatment" can now be seen as being at best naive and at worst a mark of duplicity'.[60] Rotha himself comes close to tying himself in knots when reiterating the essential difference between the newsreel and the documentary:

> The essence of the documentary method lies in its dramatisation of actual material. The very act of dramatising causes a film statement to be *false to actuality*. We must remember that most documentary *is only truthful in that it represents an attitude of mind* . . . even a plain statement of fact in documentary demands dramatic interpretation in order that it may be 'brought alive' on the screen [my italics].[61]

It is interesting to consider that in his introductory remarks to the section on the 'evolution of the documentary' in *Documentary Film*, Rotha retains an attachment to the conception of cinematic creativity as rooted in editing, a key element of his earlier thinking. He makes a distinction between the theatrical tradition of the story film—which he refers to elsewhere as the entertainment film—and an alternative approach such as the documentary. This 'proceeds from the belief that nothing photographed, or recorded onto celluloid, has meaning until it comes to the cutting bench; that the primary task of film creation lies in the physical and mental stimuli which can be produced by the factor of editing.'[62] In this way the film cannot but remain distant from reality, which would appear to give credence to Winston's objections to the kind of claims made by the documentarians with regard to their claims on and to the real.

Rotha and Grierson's versions of the evolution of documentary form are almost identical. Both identify the centrality of certain key traditions. These include the romantic naturalist tradition associated with Robert Flaherty, the man-against-nature scenario of films like *Nanook of the North* (1922) and *Moana* (1926); and the continental realist tradition which included the 'city' symphonies of Walther Ruttmann, *Berlin: Symphony of a Great City* (1927), and Alberto Cavalcanti, *Rien que les heures* (1926). Despite Grierson's position of authority vis-à-vis this perspective, Rotha actually presents a more developed history of the documentary which includes a further two key formative traditions. These are the newsreel tradition of Dziga Vertov and his Kino-Eye group in the Soviet Union, and the propagandist tradition including both the work of the major Soviets like Eisenstein, Pudovkin and Victor Turin (whose 1928 film about the Turkestan–Siberian railway, *Turksib*, Rotha regarded as marking the beginning of a new documentary method to replace the initial wave of Revolutionary-inspired works) and the British documentary movement. 'Propaganda' was regarded by Rotha as central to the purpose of the documentary film and by implication the intrinsic nature of film as a means of illumination and education and therefore a cornerstone of modern citizenship:

> By adopting propaganda as an alternative basis of production, not only might the cinema serve the greatest possible purpose as a medium of almost unlimited potentialities and its films play an important part in the life of the State and its people, but production might enter into a freedom impossible to the entertainment film.[63]

But despite the greater elaboration (and, arguably, sophistication) of Rotha's account of the history and theory of documentary, the shadow of Grierson—the self-styled intellectual leader of the British documentary movement—unfortunately falls heavily on Rotha's writing about the form, both in this book and elsewhere.[64]

In order to probe deeper into the shifts in Rotha's concept of creative cinema from *The Film Till Now* to *Documentary Film*, it is important to consider the major economic, political and social upheavals of the period. The necessity for a theoretical engagement with reality becomes increasingly unavoidable at a point in history marked by the Western economies plunging into deep recession following the 1929 Wall Street Crash, in turn fuelling waves of political unrest which saw the rise of fascism. The ascension of Adolf Hitler in Germany in 1933 not only signalled the end of democracy but also the final extinguishing of an extended period of major cinematic creativity associated with the Weimar period. A combination of state censorship, the promotion of Nazi ideology in cultural life and the exodus of film-makers to Paris, London and Hollywood, effectively brought this era to an end. The situation was little better in the Soviet Union as Stalin began to consolidate his iron grip on every aspect of Soviet life and culture. Among those to suffer was Sergei Eisenstein, who had returned to the Soviet Union in 1932, after a frustrating three years in North America and Mexico, to discover that his prestige as the Soviet Union's leading film-maker had been undermined. He was criticized as an anti-realist and a formalist at the infamous Soviet Writers' Congress of 1934 where under Zhdanov's influence socialist realism became official policy.[65]

In his autobiographical account of the history of British documentary, *Documentary Diary*, Rotha recalls his own growing horror at the developments of the early 1930s. He refers to anti-war demonstrations, the reporting of Nazi atrocities, the rise of fascist tendencies in Britain, particularly from the press barons Viscount Rothermere and Lord Beaverbrook, and the 1934 hunger march, via extracts from letters he had sent to Eric Knight. But what is a little perplexing is that very little of this radicalism finds its way into *Documentary Film*. In his discussion of propaganda as a central aspect of the potentialities of the medium of cinema, Rotha notes the successful organization of filmic propaganda in the USSR, Germany and Italy, but offers no criticism of the kind of messages being propagated.[66] Curiously, he seems to imply that, as a matter of course, state-run propaganda was preferable to that developed in the interests of private capitalistic enterprise. This is one of the major weak points in his argument in that he fails to grasp that the interests of capitalism and the state may be mutually reinforcing, if not identical.

Part of the problem was Rotha's failure to develop and articulate a coherent political position in his writing. *The Film Till Now* contains an astute understanding of the economic context of production: how this constrained and shaped the works created within it, the operation of restrictive practices such as block and blind booking and how these gave Hollywood such a position of dominance in the world market, and the monopolistic nature of the industry itself.[67] However, despite his left-wing inclinations, Rotha's expressed belief in the virtues of the social democratic state denied him the more sophisticated critical insights of Continental intellectuals such as Georg Lukács, Bertolt Brecht, Walter Benjamin and Theodor Adorno, who in the 1930s were engaged in a series of fierce debates about the relationship between aesthetics and politics in the context of the contemporary social and political crisis in Europe. Without rehearsing all the major arguments here,[68] I will draw upon some of the ideas generated by this intellectual activity, in particular the rather positive analysis of the cinema offered by Walter Benjamin.

Rotha does at times talk in terms of a class-ridden society and the perpetuation of a hegemonic social system which operates in the interest of the dominant class. He blames the formal education system, at least in part, for its tendency to serve the political, social and economic interests of the ruling class. He also acknowledges the role of propaganda, including cinema, in perpetuating the status quo:

> All institutions, whether political, sociological or aesthetic, fundamentally reflect and assist in the maintenance of the pre-dominating interests in control of the productive forces of their particular era. To this the cinema is no exception.
>
> Hence it is clear that, under present policies of production, we cannot expect any film to deal impartially with such vital subjects of contemporary interest as unemployment, the problem of the machine, slum clearance, the relation of the white man to the native, or the manufacture of armaments. To do so would be to lay open to criticism some of the fundamental principles upon which modern society stands and for which the cinema, consciously or unconsciously, must act as a sort of deodorant.[69]

His solution is to find an alternative basis to production other than profit, the point at which he invokes the concept of propaganda. In addition to apparently failing to understand the role of the state in advanced capitalism, Rotha also seems to be wilfully naive in implying that the involvement of private industry in film sponsorship escapes being tainted by the kind of self-interest he routinely and regularly ascribes to the film trade. Brian Winston picks up on this, and while he is somewhat kinder to Rotha than Grierson, the force of his argument is that the ultimate interests served in the sponsored documentary were very much those of the sponsors, which in turn undermined the documentary movement's claims to political radicalism.[70]

Of all the major Marxist intellectuals struggling with questions of the relationship between aesthetics and politics during the 1930s, Walter Benjamin is clearly the most pro-cinema as a potentially progressive mass medium. To briefly rehearse his major argument, Benjamin saw cinema, as a new technology based on mechanical reproduction, inaugurating an era of the mass appropriation of art.[71] Traditional art forms had been marked by a concept of 'aura', a transcendent sense of authenticity or authority which served to depoliticize art by removing it from material and social concerns but which, in so doing, ultimately served the hegemonic forces of reaction. Mechanical reproduction, on the other hand, destroys notions of 'aura' and 'authenticity', reversing the function of art from being based on ritual to being based on politics. Consequently, the cinema was, for Benjamin, a vehicle for the emergence of a progressive new proletarian consciousness giving objective form to the reality and aspirations of the masses.

Benjamin shares Rotha's antipathy for the organization of entertainment cinema under capitalism. He suggests that the Hollywood star system actually preserved 'aura' at the level of the individual, and as long as film was dominated by the interests of capital, then no revolutionary merit could be accorded to film other than as a criticism of traditional concepts of art. On the other hand, he does display enthusiasm for the alternative practices associated with Soviet cinema which, for Benjamin, had allowed the masses to portray themselves, primarily in their own work environment. He writes:

> In Western Europe the capitalistic exploitation of the film denies consideration to the modern man's legitimate claim to be being reproduced. Under these circumstances the film industry is trying hard to spur the interests of the masses through illusion-promoting spectacles and dubious speculations.[72]

69

This comes very close to an advocacy of the kind of documentary idea elaborated by Rotha.

Benjamin also displays an attraction to the mechanics of form and their relationship to reality, which again suggests a certain affinity with Rotha. He suggests the relationship between a painter and a cameraman is akin to that between a faith-healer and a surgeon. The painter maintains in his work a natural distance from reality (as the faith-healer is distanced from his patient with a slight mediation via the laying on of hands), while the cameraman (like the surgeon) penetrates deeply into his subject. The picture obtained by the painter is a total one, while that achieved by the cameraman consists of 'multiple fragments which are assembled under a new law'[73]—that is to say via the process of montage. This dialectical relationship between medium and reality in the case of film was, for Benjamin, crucial to its progressive nature:

> Thus, for contemporary man the representation of reality by the film is incomparably more significant than that of the painter, since it offers, precisely because of the thoroughgoing permeation of reality with mechanical equipment, an aspect of reality which is free of all equipment. And that is what one is entitled to ask from a work of art.[74]

The mechanical nature of film also allowed human beings to see things that were invisible under conditions of normal perception. Slow motion, for example, allows a contemplation of movement hidden from the naked eye. This was further proof of the cinema's revolutionary social significance: 'The cinema introduces us to unconscious optics as does psychoanalysis to unconscious impulses.'[75]

Beyond the Documentary: The Appeal of Neo-Realism

The substantial element of Rotha's contribution to film theory was effectively complete by the mid-1930s.[76] For the next thirty years his creative energies would be directed primarily towards film-making as both a director and producer of documentaries. His writing activities, on the other hand, comprised mainly film reviews or polemics on aspects of film policy. However, his sympathies lay very much with the post-World War II preoccupation with realism. This informed the assumptions of both the major British critics of the period, including Roger Manvell and Richard Winnington (whose intellectual formation owed a great deal to the likes of Rotha and Grierson), and celebrated Continental theorists such as André Bazin and Siegfried Kracauer. Most accounts of the development of pre-1970s film theory foreground a fundamental shift in emphasis from the concentration on formal properties associated with Eisenstein and Arnheim to the realist theory of Kracauer and Bazin.[77] In his consideration of the significance of Kracauer within the context of the emigration of German intellectuals to America in the 1930s, Martin Jay suggests that the eclipse of formative film theory by realist positions was in part the result of the very success of the campaign to allow the cinema the status of art: 'by the time of the realistic counter reformation, movies had indeed become films, and it was no longer necessary to defend their artistic credentials'.[78]

Rotha was a personal friend of Kracauer and in the preface to the 1948 edition of *The Film Till Now* he lavishes great praise on the latter's first major book, *From Caligari to Hitler: A Psychological History of the German Film*, written in exile and first published in 1947. More important, however, is Rotha's endorsement of Kracauer's *Theory of Film*, which he had read in manuscript form. In the foreword to *Rotha on the Film* he is particularly enthusiastic about Kracauer's statement that 'the basic aim of the film artist is to invite his audience to share in the participation of life to ultimate social benefit of that audience'.[79] In *Theory of Film*, Kracauer elaborates an uncompromisingly realist theory of cinema which begins by arguing the identity of the basic properties of film and photography. Like photography, film 'is uniquely equipped to record and reveal reality and hence, gravitates towards it'.[80] It is this ontological relationship which is central to Kracauer's understanding of the medium, and which is some way from the Soviet conception of montage. Indeed, for Kracauer, editing did not encapsulate any essential creative property of the medium but merely served to establish 'a meaningful continuity of shots'.

Kracauer identifies two major tendencies in cinema history, the realist and the formative, the origins of which he locates in the work of the Lumière brothers and Méliès. Although certain traditions of film-making subscribe to one or the other of these traditions (documentary and newsreel v. expressionism and experimental film), most embrace some combination of the two. But, for Kracauer, the basic properties of the medium necessarily mean that in order to be truly cinematic, the realist impulse had to be dominant:

> As in photography, everything depends on the 'right' balance between the realistic tendency and the formative tendency; and the

two tendencies are well balanced if the latter does not try to overwhelm the former but eventually follows its lead.[81]

As for film being art, Kracauer argues that if film does lay claim to artistic status, then this is not analogous to the other arts which by virtue of being arts are autonomous from the real. As he puts it:

> in defining [certain films] as art, it must be kept in mind that even the most creative film-maker is much less independent of nature in the raw than the painter or poet; that his creativity manifests itself in letting nature in and penetrating it.[82]

One major element of Kracauer's approach to cinema that would have undoubtedly appealed to Rotha is his ideas concerning the social potentialities of the medium. Kracauer regretted what he saw as the alienating character of modern life, a consequence of the triumph of science over religion giving rise to a dominant belief system claiming authority from the 'truths' of nature. Yet this system actually generated greater realms of abstraction and distance from the substance of that very nature—constituting what Kracauer describes as a top-down system beginning with high levels of generalities from which experience is understood. This in turn created a fragmentary world where systems of knowledge barely connect with the physical universe they are supposed to explain. For Kracauer, one possible solution to this problem lay in the possibilities of cinema to redeem physical reality. Unlike scientific knowledge (and most art), film and photography operate in a bottom-up manner, working from concrete experience towards higher levels of generality. In reflecting and revealing the world to be made up of a myriad of small moments of experience, film can allow us to rediscover the world we have lost. Such a progressive conception of the medium has a great deal in common with Rotha's own enthusiasm for the potential of documentary to inform and educate, facilitating more effective function- ing of social democracy and revealing the distortions and falsehoods perpetrated by the enemies of social democracy.

Kracauer's pessimism about the modern world and championing of realism implies an antipathy towards the kind of post-war cinematic modernism associated with Michelangelo Antonioni, Federico Fellini and Jean-Luc Godard, which sought to probe the sense of alienation and fragmentation characterizing modern life. But to do so, they used techniques emphasizing these very qualities—in the way that the expressionists developed a mise-en-scène of confusion, paranoia and madness. It is instructive, although perhaps not surprising, that despite his youthful enthusiasm for the first wave of modernism in European cinema—associated in particular with the German and Soviet cinemas of the 1920s—Rotha failed to engage with this second wave. In his post-script to the 1967 edition of *The Film Till Now*, he displays a certain ignorance regarding the revolutionary techniques of Continental film-makers. He notes his regret that neo-realism should have 'declined into the fashionable *chic* of *La Notte* (1961), *La Dolce Vita* (1960) and *8 1/2* (1963)'.[83] His response to the French *nouvelle vague* is ambivalent, praising Truffaut for his sensitivity to life but criticizing Godard's aboli-tion of narrative and what he terms 'the cult of disrespect for knowing how properly to use the medium and its instruments'.[84] Moreover his enthusiasm for the British realist films of the early 1960s omits any reference to Tony Richardson, the most radically experimental of the 'new wave' directors.

In his writings, Rotha makes no mention of the other great theorist of cinematic realism, André Bazin. But one of their major points of contact is the shared enthusiasm for neo-realism. This aesthetic emerged out of the ruins of the Italian cinema in the immediate aftermath of World War II and is associated in particular with the early films of Roberto Rossellini, Vittorio de Sica and Luchino Visconti among others. Bazin's seminal writings on neo-realism, and in particular the work of Rossellini and de Sica, are well known and form a major part of the second volume of the English translation of his essays and reviews, *What is Cinema?*.[85] The appeal of neo-realism as an aesthetic lay in its unembellished approach to filmic narrative and mise-en-scène resulting in the creation of images of the daily struggles encountered by ordinary people, featuring non-professional actors and filmed entirely in real locations. For Bazin, as well as for certain practitioners such as Rossellini, neo-realism was as much a moral perspective on the world as an aesthetic. It was this moral imperative which recommended the movement to other socially commit-ted critics like Rotha.

By 1948 Rotha was already lavishing praise on Rossellini, compar-ing him to documentarians like Robert Flaherty and Joris Ivens. It is Rossellini's extensive use of location work in *Rome Open City* (1945), *Paisa* (1946) and *Germany Year Zero* (1947) that make him such an important figure for Rotha. This forged an even more successful link between documentary and fiction than had been achieved by either the Soviets in the 1920s or by the realist British cinema during the war:

> What Rossellini has done is to blend into an indivisible unity the fictional incident from its realistic expression, and done it with immense effect because of his own dynamic and persuasive personality coupled with his inherent sense of cinema.[86]

Like Bazin, Rotha was even more impressed by the work of Vittorio de Sica[87] and his screenwriting partner Cesare Zavattini, considering them the two most significant figures in Italian neo-realism. Of *Bicycle Thieves* (1948) he writes, 'I know of no other film that catches and dramatises everyday existence and shapes it to tell a story with such subtlety, observation and penetration',[88] while *Umberto D.* (1952) is compared to Stroheim's *Greed* in its controversial closeness to the harshness of reality. Again the combination of 'real people in actual surroundings, with all the suffering and pathos and delight in small things that are true of our own lives',[89] makes this a masterpiece for Rotha.

In contemplating Rotha's enthusiasm for Kracauer and the similarities between his assessment of neo-realism and that of Bazin, we can clearly see the distance he had travelled from the thinking which informed the first edition of *The Film Till Now*. The aesthete of 1930 becomes the socially committed practitioner of the 1930s and 1940s. Undoubtedly much of the explanation for this transformation can be located at the level of Rotha's own experience and the social and political upheavals of the 1930s. These same upheavals inspired Kracauer's thoughts on cinema, in terms of both his negative reading of German expressionism, which diverted attention away from the reality of the germination of a nascent fascism, and his positive appraisal of realism and the medium's redemptive potentiality. In the preface to the 1948 edition of *The Film Till Now*, where he first lavishes praise on Rossellini, Rotha suggests that 'the film is fundamentally an art based on observation' and that 'true observation is only obtained at first hand'.[90] This is a more significant shift in his thinking, remembering that in *Documentary Film* the creative potential of the medium still resides in editing.

The ultimate shortcomings of realist film theory are remarkably similar in substance to those of the formalism it challenged. The major flaw is a similar tendency towards prescriptivism and essentialism, a theory that by its very construction simply rejected or ignored anything falling outside its parameters. Hence Bazin's rejection of German expressionism and Soviet montage cinema on the grounds that neither aesthetic trend was able to reveal the reality of the world in the way that directors like Flaherty, Murnau, Stroheim or the Italian neo-realists were able to.[91] The restrictive perspective of the champions of British realism proved equally inadequate to the analysis and understanding of the range of cinematic forms which history has thrown up, vilifying anti-realist film-makers like Michael Powell and 'lurid' popular genres such as the melodrama and the horror film.

Rotha's own writing begins to lose its vitality and perceptiveness in the light of the eclipse of neo-realism by the late 1950s. As noted above, he was unable and unwilling to understand the work of the neo-moderns and his journalism in the 1960s lacks a coherent intellectual project. His column for *Films and Filming*, for example, is something of a jumble of observations on contemporary developments in the British film industry and film culture, nostalgic reminiscence about the achievements of European silent cinema and the British documentary and the odd raving about some current objectionable film-maker or aesthetic trend. While this is unfortunate it does not detract from his considerable achievements and consistent theoretical engagement with the development of cinema over the three decades during which his major works were published.

Concluding Remarks

I hope to have demonstrated already some of the reasons why Rotha remains an interesting and important figure in British cinema history. He was both a product of and a major contributor to the intellectual film culture of the 1920s and 1930s, a culture that vigorously promoted the film as a vital and explicitly international art form. This has had a major influence on certain trends in revisionist film history including the reassessment of the 'Continental' influence in British cinema: from the early formal experiments of Alfred Hitchcock and Anthony Asquith, through the contribution of major émigré directors and technicians, to the cosmopolitan sensibility of Powell and Pressburger. Some of the foundational writings of this intellectual film culture have also been subject to a productive reconsideration, most notably in the selection of essays from the journal *Close-Up* published in 1998,[92] providing a context for the reappraisal of Rotha's own central contribution.

Rotha's writing provides a fascinating insight into the central concepts and problems exercising theorists before the emergence of the kind of semiotic and psychoanalytical approaches that have dominated English-language film theory since the 1970s. His is also arguably the major British contribution to formative thinking about issues such as film art, the importance of montage in silent cinema, the social and political purpose of cinema, and the ethics of realism. The development of his own ideas tell us a great deal about the fundamental transformations which film theory underwent in the turbulent years of the 1920s through to the 1940s, in response to industrial, technological, social and political change. Moreover, in Rotha's case this transformation is encapsulated within his own thoughts over a comparatively short period, providing valuable insight into the shift from formalism to realism, the struggle with new cinematic forms and the coming of sound, and the attempt to embrace certain continuities—in particular the centrality of Soviet innovation—as well as the more obvious discontinuities.

The on-going debates about what a meaningful and vibrant British film industry might be are also reflected in Rotha's work. He was a tireless advocate of a state-subsidized cinema that played a central role in the maintenance and development of a progressive, socially democratic national culture. These ideas are increasingly relevant in the context of a media world dominated by the ubiquitous globalization of Hollywood. This hegemony has seriously impeded the development of other national cinemas and with them alternative voices, narratives and cultural expressions beyond those of corporate America. The confrontation between Europe and the United States over subsidies, quotas and audio-visual products in the context of the GATT trade talks in the early 1990s are just one recent example of this issue.

Finally, there are elements of Rotha's theorizing which move beyond the core ideas explored in this essay, suggesting nascent elements of a more modernist sensibility. Carney and Schwartz identify various points of confluence between the new medium of cinema and the experience of modern life in the late nineteenth and early twentieth centuries.[93] These include a new fascination with movement and spectacle, an 'increased appetite for mobile, kinetic sensation',[94] and an interest in the body as a site of vision and stimulation. While Rotha's approach to cinema tends towards reflections on cerebral rather than physiological properties of the medium, there are moments of a rather different kind of understanding. His appreciation of Eisenstein, for example, incorporates a keen sense of the kinetic effects of montage (this was before the Soviet film-maker and theorist's own key writings on the subject were available in English translation):

> [Eisenstein] builds with a remarkable process of cutting; an overlapping of movement from one shot to the next that filmically gives

double strength to his images. He seldom uses images without movement or material, unless it is to convey atmosphere (as in the shots of the gods and architecture in *Ten Days That Shook the World*), which he overlaps, thus emphasising the content . . . His films can only be described as producing the sensation of throbbing, pulsating, and prickling like that of a purring piece of machinery. The spectator is conscious solely of the instance, the astonishing urge of expression.[95]

Even more interesting is Rotha's identification of the emergence of certain inherently cinematic traits in early American film defying the overwhelming and, for him, regrettable, emphasis on theatrical technique and mindless entertainment. These traits included 'slapstick'—bringing to the screen certain actions which were unreal and impossible in reality (the early Disney cartoons were also seen as part of this tradition); 'melodrama'—entailing the virtue of movement of actors and materials, (included in this category were chase films and the swashbuckling exploits of Douglas Fairbanks); and 'spectacle'— particularly in the use of natural landscapes. Although the terminology used bears little resemblance to the subsequent utilization of the three concepts, collectively they signify a sense of cinema's ability to 'move' an audience in a physiological and emotional sense. The cinema's power to induce laughter, fear, tears and elation (suggested by the concepts of 'slapstick' and 'melodrama') is clearly given a positive ascription by Rotha, countering his generally negative analysis of the relationship between Hollywood cinema and its audience. This is augmented by the appreciation of specularity, although clearly it is here that one can detect the seeds of Rotha's later elaboration of the cinema's relationship to reality.

This kind of analysis has a great deal in common with Tom Gunning's recent work on 'the cinema of attractions'. This idea, explored primarily in relation to early film (pre-1906), foregrounds the ability of cinema to show rather than to tell. Gunning examines the exhibitionism of film, its penchant for display, and the particular affect this had on the spectator:

> the cinema of attractions directly solicits spectator attention, inciting visual curiosity, and supplying pleasure through an exciting spectacle —a unique event, whether fictional or documentary, that is of interest in itself.[96]

The ramifications of Gunning's ideas for the reconceptualization of the relationship between the realist and formative tendencies of early film (referred to by Kracauer above) are clear and are explicitly raised in the article. However, 'the cinema of attractions' has a great deal more to offer in our thinking of the shifting relationship between spectacle and narrative in the feature film from the days of silent cinema to the present. These are some of the key questions Rotha obviously pondered but was unable or unwilling to comprehend fully.

While Rotha may lack the fashionable intellectual profile of Eisenstein, Kracauer, Epstein or Arnheim, his passionate and sustained engagement with cinema invokes a formative moment of critical and theoretical activity which continues to provide a great deal of insight and inspiration. Above all, Rotha's work conveys a sense of recognition of the value and potential of the cinema and the struggle to articulate this meaningfully to intellectuals, practitioners and ordinary film-goers alike. While occasionally his writing may today seem naive, misguided or even reactionary (particularly in his rigid conceptions of Hollywood cinema), what is more important is the passion, the commitment and the fundamental belief in the medium of cinema which informed Rotha's writing. As such he deserves to take his rightful place in history as a significant and multi-faceted theorist, critic, historian, propagandist and practitioner. His contribution to the development of British film culture, and film theory, is considerable and should not be forgotten.

Notes

1. Alan Lovell, 'The British cinema: the known cinema?' in Robert Murphy (ed.) *The British Cinema Book* (London: BFI, 1997).
2. Rachel Low begins her fourth volume on *The History of the British Film* with a consideration of 'Artistic and critical theory in the twenties', a period which saw cinema gain an unprecedented new level of social and cultural respectability. Rachel Low, *The History of the British Film, 1918–1929* (London: Allen & Unwin, 1971).
3. Tom Ryall, *Alfred Hitchcock and the British Cinema* second edition (London: The Athlone Press, 1996), p. 7.
4. For a full list of founder members of the Film Society see the interview with Ivor Montagu in *Screen*, vol. 13, no. 3, Autumn 1972, footnote 8.
5. From statistics provided by Montagu in 'Old mans mumble: reflections of a semi-century', *Sight and Sound*, vol. 44, no. 4, Autumn 1975.
6. Jen Samson, 'The Film Society 1925–1939', in Charles Barr (ed.) *All Our Yesterdays: 90 Years of British Cinema* (London: BFI, 1986).
7. Tom Ryall, *Alfred Hitchcock and the British Cinema*, p. 14.
8. Kenneth Macpherson, 'As is', *Close Up*, vol. 1, no. 1, July 1927, pp. 8–9.

9. Paul Rotha, 'Technique of the art director', *Film Weekly*, 12 November 1928.

10. Rachel Low, *The History of the British Film, 1918–1929*, p. 23.

11. Tom Ryall, *Alfred Hitchcock and the British Cinema*, p. 14.

12. Kenneth Macpherson, 'As is', *Close Up*, vol. 7, no. 4, October 1930, p. 234.

13. J. Dudley Andrew, *The Major Film Theories: An Introduction* (London: Oxford University Press, 1976).

14. Vachel Lindsay, *The Art of the Moving Picture* (New York: Liveright, 1970), p. 44.

15. Riccioto Canudo, 'The birth of a sixth art', in Richard Abel (ed.) *French Film Theory and Criticism 1907–1939, Volume 1: 1907–1929* (Princeton, N.J.: Princeton University Press, 1988), p. 59.

16. Hugo Münsterberg, *The Film: A Psychological Study* (New York: Dover Books, 1970), p. 74. First published as *The Photoplay: A Psychological Study* (New York and London: D. Appleton and Company, 1916).

17. See Vuillermoz 'Before the screen', in Richard Abel (ed.), *French Film Theory and Criticism 1907–1939, Volume 1*.

18. Paul Willemen, 'Photogénie and Epstein', in *Looks and Frictions: Essays in Cultural Studies and Film Theory* (London: BFI, 1994), p. 124.

19. Abel, *French Film Theory and Criticism 1907–39 Volume 1*, Introduction to Part 2: 1915–1919, p. 110.

20. Leon Moussinac, 'On cinegraphic rhythm' (1923) in Abel (ed.) *French Film Theory and Criticism 1907–39, Vol. 1*, p. 281.

21. V.I. Pudovkin, *Film Technique and Film Acting* (New York: Lear, 1949) p. xiii.

22. See various essays in S.M. Eisenstein, *The Film Form and the Film Sense* (Cleveland: Meridian Books, 1957).

23. The most interesting of these include a two-part article entitled 'What is the art of the film?', *The Film Weekly*, 17 June and 24 June 1929, which set out Rotha's ideas concerning the essence of film art and his interest in the cinematic achievements of German cinema; and two articles on the importance of editing: 'Production—off the studio floor', *The Film Weekly*, 14 October 1929, and 'Rhythm—and its creation', 21 October 1929.

24. Paul Rotha, *The Film Till Now*, fourth edition (London: Spring Books, 1967), p. 126. All subsequent references are from this edition.

25. In spite of his general antipathy towards American cinema, Rotha does identify some major exceptions, film-makers who against the odds made important and interesting films. Their number include D.W. Griffith, Erich von Stroheim, Charlie Chaplin and Douglas Fairbanks, all of whom in different ways resisted the system to produce works of sincerity and genuine creativity.

26. Rotha, *The Film Till Now*, p. 89.

27. Ibid. p. 96.

28. Ibid. p. 100.
29. The list of categories of the following:
    The abstract or absolute film
    The cine-poem or ballad film
    The surrealist film
    The fantasy film
    The cartoon film
    The epic film (including *Battleship Potemkin* and *October*)
    The documentary or interest film (e.g. *Drifters*)
    The combined documentary and story interest film (*Nanook, Storm Over Asia*)
    The cine-eye and cine-radio films of Dziga Vertov and others
    The cine-record film (reconstructions such as Dreyer's *Jeanne d'Arc*)
    The decorative or art film (many of the German expressionist features)
    The cine-fiction film
    The music, singing and dancing film
30. V.F. Perkins, *Film as Film* (Harmonsworth: Penguin, 1972), see Chapter 1, 'The sins of the pioneers'.
31. Rotha, *The Film Till Now*, p. 301.
32. Rotha, 'The films of Fritz Lang', *Celluloid* (London: Longmans Green, 1931), p. 237.
33. Ibid. p. 343.
34. Ibid. p. 403.
35. Ibid. p. 344.
36. V.I. Pudovkin, *Film Technique and Film Acting* (New York: Lear, 1949), p. xvi.
37. Ibid. p. 58.
38. Rotha, *The Film Till Now*, p. 353.
39. Ibid. p. 389.
40. Ibid. p. 221.
41. Ibid. p. 318.
42. André Bazin, 'The myth of total cinema', in *What is Cinema?* volume 1 (Berkeley: University of California Press, 1967).
43. Rotha, *The Film Till Now*, p. 408.
44. Rudolph Arnheim, *Film as Art* (London: Faber & Faber, 1958), p. 130. This is the revised edition of Arnheim's *Film*, first published in Britain by Faber & Faber in 1933.
45. Münsterberg, *The Film: A Psychological Study*, pp. 87–8.
46. Eisenstein, Pudovkin and Alexandrov, 'A statement on sound', in Eisenstein, *The Film Form and the Film Sense* (Cleveland: Meridien Books, 1957).
47. Richard Taylor, 'Introduction', *S.M. Eisenstein, Selected Works Volume 1: Writings, 1922–34* (London: BFI, 1988), p. 11.

48. From 'A statement on sound', quoted by Taylor, p. 11.

49. In this foreword Rotha notes more than once his disagreements with Arnheim's analysis—particularly his views on the 'art' film and its audience and the latter's disregard for documentary, but he does concur with the negative assessment of technological development.

50. Rotha, *The Film Till Now*, p. 402.

51. Bazin, 'The evolution of the language of film', in *What is Cinema?* volume 1.

52. Rotha, *Documentary Film*, third edition, (London: Faber & Faber, 1952), p. 25. All subsequent references from this edition.

53. See, for example, John Grierson, 'The course of realism' in Forsyth Hardy (ed.), *Grierson on Documentary* (London: Collins, 1946).

54. Ibid. pp. 30–1.

55. Rotha, *The Film Till Now*, p. 263.

56. Ibid. p. 264.

57. Ibid. p. 220.

58. Rotha, *Documentary Film*, p. 131.

59. Ibid. p. 77.

60. Brian Winston, *Claiming the Real: The Documentary Film Revisited* (London: BFI, 1995), p. 11.

61. Rotha, *Documentary Film*, p. 117.

62. Ibid. p. 79.

63. Ibid. p. 59.

64. Grierson's presence is felt particularly in *Documentary Diary*, and one is left with the rather painful sense of Rotha's desire for approval which he obviously didn't always receive.

65. See Eisenstein's essays 'Help yourself!' and 'Pantagruel will be born' in Richard Taylor (ed.), *S.M. Eisenstein, Selected Works: Volume 1, Writings, 1922–34*.

66. Rotha's enthusiasm for Soviet cinema was, however, tempered with an astute caution. On a structural level he observed that the organization of the Soviet film industry appeared to provide a viable alternative model to the capitalistic basis of Hollywood and most other national cinemas. The problem was, however, the possibility of antagonism between the aims of the Soviet government who financed and controlled the industry and individual film-makers whose artistic impulses and development had to be subordinated to, and potentially stifled by, the needs of Communism and propaganda. In this sense, the economic constraints afflicting Hollywood directors were mirrored by political constraints for the Soviet film-maker. Rotha notes that while both Eisenstein and Pudovkin undoubtedly possessed 'a marvellous degree of technical accomplishment', their continued success depended very much on their abilities to continue to work within the system. The problems faced by Eisenstein, particularly

with the rise of Stalinist Social Realism, do not need to be revisited to appreciate the prophetic nature of Rotha's observations.

67. The industrial context of the coming of sound is subject to particularly close analysis, with Rotha identifying the centrality and power of the Radio Corporation of America (RCA) and American Telephone and Telegraph (AT&T) to this process of transformation. The extensive business connections of each are examined in some detail to demonstrate the extent of capitalistic domination.

68. For a detailed introductory examination of the debates associated with these writers, see Eugene Lunn, *Marxism and Modernism* (London: Verso, 1985). Key letters from these debates are included in the collection *Aesthetics and Politics* (London: NLB, 1977).

69. Rotha, *Documentary Film*, p. 56.

70. Winston, *Claiming the Real*, Chapter 12.

71. See Walter Benjamin, 'The work of art in the age of mechanical reproduction', in *Illuminations* (London: Jonathan Cape, 1970).

72. Ibid. p. 226.

73. Ibid. p. 227.

74. Ibid. p. 227.

75. Ibid. p. 230.

76. All of his subsequent major publications were to be either new editions of his two major works, or a self edited collection—*Rotha on the Film*.

77. See, for example, J. Dudley Andrew, *The Major Film Theories: An Introduction* and Andrew Tudor, *Theories of Film* (London: Secker and Warburg/ BFI, 1974).

78. Martin Jay, *Permanent Exiles* (New York: Columbia University Press, 1985), p. 174.

79. Rotha, *Rotha on the Film* (London: Faber & Faber, 1958), p. 22.

80. Siegfried Kracauer, *Theory of Film: The Redemption of Physical Reality* (Oxford: Oxford University Press, 1960), p. 28.

81. Ibid. p. 39.

82. Ibid. p. 40.

83. Rotha, *The Film Till Now*, p. 777.

84. Ibid. p. 778.

85. Andre Bazin, *What is Cinema?*, volume 2 (Berkeley: University of California Press, 1971).

86. Rotha, *The Film Till Now*, preface to the 1948 edition, p. 55.

87. In Bazin's famous phase, 'Rossellini's style is a way of seeing, while De Sica's is a way of feeling', 'De Sica: metteur en scene' in *What Is Cinema? volume 2*, p. 62.

88. Rotha, *Rotha on the Film*, p. 145.

89. Ibid. p. 186.

90. Rotha, *The Film Till Now*, p. 52.

91. See Bazin, 'The evolution of the language of cinema' in *What Is Cinema?*, volume 1, (Berkeley: University of California Press, 1967).

92. James Donald, Anne Friedberg and Laura Marcus (eds), *Close Up 1927–1933: Cinema and Modernism* (London: Cassell, 1998).

93. Leo Charney and Vanessa R. Schwartz, *Cinema and the Invention of Modern Life* (Berkeley and Los Angeles: University of California Press, 1995).

94. Ibid. p. 5.

95. Rotha, *The Film Till Now*, p. 232.

96. Tom Gunning, 'The cinema of attractions: early film, its spectator and the avant-garde' in Thomas Elsaesser (ed.), *Early Cinema: Space, Frame, Narrative* (London: BFI, 1990), p. 58.

ROTHA'S WRITING

I

THE ART OF THE FILM
THEORY AND CRITICISM

The selected writings in this section chart the initial emergence and subsequent development of Paul Rotha's conceptualization of 'the art of the film'. His writings were first published in the late 1920s in journals and magazines like *The Connoisseur* and *Film Weekly*. It was in the pages of the latter publication that his theory of film began to be expounded, culminating in the first major statement of his ideas in *The Film Till Now*. Parts of the central argument of 'The development of the film as a means of expression' (1930) had already been aired in short articles published in *Film Weekly* in 1929.[1] For Rotha, the development of film as an expressive art had been severely hampered by its unique relationship to the real, which restricted the imagination of film-makers to either detached scenes of 'real life' or, in the case of 'the story film', equally sterile filmed scenes from theatre or 'living photography'. But he proceeds to identify key landmarks in a more productive engagement with the medium's true potential, beginning with breakthrough films like *The Cabinet of Dr Caligari* (Robert Wiene, 1919), the first time in history that the director had worked *through* the camera, and *The Last Laugh* (F.W. Murnau, 1924), an expression of the film in its purest and most unified form. But it is the experiments of the Soviet film-makers that Rotha considers 'the most momentous advances' in film art, and in particular their preoccupation with the creative possibilities of editing.

As is noted elsewhere in this volume, Rotha's initial theory of film embraced Pudovkin's idea that editing constituted the very essence of the filmic medium. The articles 'Production—off the studio floor' and 'Rhythm —and its creation', which appeared in *Film Weekly* in October 1929, constitute Rotha's first attempts to expound a theory of this centrality of 'constructive editing and cutting'. Rotha's contrasting attitudes to the development of the medium in the United States and Continental Europe is also evident: American productions are occasionally 'saved from sheer mediocrity by clever cutting'; while European film-makers recognize that editing constitutes the essential art of the film. The second article concentrates on the techniques of Soviet editing in a succinct statement of the centrality of rhythm to the overall design and unity of film art. So crucial was editing to Rotha that in a review of the Soviet film *The Living Corpse* he totally ignores the input of the director, attributing the entire creative credit to Vsevolod Pudovkin's editing.[2]

While Rotha regarded American films as largely assembly-line fodder, produced solely for profit, the American cinema was not devoid of interest. In *The Film Till Now* he acknowledges the emergence of certain inherently cinematic traits in early American film which defied the overwhelming over-emphasis on theatrical technique (see p. 77 of this volume). Some of these virtues are elaborated in 'The magnificence of Fairbanks' (1930), the rhythmic beauty and perpetual movement of the star rendering him a quintessentially cinematic phenomenon; while the review of *City Lights* (1931), considered by Rotha to be Chaplin's greatest achievement, explores the subtlety and depth of the silent comedy and champions Chaplin's decision to hold out against the tyranny of synchronized sound.

But for Rotha, the vanguard of developments in film art remained firmly located in Europe. And despite emerging political problems in both countries, the Soviet Union and Germany continued to provide the most fertile soil for such experimentation. The review of Alexander Dovzhenko's *Earth* (1931) allowed Rotha to champion a very different kind of film technique to that associated with Eisenstein and Pudovkin. In this instance the centrality of montage is replaced by a more gentle and contemplative approach to the representation of rural life in a rapidly changing Soviet Union. Equally interesting is the retrospective reminiscence of Pabst, written in 1967. If Dovzhenko's virtue was a poetic rendition of the natural world, then G.W. Pabst's great achievement was the ability to blend elements of fact and fiction in features like *Westfront 18* (1930) and *Kameradschaft* (1931). For Rotha, what distinguished Pabst was his ability to make films which eschewed glamour and artificiality in the interests of social and emotional truth. In this sense his work is retrospectively regarded by Rotha as anticipating the later achievements of Italian neo-realism.

Having initially rejected realism as a stumbling block, Rotha developed an acute interest in the potential of film art to express reality. While this could occasionally be done within the confines of fiction, a more appropriate form was provided by the documentary. By 1931 Rotha had become closely associated with the emerging British documentary movement and his first film, *Contact*, appeared two years later. He was strongly influenced by the ideas of John Grierson and these provided a framework for his major survey and theoretical analysis, *Documentary Film*, which was published in

1935. 'Some principles of documentary' explores the strengths and weaknesses of the major traditions of the form including the romanticism of Robert Flaherty, the 'symphonic' approach of Continentals like Walther Ruttmann, the 'newsreel tradition' associated with the Dziga Vertov group in the Soviet Union, to the propagandist tradition of both Eisenstein and Pudovkin and the emerging British documentary movement. In different ways, all of these traditions evade the problems of contemporary life. Consequently, it is the need for social analysis, for the documentary to relate real human beings to their environment and to address the realities of the modern world as they are experienced, which Rotha presents as the major challenge facing film-makers. The related problem of how to effectively portray the individual (as opposed to stereotypes or undifferentiated members of the crowd) in cinema is the central focus of 'Films of fact and fiction' (1938), with particular emphasis on Soviet cinema and the British documentary. While Rotha remains committed to the art of the film, he comes close in both of these last two articles to suggesting that an over-investment in technique works against the film-maker's ability to interpret and analyse reality, alluding to what is an inherent tension in Grierson's famous formulation of the documentary as the 'creative treatment of reality'.

For most of the 1930s and 1940s Rotha channelled his major creative efforts into directing and producing documentaries. However, he retained an interest in developments in the feature film, particularly films which engaged in some way with real social experience and the problems of everyday life. It is unsurprising, therefore, that he should be so enthusiastic about the emergence of a neo-realist aesthetic in Italy in the aftermath of the war. While he admired Rossellini, it was the more intimate work of Vittorio De Sica and Cesare Zavattini which Rotha found most rewarding. The short reviews of *Bicycle Thieves* (1950) and *Umberto D* (1955) represent an articulation of this enthusiasm for a new kind of engagement with the minor daily events in the lives of people struggling against the kind of adversity which was only too real for many people in Italy and elsewhere after World War II. Neo-realism also proved to be a major influence on Rotha's film-making. It is arguably no co-incidence that he should direct his first feature film in this period. Released in 1951, *No Resting Place* tells the story of a family of Irish tinkers in a style which employs all the hallmarks of the Italian masters: the slightness of the story, the close relationship of character to environment, the interest in the everyday, and the restrained camera and editing technique.

Notes

1. Paul Rotha, 'What *is* this *art* of the film?', *Film Weekly*, 17 June 1929: part two continued in 24 June 1929 issue.
2. Paul Rotha, 'Constructive film "editing" ', *Film Weekly*, 29 July 1929.

The Development of the Film as a Means of Expression (1930)

(From *The Film Till Now*)

When considering the commercialism which surrounds the producing and exhibiting of any one film, the unscrupulous dealings and double-crossing which occur when a production is launched, it is surprising to discover how far the cinema has really advanced as a medium of dramatic expression. It has been seen how the film began its career and how it became popular with the public, but it is well to remember that the child film was nursed by a company of 'fur-dealers, clothes-spongers, and grocers' (to use the words of Mr Messel[i]) in whose hands it could hardly have been expected to rise above the lowest form of entertainment. Moreover, and the fact must be stressed, the primary aim of film producers is to make the maximum of financial return in the shortest possible time, a method hardly congenial to so intricate an art as the cinema.

The later part of this survey will show some of the real functions, capabilities, and potentialities of the film as a medium of expression, considered apart from any commercial point of view save that of general appeal. It is the aim here to preface these theories by actualities, to reinforce the potentialities of the cinema by analysis of the progress of the film until now, examining influences and estimating their worth, selecting some tendencies and rejecting others.

It is essential, in the first place, to assert that the film is an independent form of expression, drawing inspiration with reservation from the other arts. Furthermore, it should be remarked that the attributes of the film are derived from the nature of the medium itself, and not from other matters of subject, story-interest, and propaganda. It should also be remembered that the film is essentially *visual* in its appeal; and that light and movement are the two elements employed in the creation of these visual images. As I shall demonstrate later, the abstraction of the 'absolute' film is the nearest approach to the purest form of cinema, far removed from the commercial film, and descriptions will be given of their 'simplest' methods of psychological appeal through the eye to the mind of the spectator. Following this, there will be determined the other forms of cinema, descending in aesthetic significance through the epic and art film to the ordinary narrative film and the singing and dancing picture.

The scientific and mechanical advance of the cinema has developed with marked rapidity as compared with aesthetic progress, which has been either backward, or, in all but a few studios, absent. I have yet to explain that perhaps the greatest handicap imposed on aesthetic progress was the camera's misleading faculty of being able to record the actual. At an early stage, it was found that the camera was capable of registering a credible record of real scenes and events, thereby becoming a valuable asset to education, a reliable means of historical reference, and a potential method of discovery in the sciences. When put to these uses, the realistic properties of the film were good. Even to-day, the newsreel and topical budget are always welcome events in the evening's programme, especially when heightened in effect by sound. It must be emphasised, however, that no narration of story, or expression of dramatic theme, has place in this form of cinematic record. The appeal is purely *interest*. The audience is not asked to participate in the emotional feelings of stout gentlemen in top hats launching liners, or His Majesty opening a new home for destitute orphans. The audience watches the incidents with interest and listens to the dialogue in much the same way as it reads the evening paper. But when the camera came to be employed for the telling of a fictional theme, its realistic photographic powers were used instead of the creative imagination of the director, who failed to express the story *through* the camera. The latter almost at once became an instrument of photographic realism rather than a medium for the expression of creative imagination. Its real powers of distortion by means of exaggerated camera angle, slow-motion, and 'masking', and of transposition were completely neglected in the hasty striving after the obvious goal of realism. The power of the camera to record the actual on the screen fooled the audience into believing that its sole pleasure lay in the recognition of familiar things. Thus, at the outset of the story-picture, the film began its career on a false basis and it hardly need be stated, has continued along these wrong lines (with a few notable exceptions) until the present day, when the dialogue film is further extending the desire for realism, as are also the stereoscopic screen and the colour film. The exact replica of an object, accurate in every detail and measurement, cannot give the same emotions of pleasure as the real object. A photograph of a person is a very poor substitute for the actual being. It lies in the hands of the creator to utilise his imaginative powers in the creation of the replica, which is his impression, expression, or mental rendering of the subject. Because a picture is 'lifelike', it is not necessarily an exact rendering of the original. It is rather the artist's interpretation of the original, in which he has emphasised the salient characteristics. The spectator at once seizes upon the latter and recognises them as being akin to his own thoughts about the subject, which perhaps have been subconscious in his mind until the picture has brought them into sudden understanding. Further, the artist's conception may suggest thoughts about the original of which the spectator had no previous knowledge. This is particularly applicable to the film with its power of emphasis by the close-up. The very presence of commonplace objects takes on a fresh meaning when shown enlarged on the screen, when emphasised as playing a part in the whole pattern of life. And, above all, it is essential to remember that a picture can be a non-representative, as well as a representative, record of an object.

But it will be understood that actual progress of the film along its proper path has been slow, and is only defined in a small percentage of the many thousands of productions realised up till now. Mr Charles Marriott has suggested that 'art is a matter of the medium in which it is executed and a just balance between using that material in the imitation of nature and of abstraction, the degree of naturalism and the degree of abstraction being limited by the material.' This matter of 'the medium in which it is executed' cannot be stressed too much with regard to the cinema, for only on rare occasions is the film used rightly as its nature demands. The pleasure of film appreciation lies in the recognition of small developments, which do not often comprise the whole. It is rare to find a film that is in itself a step forward. Indeed, sometimes it is a reward to find one single sequence in a movie which suggests an advance in the film's capabilities. However discouraging the present position of the film may be, the worst director may unconsciously put forward a fresh idea of interest. Someone has got to go on making movies, even if they do not stop to ask themselves whether progress is being made.

With the production in 1903 of *The Great Train Robbery*, the story-film was launched on its long and prosperous career. The incident, or action, of the film became of first importance. An excellent example, which shows clearly how mistaken were the ideas of the pioneer directors, was seen in the *Comédie Française* films of 1908. Members of this celebrated theatre were persuaded to perform famous scenes from several of the French classic dramas, including episodes from *Tartuffe* and *Phèdre*, and to act them as they would on the stage, exaggerating their gestures into the lens of the camera. It was calculated by the promoters of the scheme that the appeal of the well-known scenes, coupled with the popularity of the celebrated actors and actresses, would achieve a wide success. The fallacy of the idea is obvious, of course, and the result was quite ineffectual. But it suggested to Adolf Zukor the great possibilities of famous plays and famous players, which, as is now well-known, developed into Famous-Players and later into the Famous-Players-Lasky Film Corporation, one of the biggest producing concerns in the world. From the time of the *Comédie Française* effort onwards, it became a natural course of events to appropriate subjects and persons hallowed by public approval, with complete disregard of their suitability, and to adapt them to the screen. This process is as common, if not commoner, to-day as it ever was. Stage stars are filling the film studios because of the dialogue cinema; any best-seller novel is bought for the screen; any name that comes into the public eye is snapped up for the movies. What of Elinor Glyn, Aimée Macpherson, Philip Yale Drew, and in the past Jack Dempsey, Georges Carpentier, and Steve Donoghue?

Gradually the acted story became the *raison d'être* of the film. Stage technique was modified, the gesture still being used in relation to the spoken word, and 'acting' became one of the necessary talents of the movie star. Upon this type of stagy performance, good photographic looks and the power of suggesting sexual passion has the infamous star-system of Hollywood grown up, a system that has been slavishly copied in this country. Quite frankly, this sort of thing is not film at all but merely 'living photography'.

Despite all opposition, the inherent assets of a medium inevitably assert themselves, and, in the case of the film, some of its simpler resources began to show at an early stage. This was not due, however, to any deep thinking on the part of the 'fur dealers and clothes-men', but to a natural course of development. They were to be found principally in the slapstick comedy, the melodramatic thriller, and the spectacle film. Of the three young tendencies, slapstick is the most interesting, for it utilised the fantasy capabilities of the cinema. It brought to the screen things that were unreal and impossible, but verified them by actual vision. All the devices of the camera, such as slow-motion, ultra-rapid motion, abrupt cessation of movement by camera stopping, and distortion, have their direct use in slapstick for achieving comic effect. This has now been augmented by the introduction of sound, which is capable of adding largely to comedy effect. In particular, reference may be made to the *Mickey Mouse* cartoon films, perfect examples of the sound and visual cinema. In an exceptionally early fragment of film prior to 1900, which was included recently in a souvenir film, *Royal Remembrances*, a motor-car ran over a policeman who was smashed by the impact into small pieces which subsequently rejoined themselves. This may be seen as an early example of consciousness of the capabilities of the medium. Years later, the same cinematic trick of breaking an object into pieces and re-assembling the fragments into a whole, was used for dramatic purpose in Eisenstein's *Ten Days that Shook the World*. The gigantic symbolic statue of the Czar fell and crumbled only to come together again with the assembly of the Kerensky Provisional Government. In devices of this kind, the mind of the audience is held between the fact that they know the incident which they are seeing is in reality impossible, and the veritable fact that there it is in actuality before their eyes. A wonderful state of mind with which to conjure! The great asset of the melodramatic thriller was its movement, exemplified in the chase-and-escape element, which displaced dull literary story-interest. The emotions of the audience when witnessing these melodramas of speed were roused to excitement by the action, and not by the meaning of the story. It was this call for movement that developed the faculties of the scenario-writer, who learnt to employ the film's capacities for parallel action and 'last-minute-rescues'. The value of the high-spot climax was appreciated and was led up to by the chase. It was from these melodramas and Westerns, with their essential fast movement, that the Americans learnt their slick flashiness which is the hallmark of their movies to-day. On the other hand, this feeling for movement has led to the false assumption that American films have tempo in comparison with the early German and Swedish productions. It must always be stressed that movement of actors and material is only one form of cinematic movement. The function of editing is equally as important, being the intrinsic essence of filmic creation.

In the middle of the striving for photographic realism, there came the first real aesthetic advance in the cinema. Just after the war, the first genuinely imaginative film made its appearance amongst the hundreds of formalised movies. This break in the monotony, this gleaming ray of light, deserves our closest attention.

Like a drop of wine in an ocean of salt water, *The Cabinet of Doctor Caligari* appeared in the profusion of films during the year 1920. Almost immediately it created a sensation by nature of its complete dissimilarity to any other film yet made. It was, once and for all, the first attempt at the expression of a creative mind in the new medium of cinematography. Griffith may have his place as the first employer of the close-up, the dissolve, and the fade, but Griffith's contribution to the advance of the film is negligible when compared with the possibilities laid bare by *The Cabinet of Doctor Caligari*. Griffith and his super-spectacles will disappear under the dust of time, if they have not already done so, but Wiene's picture will be revived again and again, until the copies wear out. In ten years this film has risen to the greatest heights, as fresh now as when first produced, a masterpiece of dramatic form and content. It is destined to go down to posterity as one of the two most momentous advances achieved by any one film in the history of the development of the cinema till now. *The Cabinet of Doctor Caligari* and *Battleship Potemkin* are pre-eminent.

Made for the Decla producing firm by Robert Wiene, of the Sturm group in the Berlin theatre, during 1919 (a period, it will be remembered, when expressionism and cubism were the doctrines of the advanced schools of the drama, the novel, painting, and sculpture in Germany, France, and Russia) *The Cabinet of Doctor Caligari* was released in March of the following year. It was handled in Britain at a later date by the Philips Film Company, now extinct. Wiene was almost an amateur in film production. The architects or designers, Walther Röhrig, Herman Warm, and Walther Reimann, were three artists absorbed with ideas of cubist and abstract art. It is only natural to assume that their intelligence saw in the making of a film an adventure in a new medium, a form of expression which they must have realised was wider and more receptive than the static stage and canvas, but an expression which to them at that date bore a distinct relationship to the other arts. It is not surprising, therefore, that *The Cabinet of Doctor Caligari* is in some places more theatre than film, and that there is a distinct tendency throughout to illustrate the subtitles with pictures. These faults, apparent now with a heightened knowledge of the film's capabilities, must be allowed for in the appreciation of the meaning of this remarkable picture. In technical accomplishment of camerawork, the film made little real progress. The photography, by Willi Hameister, revealed no new suggestion of camera-angle, all the scenes apparently being taken from a normal eye-level. Dramatic mood was achieved by contrasted lighting effects and by the design of the settings. Long shots and medium shots predominated, masked close-ups occasionally being used, and the old iris-in and iris-out method of beginning and ending a sequence was adopted throughout. The latter camera device was notably used for emphasising important matter, by opening or closing on to a face or a light, or on to the revolving roundabouts. These openings were not always circular in shape; the view of Holstenwal was discovered to the audience by a diamond-shaped iris, suitable to the twisted and angular houses of the distorted town.

The progress lay, rather, in the tremendous problem of how the camera was to be used. The result of Wiene's thought was sufficient to stagger the film production of the two continents out of its comfortable peace and calm.

In 1919, *The Cabinet of Doctor Caligari* put forward these dominating facts, which have lain at the back of every intelligent director's mind to this day: that, for the first time in the history of the cinema, the director had worked *through* the camera and broken with realism on the screen; that a film, instead of being realistic, might be a possible reality, both imaginative and creative; that a film could be effective dramatically when not photographic; and finally, of the greatest possible importance, that the mind of the audience was brought into play psychologically.

As a film, *The Cabinet of Doctor Caligari* asked everything of its audience. They were to take part and believe in the wild imaginings of a madman. They were to share his distorted idea of the professor of the lunatic asylum in which he (the lunatic) and they (the audience) were confined. The theme and the conception were absolutely remarkable.

The scenario was written by Carl Mayer and Hans Janowitz, and even now contains brilliant and absorbing story-interest. The continuity, perhaps a little difficult to follow, was well constructed and flowed with adequate smoothness. It is curious to note that after seeing *The Cabinet of Doctor Caligari*, it is the story, and its remarkable unfolding, which principally holds the imagination.

The settings, which were almost entirely composed of flat canvas and hanging draperies, furnished with such simple objects as ladder-back chairs and stuffed horse-hair sofas, were painted with two intentions in mind: primarily to emphasise the distortion of the madman's mind through whose eyes they were seen, and secondly to provide interesting decorative values of tone varying from rich velvety blacks to the purest whites. Wherever possible, the design and layout of the set enhanced the dramatic content or meaning of the scene. In the linear design of the painted floors, for example, the prominent, usually straight lines of pattern led the eyes of the spectator direct to the figures or objects of significance. The walls of the prison cell were arranged and painted in tall perpendicular planes, emphasising dejection. The prisoner, seated cross-legged on the floor, was the point to which all lines of the painted floor-pattern converged. Again, the warped and angular branches of the trees in the landscape strengthened the dramatic escape of Cesare bearing away the body of the unconscious Jane. The stool upon which the official-bound Town Clerk was seated was at least six feet high, symbolising both bureaucracy and the difficulty that Caligari had in obtaining attention. These are but a few examples of the emphasis of dramatic content by means of pictorial composition and settings.

The lighting, also, was arranged from this point of view, in complete co-operation with the designers. When the murder of the Town Clerk was discovered, a magnificent scene was shown of a darkened room, its walls sombre and angular, with the single source of light directed on to the beautifully grouped draperies of the white sheets. No corpse was visible, only the motionless figures of the policemen in the half-light, but there was no doubt as to the content of the scene. Although the *décor* was largely angular, at times contorted and twisted arabesques, Matisse-like, aggravated the scene, as when Cesare made his nocturnal entry in Jane's bedroom.

Of the acting there is not a great deal to he said, for the parts did not call for any great emotional skill beyond melodrama. This type of acting, together with heavy makeup, was characteristic of the atmosphere of the film. The titles, in accordance with the feeling of the whole, were irregularly lettered and strangely set out.

It may, perhaps, be asserted that this film has dated. Technically, as regards camerawork, stock, lighting, this is correct and naturally inevitable. But in meaning, content, suggestion, treatment, and above all entertainment, *The Cabinet of Doctor Caligari* is as convincing to-day as when seen years ago. It is true, also, that surrealism and neo-realism have superseded expressionism in the minds of the *avant-garde*, but this does not alter the fact that expressionism plays a large part in the film. Nevertheless, it is curious to remark that although *The Cabinet of Doctor Caligari* was a revolution in cinematic tendency, it has never been directly imitated or copied. *Raskolnikov*, directed by Wiene in 1923, and based on Dostoyevsky's novel *Crime and Punishment*, was assisted in dramatic emotion by Andrei Andreiev's cubist architecture, but could hardly be called an imitation. Rather was it an essay by the same director in a similar vein to an earlier success.

Comparison has also been falsely drawn between *The Cabinet of Doctor Caligari* and *Aëlita*, a film made in Soviet Russia by Protazanov with cubist settings. This is a delusion, for the sets and costumes of *Aëlita*, on which it is assumed the comparison is founded, were designed fantastically in order to express an imaginary idea of the planet Mars, and not, as in *The Cabinet of Doctor Caligari*, to emphasise the thoughts of a distorted mind. The cubist setting for Wiene's film was used purely because the audience were asked to imagine themselves thinking a madman's thoughts through the medium of the camera.

As a document of cinematic progress, the value of *The Cabinet of Doctor Caligari* increases year by year. Since its first showing, over ten years ago, it has been mentioned and referred to, criticised and revived, times without number. It has become celebrated. Practically all those who were connected with its production have become famous. There is no need to trace their course and recent successes; they are too well known. Only one word need be added, Robert Wiene never repeated his achievement. It is his sole work of genuine merit.

Although the appearance of *The Cabinet of Doctor Caligari* set working the brains of people both in and out of the film industry, and although it was a clear finger pointing one path for the cinema, one film, however great, cannot change the output of vast producing concerns. With its new ideas on the use of the camera as an instrument of expression, Wiene's film certainly influenced some of the more advanced American directors, but taken as a whole the productions of Hollywood remained on their former level. What *The Cabinet of Doctor Caligari* did, however, was to attract to the cinema audience many people who had hitherto regarded a film as the low watermark of intelligence.

Not until 1925, however, was a film to appear which wholly justified the position of the cinema. During the intervening period many remarkable films were realised, chiefly in Germany and in Sweden, which evidenced that brains were at work in Europe, but these were of less significance than would first appear. They naturally have their place in the gradual development and will be found dealt with more fully at a later stage. In 1925 *The Last Laugh*, the joint product of Murnau, Mayer, Freund, and Jannings, definitely established the film as an independent medium of expression. Unlike *The Cabinet of Doctor Caligari*, it had nothing in common with the theatre, but made full use of the resources of the cinema as known at that date. It was a remarkable example of filmic unity, of centralisation of purpose and of perfect continuity. It was made without sub-titles, with the single exception of a director's note, which changed the natural sad ending into a happy one, a superbly handled concession to the public. Everything that had to be said in this thematic narrative of an old hall-porter was said entirely through the camera. Not a written or spoken word was necessary to the correct unfolding of the theme. By psychological understanding, every action suggested a thought to the audience, every angle a mood that was unmistakable in meaning. *The Last Laugh* was cine-fiction in its purest form; exemplary of the rhythmic composition proper to the film.

After this date, 1925, the German cinema, to which students of the film were looking for further progress, began to decline, largely on account of the general exodus of talent to Hollywood. The art film (decorative in treatment and enveloped in an architectural environment of studio structures), for which Germany had built herself a reputation, was a commercial failure. The superb efforts of German creative directors drained the coffers of the industry, an unfortunate but indisputable fact. An argument for the failure of these films is the knowledge that the cinema is essentially modern, and modernism is, above all things, anti-romantic and experimental, reflecting as it does the spirit of the age. The German decorative films were for the most part romantic and spectacular, with a natural tendency towards the German love of the theatrical and the splendour of pageantry. Their tone was on a grand scale, at once serious minded and splendid, far from the superficiality of the American movie to which audiences were accustomed.

About this time, between the appearance of *The Cabinet of Doctor Caligari* and *The Last Laugh*, the wide-felt influence of psycho-analysis, which had swept over the post-war schools of painting and literature, was making its mark on filmic treatment. Many films, both from France and Germany, bore effects of psycho-analytical study, particularly those by directors who were striving after naturalistic methods, such as Lupu Pick, Karl Grune, and G.W. Pabst. There will be seen in the later section dealing with film psychology the important part played by the 'ineptitudes' of life in the revealing of inward phenomena. An early example of this groping idea was found ingenuously in *Doctor Mabuse*, but unfortunate as parts of this melodrama were, there is no doubt that Fritz Lang was feeling along the right lines. During this stage also, the machinery complex, which had occupied the Vorticists before the war, re-arose in a glut of composite shots of trains, trams, factories, and all types of machinery. At one time it was almost impossible to see a film without a double, triple, or quadruple exposure shot of wheels. For some years, expressionism also had its sway with the German film, despite an occasional breakaway into isolated individualism. The Expressionists were interested in Man in general and not in the Individual. Although they made use of the representation of characters, the result was not regarded as personal experience but as the essential experiences of humanity. Thus, it was usual to find themes woven around the Man and the Girl, as in Grune's *The Street*, Pick's *New Year's Eve*, Czinner's *Nju*, Lang's *Destiny*, with additions in the form of Death The Stranger and The Prostitute. It is of importance to note that nearly all these films were entirely studio-made, whole palaces and streets being built, providing a feeling completely different from the open-air films taken on a real location.

Some time later, the theme interest seemed to have been focused on individuals again and their peculiar characteristics, as with Pommer's jewel thief and policeman in *Asphalt*, and the two men and the wife in *Homecoming*. This was a swing round to the partial admission of the star system, a feature of the Americanisation of the German studios. Very different in texture, for example, was *The Hungarian Rhapsody* in comparison with the moral seriousness of *The Wild Duck*. There was a tendency towards individualism in the new German film and a feeling for a more materialistic spirit which was progressive. The first may be said to have been due to America; the second to the influence exerted by the Soviet films in Germany.

In contrast with the heavy morbidness and slow technique of the Swedes and Germans, the French school was marked chiefly by its directors' nineteenth-century delight in classical compositions and its continuous leaning towards spectacle. French films were roughly divided into two classes: the *avant-garde* of the *jeunes cinéastes* and the commercial film on the lines of *Atlantide, Michael Strogoff* and *Casanova*. Whereas the Germans had sought to gain their effects by a theatrical, traditional form of acting in conjunction with an environment of studio structures, the French experimentalists attempted the creation of atmosphere by a series of succeeding exterior compositions, usually of great pictorial beauty but non-dynamic. Nevertheless, although many of the *jeunes cinéastes* toyed with the cinema as their fathers had dabbled in their *ateliers*, several developed into directors of remarkable talent, as for example, René Clair, Jean Epstein, and Jacques Feyder, whose work must be considered apart from the usual *avant-garde* kindergarten product.

Meanwhile, it must be remembered that America was producing films in vast quantities during the years that the cinema was discovering its aesthetic qualities in Europe. The American cinema as a whole naturally demands wide investigation, which will follow at a later stage, but at the moment it is important to mention two outstanding tendencies that had grown up in Hollywood. A school of light, domestic, drawing-room comedy, displaying a nicety of wit and intelligence, had developed, to be carried eventually to as high a degree of perfection as this lighter side of film allowed. It had its origin in Chaplin's memorable satire *A Woman of Paris* (1923), as well as in Ernst Lubitsch's brilliantly handled *The Marriage Circle*, made in the following year. It was probably the result of a fusion between the existing school of Hollywood bedroom farce and the imported European talent, the latter being exemplified primarily by Lubitsch. Along these lines the majority of Hollywood's clever young men worked with a superficial skill, to produce many effervescent comedies and farces, sparkling and metallic, which provided light entertainment for the audiences of many nations.

In contrast with this movement in the studios, there had appeared a small group of directors who showed a preference for constructing their films around natural incidents and with real material; a tendency that had possibly grown out of the early Western picture. Robert Flaherty, Ernest Schoedsack, Merian Cooper, Karl Brown, and William Howard formed the nucleus of this group, to whom there should be added James Cruze, John Ford, and Victor Fleming, by reason of their isolated pictures which fall into this category. To Flaherty, however, must be given the full credit for the first film using natural resources, the inspiring *Nanook of the North*, in 1922, followed later by the beautiful *Moana*, in 1926. Other remarkable pictures characteristic of the natural-istic movement to be noted were *Grass, Chang, Stark Love*, and *White Gold*, all films that stood out sharply from the common run of American movies.

Apart from these two tendencies, only the work of Erich von Stroheim, King Vidor and Henry King, and the individualistic films of Chaplin and Fairbanks, emerged with real seriousness from the mass of machine-made movies up till the time of the dialogue film. In-vestigation of these, together with less interesting work, will follow.

Acknowledging the theoretical excellence of Pabst, the importance of Carl Dreyer's *La Passion de Jeanne d'Arc*, Clair's delightful comedies,

Feyder's impressive *Thérése Raquin*, and the domestic comedies of the American school, the most momentous advances of the cinema during recent years have shown themselves in Soviet Russia. Although the value which the Soviets attached to the resources of the film, and which they have developed with such skill, is constantly stressed in these pages, it must not be forgotten that the intensity of purpose so predominant in the Soviet film has been brought about by changed social conditions and political events since the revolution in 1917. Early Soviet pictures, such as *The Postmaster* and *The Marriage of the Bear*, contained little of the filmic creation of the present productions. When analysing the contemporary Soviet film, it has firstly to be understood that a production is seldom launched unless the thence contains some definite sociological or political meaning; because the Soviets have realised more than any other nation how powerful an instrument of propaganda is the cinema. It is partly out of the desire to express these contained ideas with the utmost possible conviction, and partly out of the exceptionally brilliant skill of the foremost Soviet directors, that the modern state of technical perfection in the science of the film has been reached. There has been a tendency in Britain and elsewhere, however, due to the always hasty enthusiasm of the intelligentsia, to call any film coming from the USSR a masterpiece. This is very far from being the case, for actually there are not more than about half-a-dozen really brilliant film directors in Soviet Russia. There are, of course, many second and third-rate directors, as there are in Germany or America, but it has become fashionable to raise their work to unusually high standards in London. The whole situation is rather reminiscent of that when the intelligentsia 'discovered' Russia in the first decade of this century; when it became the fashion to read Chekhov, Dostoyevsky, Gogol, Gorky, and Turgenev without discrimination as to their merits; when no studio was complete without its samovar, and ikons were all the rage for interior decoration.

Every Soviet film is, to put it crudely, a picture with a political purpose, and it is the duty of a Soviet director to express that purpose as clearly, powerfully, and vividly as possible. Added to which, it must be remembered that the cinema in Soviet Russia has been fortunate in having the wholehearted support of the Government, whose leaders have at all times fully recognised the value of the film for spreading their principles. Lenin regarded the theatre as a potential microcosm of the whole theories of Bolshevism, and determined to build a new theatre in Russia which would serve as a practical model for the people to learn from and to copy. The cinema, by reason of its limitless range and commercial superiority over the theatre, lent itself to the same idea. It will be recalled, for example, that the Government commissioned several films to be made in order to commemorate the tenth anniversary of the Soviet *régime*. *Ten Days That Shook the World* (original Soviet title, *October*) and *The End of St Petersburg*, were two of the results. Out of their efforts to meet this demand, Eisenstein and Pudovkin built up a form of film technique that is now unequalled for dramatic intensity. The same applies to more recent directors, to Dovzhenko, Ermler, Raizman, and Turin.

It is certain that the first Soviet experiments in film editing, employing strips of celluloid as the basic material, which is the foundation of almost all their film technique, were due to Lev Kuleshov, an instructor and film director in Moscow. From his original theories regarding the relation and inter-relation of pieces of film, which we may place about 1922, there have been developed the principles of constructive editing. Pudovkin, having studied for a while with Kuleshov, carried the idea further by devoting himself to using raw material as the foundation for his filmic working; whilst Eisenstein, having made his first mass film, *Strike*, in 1924, proceeded to enlarge on his ideas of 'intellectual cinematography'. To these directors must be given the credit for the most advanced forms of contemporary cinema and their theories are to be seen reflected in the work of almost all the lesser-known Soviet directors. From 1924 onward, therefore, the most interesting developments in the cinema have taken place in the USSR, and it is to this newly-constructed country that we must turn for modern tendencies towards progress.

Of the film to-day, I find it hard to write, let alone to tell, for the unbalanced state of the whole industry, together with the sweeping tide of the noisy dialogue film, are movements which strangle at the outset any attempt at progress in the cinema. To find the proper film it is necessary, first, to brush aside the sweepings from America and Britain, dissect the films from France and Germany with an open eye for second-hand virtuosity, and regard the new Soviet pictures with reservation in case they may be resting on their past successes. Of the wedded synchronised sound and silent film, co-ordinated into a filmic whole, there is as yet no concrete example, though one waits in anticipation for Pudovkin's *Life Is Beautiful*. It is possible only to watch the dialogue film and utilise one's imaginative power. Of the silent film but few examples come laggardly to Britain, often enough to be hidden away unseen. Occasionally a few of these may find their lonely way to the Film

Society, or to the affectionate screen of what is, at the moment of writing, London's only loyalist, the Avenue Pavilion.

Of the feeling prevalent on the Continent it is difficult to say, for news is rare of the silent film, and words and static photographs are inadequate to express the dynamic of film technique. The ever-moving theme, the relation and interrelation of thought expressed in moving images, is too elusive to be captured in print. It is, perhaps, only possible to sum up by disconnected statements of ideas, reactions, and observations.

The predominant characteristic of the film to-day is the growing tendency to find filmic expression by means of climactic effect. This process of image construction is the basis of Soviet technique, and has spread with rapidity into the minds of the more advanced German and French directors. There seems, moreover, to be a distinct striving after some form of arithmetic or geometric progression in the arrangement of visual images during editing, in the relation and interrelation of film strips. There is also a tendency to shorten the approach to a scene by the elimination of the long shot and the increased use of the close-up. The psychological effects made possible by the introduction of varied cutting by the Soviets is in the process of being carried to an advanced stage. Cross-cutting and intercutting are being utilised more as a method of insistence on the main object, than as the old-fashioned even distribution of dramatic suspense of the 'last-minute-rescue' variety. Symbolic inter-cutting is being employed as an aid to the emphasis of the central theme, as with the statue of Peter the Great in *The End of St Petersburg*. It is a dual theme of symbol and individual, connected mentally by association of ideas and visually by similarity of the shooting angle. It is being found that emotional effect is to be more easily reached by an intercut comparison to a like emotional effect.

There seems prevalent in the film to-day a more sensitive feeling for the association of ideas, which is finding filmic expression in terms of contrast and comparison, mental and visual. There are directors who in their work seek to establish by suggestion, contrast, and comparison, what may perhaps be called a continuity of human thought. One is emotionally conscious that the content of a theme is constantly ranging over more than one idea at the same time, a double purpose of mean-ing for the expression of which the natural resources of the film are admirably suitable. This affinity of ideas is marked by a connecting link, which may be said to be, in its terms of contrast and comparison, the essence of filmic treatment, both in the mental association of ideas by symbolism and by the actual visual likeness of one thing to another.

Contrasts appear to take on various aspects. The contrast of space between the interior and the exterior; between the close confinement of walls and the spreading horizon of a landscape; between the occupied and the unoccupied; between the full and the empty. The contrast of size, between the thick and the thin, the long and the short. The contrast of shapes, between the square and the circle, between a top hat and a cloth cap. The contrast of likenesses, so well exemplified by Vertov's gas mask and skull. The contrast of extremes, between the worker under-ground and the top of the factory chimney. There is an association of ideas between the mouth of a bugle and the muzzle of a gun. There is a comparison of likeness between the poise of an athlete and the balance of a horse. There is a similarity of motion between the stroking of one's hair and the stroking of a cat. There is the comparison of form, used so much for easy transference of thought in dissolves and mixes. All these factors make themselves apparent in the uses of cross-cutting for effect. They are filmic methods of strength, emphasis, enforcement of meaning by the association of ideas.

To be considered further but not necessarily to be accepted, there are the new theories of montage construction that have been put forward by Eisenstein. These embrace an entirely fresh method for the determi-nation of the relation that lies between the film strips in the assembling of a picture from its contributory lengths of frames. Eisenstein seems concerned with the disposal of the old, orthodox principles of editing (i.e. according to the time lengths of shots, the relationship of shapes, the association of ideas, etc., all of which produce sensations in the minds of the audience, ranging from sudden shock to smooth transfusion according to the will of the director) by the adoption of a new method which will be governed by the physiological sensations produced by over-tones of the visual and sound images. He is experimenting with the arrangement of shots, scenes, and sequences according to their degrees of emotional pathos by creative impulse, calculating to arouse the nervous reflexes of the spectator into responsiveness. He believes that, instead of an audience seeing and hearing a film, they should sense it; sense being the clue to the fourth dimension or over-tone, to be found in the beats of music and in the interval that exists between one visual image on the screen and another. On the assumption that both visual over-tones and sound over-tones are magnitudes of the same dimension (time) and that both are physiological sensations, he proceeds to new methods of filmic construction by a process of tonal and over-tonal montage. Naturally one awaits practical expression of his theories with interest before offering comment; other, that is, than those made manifest by certain portions of *The General Line*, which were not concerned with sound reproduction.

In actual production there is a welcome tendency towards the use of real material in place of studios and professional players. The cinema shows distinct signs of becoming film instead of theatre. Outside the USSR, Jean Epstein, John Grierson, and Hans Richter are seeking subjects in the commonplace instead of the artificially constructed, and there are also the few natural resources films in America. But these examples of the real film are but drops in the ocean of the movies of the world, overshadowed and dwarfed by the menace of the dialogue cinema.

Ridiculous as it may seem in the short span of life during which the film has existed, the process of misuse of the medium is repeating itself. General tendencies at the present moment show the misconception of the film to be greater and more difficult to unlearn than ever before. Directors as a whole are still only beginning to understand the potentialities of the film as a medium in itself. Its limits and delimits still present a broad field for investigation. It is just being realised that mime and gesture and the consciousness of the inanimate transmit an international idea; and that the pictorial meaning of the film is understandable to all according to their powers of sensitivity. But the main object to-day appears to be the synchronisation of the sound of the human voice with the photograph of the moving lips, and to reproduce the sound of visual objects in order to make them seem more real. That this is the desire of the American producers and directors is apparent from their advertisements. In brief, the introduction of the human voice merely relieves the director of his most serious obligation, to convey meaning to the mind by means of the resources of the visual cinema. The act of recording dialogue is *not* a further resource, as some theorists like to imagine. The dialogue film at its best can only be a poor substitute for the stage. From an aesthetic point of view, sound can only be used to strengthen symbolism and emphasise dramatic action, and experiments on these lines will be successful and justified.

On the heels of the usurping dialogue film comes the introduction of the stereoscopic screen and the colour film. Both of these inventions, wonderful though they may be in themselves, seek to achieve the realism so antagonistic to an imaginative medium. The cinema, with the addition of these new inventions, will degenerate into theatrical presentation on a large and economic scale. The true resources of the film will be swept aside in the desire for a straighter and more direct method of story presentation. The duration of time that a visual image is held on the screen is already becoming longer. As Mr Eric Elliott has so truly written: 'given a large stage scene with three dimensional effect, combined with colour and oral dialogue, it is tempting authors and producers to 'put across' the sustained dramatic situation of the theatre proper.'[ii]

Thus, there are few films which stand alone as achievements of real cinema, whilst there are many that miss greatness because of the negligence of the director or the obstinacy of the producer. Rare indeed is it to meet with an intelligent and sympathetic film producer; frequent indeed is it to meet upstart producers who make illegitimate claim to a knowledge of the film, riding roughshod over the conceptions of the director. If a film is to be a unity, clear cut and single-minded, the director alone must preconceive it and communicate its content to the audience through groups of interpreters of his vision, under his supreme command. The construction of a film from the first conception to the final product must be under the absolute control of the director. This is unhappily far from being the case.

But good films have been produced and good films will he produced in the future, although the opportunities to-day are more remote. Was it not René Clair who said that the zenith of the film was passed a few years ago? Yet, in Bryher's *Film Problems of Soviet Russia* (Pool, 1929), Pabst is said to have observed that 'Russia has taken one road and America has taken the opposite, but in a hundred years both will meet. England has taken neither, but will work out her own salvation independently, and in the end she will arrive at the same result.' This may be so, but I find it hard to agree when considering the present circumstances. Again, Mr Chaplin has written that '. . . it has been from the film itself, a device offering constant provocation to the imagination and senses of rhythm and colour that the sheer strength and crude grandeur of the motion picture industry have come. A giant of limitless powers has been reared, so huge that no one quite knows what to do with it. I, for one, am hopeful that Mr Wells shall settle the question for us in his next novel.'[iii]

Mr Wells has written that novel, but the question is no nearer being answered. *The King Who Was a King* was full of a thousand ideas, gleaned from a scrutiny of the output of Germany and America, but there was precious little in the book that had direct bearing on the position of the film itself. I believe that Mr Wells saw and realised the greatness of the film medium, but did not know quite what to do about it. And in any case his outlook was literary and not filmic.

For the most part the cinema still lies in the hands of those who desire to make it the means of the greatest possible financial return in the shortest space of time. One looks, therefore, to those in whose power it is to keep steady the direction of the advance of the film. To Chaplin, Fairbanks, and Flaherty in America; to Soviet Russia; to Pabst, Richter, and Pommer in Germany; and to the young men of France. With their wholehearted and enthusiastic support, the film can be diverted from the abyss towards which it is heading.

Notes

i *This Film Business*, by Rudolph Messel (Benn, 1928).
ii *The Anatomy of the Motion Picture*, by Eric Elliot (Pool, 1928).
iii In the foreword to *Films: Facts, and Forecasts*, L'Estrange Fawcett (Bles, 1927).

Production—Off the Studio Floor (1929)

(From *The Film Weekly*, 14 October 1929)

Many times I have been told that the great general public is not interested in the theory of films for which they pay to see; nevertheless, I am convinced from experience that there are a considerable number of people who are intrigued to know *why* and *how* they enjoyed this or that film. America claims to produce pictures that are of 100 per cent entertainment value, which means that their ingredients have been mixed in calculated proportions based on the statistics of exhibitors, who claim to have studied the wants of their audiences. For example, a film containing 50 per cent sentimentality, 30 per cent thrill (including at least two 'high spots') and 20 per cent strong, human drama, would be a sure box office attraction *before production*, and with the inclusion of a sex-appealing star, good photography, and technical accomplishment, would be guaranteed to make money for its producers. 'That', they would reckon, 'will pull big stuff in London.' Or, with a different proportion of ingredients, 'That will go over like hot cakes in the Middle West.'

Thus the human emotions, which when stirred produce enjoyment, are carefully analysed and played upon by the great producing firms in order to make money. Witness *Ben Hur* which drew its thousands to the Tivoli because of its 'high spot' chariot race and sea battle, a point that is given emphasis by the fact that outside the theatre a programme of events was exhibited, declaring '3.05 pm, the Great Sea Battle' and '4.28 pm, the Stupendous Chariot Race,' or words to that effect, printed in large red type to contrast with the lesser events of the picture. Similarly *The Trail of '98* is being advertised to exhibitors throughout England as being box-office value *because* of 'the snowslide where men, horses and dogs are lost as the avalanche buries them beneath tons of snow', and *because* of 'the White Horse Rapids, where the tiny boats were tossed about like driftwood among the mountainous waves that tore along at express-train speed.'

It may seem a far cry from these points I have raised to the theory of constructive editing and cutting, but when it is understood that editing is largely a matter of arranging sequences of film, capable of producing varying degrees of emotional reaction in their most effective order, and that the strength of these reactions is governed by the *tempo* of the cutting (i.e., the variation in length of the strips of film), then indeed, will be apparent the intimate relation that exists between this assembling, which has been so aptly called *montage* by the Russians, and the production 'according to formula' methods of America. I will not say that the editing and cutting of a film are entirely responsible for its being enjoyed or disliked, since the cross-currents of favourite stars and well-known stories are capable of producing bias, but I do believe that the quality of a picture is to a large extent dependent on them. There have been, for example, many American films that have been saved from sheer mediocrity by clever cutting. The slick Rod la Roeque and Richard Dix comedies are a case in point.

By editing, the very nature of a film can be moulded in a hundred different ways to express a hundred different meanings. It is well known that von Stroheim 'shot' so much film of *The Wedding March* that he offered to make two completely different versions of the original theme for his company. As it stands, the copy shown recently fails principally because of its *undecided* cutting and because the task of choosing and assembling 8,000 feet from the 200,000 'taken' proved impossible save at the cost of unity. The original conception of *Metropolis* was entirely changed by the English editor, Channing Pollock, and in the opinion of those who saw it in Berlin the English copy was far inferior to the Continental version. Such examples as these give some idea of the all-powerful part played by editing and cutting in picture making.

It is obviously impossible to generalise on the theory of editing and cutting, for the method adopted must be controlled by the nature of the material to be assembled. The practice in America is often to employ special cutters, who set to work on the negative as soon as it comes from the laboratory and produce films like ready-made clothing. This is a direct contrast to Continental methods, where the director considers the assembling of his film to be of almost greater importance than 'shooting' it and would not countenance it being cut by other hands than his own. This, of course, is aesthetically correct, though not perhaps a commercial outlook. A director presumably wishes his film to be a work of art, or at least of 'high intrinsic value,' whilst his firm desire it to be a money-making feature. The result being that one of the two objects is usually achieved. It is either a *Jeanne Ney* or a *Beau Geste*. That it can be both has yet to be proved. Again there was *Vaudeville*.

Rhythm—and its Creation (1929)

(From *The Film Weekly*, 21 October 1929)

From the point of view of the art of the film it is interesting to examine the basic rules of editing and cutting as understood in Russia, where this side of film technique has developed almost exclusively. First, the aim of Russian directors has been to express the actual reaction of a participant in the scene shown on the screen. This means that the camera is used as a mind as well as an eye, an idea, by the way, that has not occurred to British directors. If is did, it would probably upset their own theories. Secondly, a 'shot' is seldom repeated if taken from the same angle, unless it is desired to emphasis a special point of view. Thirdly, a 'shot' is held only long enough on the screen to be taken in by the audience. Fourthly, short cutting, being the use of small strips of film varying from perhaps six to sixteen frames and usually 'close ups,' in rapid succession, is employed to create a 'high spot' emotion. This has been foolishly called screen-hysteria. Fifthly, long cutting for obtaining a sad or soothing effect. By varying combinations of these methods of cutting almost any human emotion can be reached and made to react.

The assembling of strips of film is controlled by rhythm, which is present in many forms. An example is the contrast of action. In order to gain the greatest possible effect on an audience of a cavalry charge, for instance, alternate 'close ups' are shown in quick succession of the hoofs of the horses in fast action over the cobblestones and the motion-less bronze hoofs of an equestrian statue. The alternative cutting from swift action to solidity when repeated achieves a remarkable dramatic feeling of intensity. In the night club scene in *Crisis* Pabst wishes to get over on his audience the emotions raised by syncopation, dancing and jazz. He obtains this by taking a 'shot', with his camera travelling backwards, of a pair of exhibition dancers moving forwards with typical

Charleston steps, cutting alternately from their heads to their feet. In this way an effect is given which is impossible with a straight 'medium shot.' During the opening sequence of *Berlin* Ruttmann wished to express the rhythm of a moving train. He inter-cut short 'shots' of the wheels, the telegraph wires, and the rails, with a longer 'shot' of the coupling between two of the carriages, obtaining thereby an effect of 'three shorts and a long', so to speak, on the audience, causing them to experience an emotion that they must have realised in actuality. Just as rhythm governs these shorter sequences, so rhythm controls the design of the film as a whole, even to the inclusion and correct placing of the titles, and is thus the unconscious cause of enjoyment. From this it will be seen that the removal of a sequence or sequences of 'shots' in order to meet censorial requirements, can upset the complete balance of a film, even as would pieces of stamp paper stuck over the nude parts of pictures in the National Gallery destroy the appreciation of them as compositions.

Among the problems raised by editing and cutting, it is interesting to analyse that of camera 'panning', by which it is understood that the camera pivots, say, from a person on one side of a table to someone on the other, giving in between a panorama of the side of the set. The movement must obviously be fairly slow on account of the unpleasantness caused to the eyes of the spectator, and hence tends to slow up the action of the sequence in comparison to the method of cutting direct from one person to the other without waste of time. Similarly a travelling 'shot' bridges the gap between a 'long shot' and a 'close up' by movement rather than by cutting. Much is to be said for both these forms of technique, and their faults and their merits were to be well seen in *Piccadilly* where much of the action was slowed up by clever 'panning' with the result that people complained that the film dragged. As in long and short cutting, the nature of the action must decide which method is preferable. Great care should be exercised in choosing the exact points at which a travelling 'shot' should be cut. I do not believe that the audience should be made deliberately aware of the camera's movement as in *The Patriot*, where the start and finish of the 'shot' were apparent. This surely destroys the illusion built up by the whole art of the cinema. A travelling 'shot' should begin and finish with the camera in movement.

Another important point is the correct placing of a 'flash back' in order to gain the greatest effect and yet not unduly startle the audience. Much discussion, for example, was raised by the 'flash back' in *The Last*

Command from Hollywood to 'Imperialist' Russia. Was this the exact place to change over to the story within a story? To explain why and how the poor old general was in Hollywood? This is a matter of pure editing.

I have mentioned the placing of titles in relationship to their sequence as a matter of editing. This is a subject on which Pudovkin has again experimented. It is not necessary to show a 'close up' in conjunction with a dialogue title unless it is of vital importance to emphasise who is speaking the words. Of interest, too, is the splitting of a title, which can add tremendous power to its meaning. A title begins, is cut to a sequence of relevant 'shots'. The title continues, is again cut to the pictorial realisation. The title ends, and is followed by more 'shots'. Greater stress of meaning is gained by this splitting of a title than would have resulted from a single jumble of words. Simple repetition of a title at spaced intervals is again effective, as was seen by the title 'mother' in the film of that name.

Again I would like to touch on the importance of the scenario in connection with editing and cutting. That the scenarist should incorporate these in his script I hold to be absolutely necessary. During the 'shooting' of the material on which the director will eventually use his skill of *montage*, he must have a conception of his desired results after editing and cutting in his mind. He cannot, just for the sake of it, vaguely 'take' miles of film with the hope of editing it into shape afterwards, which is the damning fault of *The Wedding March*. When he comes to assemble he will probably find that, despite all his mass of material, he has not obtained the two most vital scenes in his continuity of building up an effect. It is essential for a director to begin with an almost complete visualisation of the whole, which is only possible with the aid of a detailed 'shooting' script and the knowledge of *how* he is going to express his conception by means of editing and cutting.

Lastly, in England the theory of *montage* is as yet under-developed and, unfortunately, shows the tendency to remain so. Perhaps one of the most vital causes of this backwardness is the apparent blindfolded attitude of critics towards editing. I quote a recent example:

> There is too much terminological bluff in connection with German and Continental films . . . We had Pudovkin here . . . talking about *montage*, the business of assembling all details of a story in order to

get the best climatic effect. . . . *Montage* and all the rest of it can be safely dismissed as methods of frightfulness.'

I can only add that this type of 'criticism' which reveals a lamentable state of mentality, can also be safely dismissed as valueless and detrimental to the progress of films in this country.

The Magnificence of Fairbanks (1930)

(From *The Film Weekly*, 10 May 1930; reprinted in *Rotha on the Film*)

Remarkable as it may be, Douglas Fairbanks, an acrobat who is unable to put drama into his gestures or emotion into his expressions, is one of the few really outstanding figures in the art of the American film. But then I have always held that 'acting' in the theatre sense is unnecessary and superfluous in the cinema. Fairbanks, by reason of the rhythmic beauty of his graceful and perpetual movement, is in my estimation utterly a product of the medium of the film. True, he has no talent other than his ever-present sense of action to support my claim, save perhaps a flair for showmanship so well exemplified in the recent *Taming of the Shrew*, but surely this marvellous feeling for natural rhythm, in the curves of his leaping from place to place, in the panther-like motion of his swinging stride, even in the rippling muscles of his superb form, marks him as a pure child of the cinema.

Alternatively bandit, pirate, freebooter, *lantsknecht*, knave, outlaw, or musketeer, he is always the same invigorating, stimulating, disreputable, defiant and attractive Douglas Fairbanks—the Essence of Heroism.

Added to which, he is wise enough to know his limitations. He never attempts, like so many celebrities, things which are impossible or outside the scope of his specialised skill. I am certain that he realises only too well that he is neither an actor nor an artist in the accepted understanding of the terms. On the contrary, he is something of far greater importance to the cinema—an acrobat of amazing accomplishment.

In all of Fairbanks's films every action, however small and insignificant, is the direct result of forethought and plan. I am convinced that he sees a foundation for rhythmical movement in almost every situation in the past and in the present. And just as Chaplin learned to walk the tightrope for the making of *The Circus*, so Fairbanks has learned to fence, to handle a whip, to throw a lariat, to cast a bolas, in order to meet the demands of the numerous roles he has played. This thoroughness is due partly to Fairbanks's tremendous enthusiasm for everything he does and partly because he sees in these accomplishments a basis for filmic movement, beyond mere acrobatic trickery. He realises that such actions are superbly graceful in their natural perfection.

At heart, Fairbanks is a complete romanticist. He delights us equally in the swing of his cloak, the fall of an ostrich feather from his hat, the hang of his rapier, the slender form of his doublet, the tilt of his curving spurs, as in the single movement with which he mounts his famous white horse and in his innumerable hairbreadth escapes. I recall particularly the prologue to his early picture *A Modern Musketeer*, which he elaborated later into the famous *Three Musketeers*, the sheer delight of *The Black Pirate*, and the inimitable bravado of *Robin Hood*.

In all his costume films he extracts the utmost from the clothes and environment offered by the period he has selected. His Petruchio in the *Taming of the Shrew*, clad in rags, applecore in hand, jackboot on head, propped against a column of the church, was to me a symbol of the romanticism of Fairbanks. It needed a brave man, a born hero, to carry off that crude costume. Nobody can deny that Fairbanks was magnificent. I can think of no other actor in the cinema who could have achieved so much bravado with so little concern.

The dominant note of all his pictures is his personality. Although none of them has been nominally directed by him, nevertheless his is the controlling mind underlying every detail. The spirit of Fairbanks is reflected in every factor of his productions; behind each movement, the construction of escapes and thrilling incidents, the design of the sets, the choice of the cast, the making of the costumes. Even the technical perfection of the camerawork and the drama of the lighting bear the mark of his discriminating judgement. The romantic mind of the man governs the architecture of the whole.

All the essential attributes of the cinema go to help the movement that envelops his pictures. The very properties of the camera, its device of slow-motion, add grace to his sweeping jumps, although he has yet to employ a smoothly moving camera to follow his actions. I would like his every swift move caught by the eagle-eye of a travelling camera, in the manner of the Germans.

In furtherance of his thoroughness, it has always been his principle to employ experts for the production of his films. He habitually surrounds himself with persons who make claim to artistry. He brought Maurice Leloir, the Frenchman, one of the greatest experts on historical costume, to Hollywood to supervise the costumes for *The Man in the Iron Mask*. He used the settings of William Cameron Menzies, one of the best art directors in Hollywood, and took Laurence Irving, a young British designer for the theatre, to America to assist on the architecture used in *The Taming of the Shrew*.

And now, after rumours have been spread for months, we learn that Fairbanks is increasing his interest in the Russian cinema and in particular in the work of the celebrated director, Eisenstein. Some years ago he is reported to have said that *Potemkin* was the greatest film he had ever seen. Both he and his wife visited Russia in 1926.

In displaying this interest in the technique of the Russians, Fairbanks is making a move that may lead him direct to the height of his fascinating career. I have followed his development from the early days of the 'moral uplift' pictures of the *Say Young Fellow, Reaching for the Moon, Down to Earth* and *He Comes Up Smiling* type through the cowboy 'out-of-doors' series of *The Man From Painted Post, The Lamb, Knickerbocker-Buckaroo* and *Arizona*, which culminated in the ever-memorable *Mark of Zorro*. Later there came the big spectacular films, *Three Musketeers, Robin Hood, Thief of Bagdad, Don Q, The Black Pirate, The Gaucho, The Man in the Iron Mask* and the recent dialogue picture *Taming of the Shrew*.

But there are two principal movements in cinema: that of the players and objects and that of the film itself through editing. Fairbanks has supreme mastery over the former. The Russian directors have alone reached a state of perfection in the latter. A fusion between the two *must* result in a film of brilliance.

City Lights (1931)

(From *Celluloid*)

During the thirty odd years for which the cinema has existed as a medium of expression, no other film has received such advance publicity as that accorded *City Lights*. No film has ever been more eagerly awaited by the general public, the small-witted intelligentsia and the film trade itself. Fanned to a pitch of semi-hysterical anticipation by the Press, the cinema-going public was prepared to find in Chaplin's new comedy a masterpiece of humour, eclipsing the brilliance of both *The Circus* and *The Gold Rush*. And, moreover, certain among this public expected a promised relief from the unceasing dialogue of the talking film.

For Chaplin's unwavering adherence to the film without speech but with a synchronised musical accompaniment had for three years been the subject of discussion and the butt for hostile criticism. When the tidal wave of dialogue swept through first the American and then the European studios, there was a considerable amount of speculation as to whether Chaplin would employ the spoken word or remain silent. By some it was rumoured that his voice did not record well—an assertion that has long since been disproved—by others that he feared to lose his world-wide reputation if he spoke; whilst in truth Chaplin merely stood fast by that marvellous natural instinct for the cinema which he has always possessed since the Keystone beginnings, and which is shared by other eminent film personalities who know enough of their medium to realise that speech is fundamentally foreign to the cinema.

The importance attached by most of the American film producers to Chaplin's decision with regard to dialogue cannot be over-estimated. Not that it was prompted by any real desire to see the cinema continue along its right curve of development, but because Chaplin, it must always be remembered, has a very wide appeal throughout the world, wider probably than that of any other film actor, and the bookings on his pictures represent considerable financial profits. Quite apart from Chaplin's status in the art of the cinema, producers cannot afford to ignore his box-office attraction, and it is not unreasonable to suggest that practically the whole of Hollywood hung in suspense with bated breath and quivering bank balances to watch the public's reception of a film without speech.

In order to realise the significance which the showing of *City Lights* was to have, it will perhaps suffice to mention that during 1930 an average of one hundred and twenty telephone calls per week were made to the New York office of the United Artists Corporation by people interested to ascertain the date of the first presentation. No film as yet distributed by that company at that time had ever drawn so many requests for advance bookings from exhibitors in every part of the world. It is to the point, also, to recall that *The Circus* still holds the record takings at the Mark Strand Theatre in New York, receiving £16,200 in one week, just four times as much as the film which had been showing the previous week. At the Dominion Theatre, London, *City Lights* took £12,200 in its first week in February of this year. Some slight idea as to the extent of Chaplin's commercial value and of the importance accorded by producers to the making of *City Lights* may be gathered from these figures.

And not only because of its promise of no speech has *City Lights* assumed world-wide notability. In the trade it has caused confusion and bad blood, for Chaplin's terms of renting have been the subject of heated argument, to which at the time of writing no satisfactory decision has been reached. Bitter to the last and jealous of his vast appeal, irritated possibly that his retention of subtitles suggests a triumph over monotonous dialogue, the trade watches Chaplin as if waiting for the chance to tear him down. By their refusal to accept his terms for the picture, certain circuits of cinemas may hope to boycott *City Lights*, for if they can succeed in beating down Chaplin it may affect the renting prices of pictures for some years to come. Even the popular Press shares this jealousy of Chaplin, and during the presentation of *City Lights* in London several cruel and singularly small-minded articles appeared calculated to disturb his well-earned success.

It is obvious that Chaplin would not have challenged the film companies of America and Europe on the battlefield of speech and silence without a great deal of forethought. A man who has spent eighteen years of his life achieving greatness in one medium and with his responsibilities would not, in the face of the universal adoption of the talking picture, spend three years and the larger part of his money on the production of a synchronised film without being absolutely confident as to the correctness of his beliefs.

From the time when the recorded voice was first employed in conjunction with screen images, Chaplin must have observed the futility of the attempt. But it is one thing to realise an absurdity and quite another to ignore it, or even to be in the position to pass it by with contempt. In all probability Chaplin, being an independent producer-director, was the only man in Hollywood who could afford to be guided by his own convictions. Unlike other directors, he was not obliged to carry out the instructions of a production-committee. He was free to stand by his decision that dialogue was a menace to the screen's power of expression. He was free to establish his belief in himself and his belief in cinema before the assembled audiences of the world. And, above all, he was free to retain the universal appeal of his language, the visual appeal of acrobats, dancers and clowns, in fact the integral essence of slapstick; whilst the remainder of the industry had crippled its markets in spite of the futile attempts to make multilingual pictures.

The idea underlying the theme of every Chaplin film is easily comprehensible to anyone, irrespective of nationality, to a greater or lesser extent of understanding according to their sensitivity. This simplicity of appeal is more apparent in the love story of *City Lights* than in any of Chaplin's preceding pictures. And because the appeal is based quite logically on the fundamentals of the science of the cinema—movement expressed in terms of pictures set to a perfectly fitting accompaniment of musical sound—it is wider than that of the dialogue film with its limits of nationality. Moreover, *City Lights* possesses two qualities without which no film can be really successful—imagination and inventive power —both of which have been almost wholly absent from the cinema during its dialogue phase. For three years, at least ninety five per cent of the world's film output has been concerned with the spoken word; it was left to Chaplin, the foremost director in America, to exert his influence and prove that the pursuit of speech was unnecessary. Undoubtedly *City Lights* will enjoy wide success, particularly because it is the work of Chaplin, but still more because it provides the relief from speech for which the majority of people have been waiting with such remarkable patience.

A slender thread of narrative usually supplies the story-interest of a Chaplin film, a simple theme drawn from the dozens which comprise the complexity of living from day to day. Around this central motif are hung innumerable comic situations, mere incidents to provoke uproarious laughter resulting from Chaplin's amazing faculty of invention. But however amusing these comedy gags may be in themselves, never for one moment does Chaplin forget the main theme of his picture.

The love of a penniless tramp for a beautiful but blind flowergirl which forms the story of *City Lights* has by now become celebrated. Yet I would again remark on its extreme simplicity of construction and the perfectly straightforward manner in which it is unfolded to the audience. The continuity has the admirable smoothness which we have come to expect from Chaplin; its merit will be revealed by a comparison with almost any talking film of to-day.

Opening with a magnificently conceived scene of the unveiling of a statue to 'Peace and Prosperity' by the eloquent officials of a large city, we discover Chaplin recumbent in blissful unconsciousness in the lap of the central figure. (Incidentally, how delightful is this burlesque on statues and how typical is this particular one of the sort that most citizens admire!) After immoderate laughter as we watch his efforts to descend from his couch, he escapes the inevitable arm of the law and wanders aimlessly along the streets, pausing here and there to inspect an artshop's window, until passing conveniently through the doors of a stationary car, he encounters the dream of his life, the flowergirl by the railings. We are enchanted by his immediate adoration but suddenly we touch pathos as he realises, almost clumsily we think, that she is blind. A moment of prickling emotion (for right at the beginning we are convinced of the hopelessness of his love) when unwittingly she empties the dirty water from a vase over him as he sits by the railings watching her actions, and then he is away into a rapid series of gloriously funny situations with his suicidal millionaire friend, who whilst drunk adores him but when sober completely forgets his existence.

Onward through a succession of brilliant gags until again we meet the flower girl and Chaplin becomes her beloved friend. By all manner of clever contrivances, suggested by the use of sound, she is made to imagine him a rich and handsome young man. Why should she not, when he buys every flower in her basket with money borrowed from the drunken millionaire? Only we and Chaplin share the tragic truth and scent the coming disillusion.

Having established his love, again he plunges into slapstick with that wholeheartedness which is essentially Chaplin's, until we return to the girl and learn of her distress. Money is needed for rent and Chaplin, determined to preserve his position in her estimation, sets out to earn the required amount. But inevitable misfortune awaits him at every turn. He becomes a street-cleaner only to be dismayed by a procession of circus animals; he enters for a boxing contest with deplorable results; but eventually, after horrible suspense, he exacts not only the rent from his millionaire friend but enough to cure the flowergirl of her blindness.

For a while he goes to prison for having robbed the millionaire, who unfortunately becomes sober enough to deny his gift. Then, after months have passed, he is released, and we follow him slouching once more along the side-walk. By chance, the victim of a newsboy's peashooter, he pauses beside the flowershop in which the girl, now cured of her blindness, is installed. Taking pity on his dilapidated appearance, she gives him a flower. He stares at her with bewilderment—fear in his eyes as to what she will think if she sees in him her benefactor. Still without knowing him, she jokingly gives him a coin so that he may pay her. As she takes it from his hand, she suddenly recognises the familiar touch. She gazes perplexedly at this odd little man, scarcely believing her eyes, whilst he waits her decision. Then, as his expression is still that of hope as she looks at him with confusion, we slowly fade to a dark screen with a close up fixed in our minds that is amongst the few to be remembered for ever.

It is quite beyond my power adequately to describe the emotion aroused by this moment of terrible intensity and agonising suspense. Coming at the close of the picture, after all that has gone before, it lifts the cinema high above its companion arts. In no other medium could such suffering be so strongly and feelingly expressed, especially in one that counts the spoken word among its attributes. Here, as at a hundred other places throughout the film, we breathed a prayer of thankfulness for Chaplin's silence. All the pathos in the world is on the screen in this concluding shot of the most fragile love story that has as yet been conceived in the cinema.

That is the story of *City Lights*: it would seem a slight skeleton for what is in my opinion one of the most moving and certainly one of the most entertaining films produced during the dialogue period. But in its slightness rests its power—the power of simple appeal—as the expression of a single personality.

Chaplin is Chaplin to all mentalities and to all classes. The fact that he delights the severest critic does not affect his world-wide popularity. He has always appealed to a vast number of filmgoers who revel principally in his comicalities, in the sight of his bowler hat and his big boots, in the succession of ridiculous situations into which he wanders, and in the diversity of funny characters against whom he pits his ingenuity. I do not think that the great masses which flock to his films see deeply into the pathos underlying these humorous adventures, but there is no reason why they should not enjoy his pictures, as indeed they do, to their hearts' content.

The truth is that a Chaplin film touches so many aspects of life that every kind of mentality can find something of particular application to its own existence. The profundities of *City Lights* are so deep down that few probably of those who have seen it have plumbed it to the depths. Delight for the masses, by which we mean entertainment, lies easy to behold on the surface. Everyone can see the humour of *City Lights*, especially when the gags are so well invented. You, I and the man next to me, all laugh when Chaplin swallows a toy whistle out of a cracker and it sounds its doleful note every time he hiccoughs. He is a figure of fun to the meanest intelligence. When the flowergirl drenches him with water because she is blind we burst into laughter, but our mirth is checked abruptly as the significance of the incident dawns on our mind. For a moment, perhaps, we are sad and then Chaplin, with his genius for timing the exact length for which to hold a mood, whirls us away into pure slapstick.

Yet when the picture is finished, we are left buoyed up by hope and enthusiasm, for despite his pathos Chaplin's spirit of endurance is never allowed to flag. Failure after failure reward his efforts, his well-meaning intentions are frustrated by wrong interpretation, but still his energy persists and he conceives some fresh miracle of ingenuity by which to attain his ends. We laugh as we watch his discomfiture, but we know that it might well be our own.

The most conspicuous quality in the direction is Chaplin's honesty of treatment. He is perfectly frank in the handling of each scene, using only the bare essentials of the material to convey his meaning. Never by any chance does he attempt to be clever or to achieve an effect by any but straightforward methods. No incident catches our eye without it playing to the full its part according to plan. No object, however small, claims our attention unless it is related to the content of the scene. Everything that comes within range of Chaplin at once assumes importance. A flower, a banknote or a horseshoe becomes alive as soon as touched by Chaplin, alive in our imaginations as well as alive in its own surroundings. He constructs his situations with a minimum of detail but every object must have its value or else its presence on the screen is a waste of time. Immediately he makes contact with an accessory there springs up an intimacy between that thing and himself. Its place in that particular scene instantly becomes apparent to us. Yet again I would stress that this simple understanding of all Chaplin's actions is not restricted to any one class or nationality; his thoughts and ideas are universal, which makes him the world power that he is.

In my estimation, though here I am at variance with many critics, *City Lights* is Chaplin's greatest accomplishment. For me it contains more creative work, more subtlety of direction and more evidence of singleness of purpose than any of his earlier pictures. It is more direct in its appeal and more comprehensive in its meaning than many of its predecessors. It is so obviously the untouched work of a brilliantly creative mind, although perhaps this is more noticeable to-day when so much mechanical product is around than when we saw that earlier masterpiece *The Gold Rush*. It seems so happily unsullied by any commercial artifices and is, of course, the better entertainment because of this. Chaplin does not think in terms of box-office values: he bases his work on a knowledge of the impulsive and natural behaviour of the ordinary human mind, which is, in effect, entertainment value. He foresees how his audience —whether in London, Lapland or Liberia—should react to any given scene and takes infinite trouble so that the construction of this scene is such that the audience cannot fail to react as he desires.

To a sensitive mind the tragedy of *City Lights* is devastating. The humour lies there on the surface, easily picked up and not long-lived, but the pathos of the whole theme and the pathetic mood of one or two individual scenes is too deep down to be lightly forgotten. I admit that I am moved beyond words by the scenes of the dilapidated but happy Chaplin and the exquisite beauty of the blind flowergirl. They move me a thousand times more than the tractors of the Soviets, Clarence Brown's Garbo, or Anthony Asquith's machine-gun. Yet I have met people who have been bored to death by *City Lights*. I even know a scenario-writer who was unable to sit through the picture.

Conceived from a multitude of aspects, every sequence and every scene, every shot and every detail of *City Lights* has been deliberately and carefully preconceived in the preparation. Chaplin is fortunate in possessing a wonderful sense of visualisation. Whilst working on a set he can look far ahead on to the screens of the world and into the minds of his audiences. It is almost impossible to pick out a single shot from this film and maintain that it would have been more effective if taken otherwise. Similarly, the time-lengths of his shots on the screen are right to the fraction of a second, never a frame too long or too short. I should imagine that he assembles his shots purely on the spur of the moment. He certainly does not cut according to any orthodox formula arrived at by involved arithmetical calculation. He judges the screen-length of a shot by watching its projection, as is customary with most American editors; but so good is his technique that we in the audience forget that we are seeing reels of projected celluloid.

I have already spoken of his amazing inventiveness of detail: in *City Lights* he excels himself. The picture is filled to overflowing with evidence of his imaginative power. To take the humorous gags alone, what could be funnier than the toy whistle, the mixing of the paper streamers and spaghetti, the ascending and descending pavement lift, and the superbly staged boxing match? It would seem incredible that such simple yet, at the same time, cunningly ingenious situations have not been made use of before, but I cannot recollect having seen them. Admittedly, much of the humour of these incidents is supplied by the accessory objects employed by Chaplin, or rather I should say by the way in which he fits them to his purpose. As Gilbert Seldes has pointed out, we must never allow ourselves to forget that Chaplin owes his existence firstly to the attributes of the camera and secondly to the choice of Mack Sennett. We can never separate him from the Keystone comedy from whence he sprang and of which these accessories are a part, and it would be fallacy to attempt to do so.

On the other hand, take the scene when he is visiting the flowergirl's home. With infinite delight he presents her with a plucked duck, claps an imaginary gun to his shoulder, takes aim and clicks his tongue. She at once thinks that he, as her young and handsome hero, shot the duck. But unfortunately she begins to stroke the bird and he, anticipating the result, rapidly seizes it and places it aside before the mischief is done. His pantomime here in illustration of how he brought down the bird is little short of marvellous. It is almost comparable with the ever-memorable Oceana Roll in *The Gold Rush*. Yet another piece of detail of the thousand that comprise this fabric of laughter is his last gesture as he is clapped into gaol—a flip of his heel to send his cigarette-end spinning with gay abandon into the air, summing up in one action his whole attitude towards life. And so on throughout the picture, touch after touch of magnificent imagination. Perhaps it is the surety of his actions which compels our admiration.

On the synchronised musical accompaniment to *City Lights* I have not much to comment. As a critic wrote at the time of its première, the music arranged by Chaplin fitted the picture like a glove, and I can imagine no better description (*The Times*, February 28th, 1931). It will suffice to say that it is never obtrusive and always has as its aim the emphasis of the mood of whatever scene it is accompanying. On the other hand, it must not be thought that this score is a definite indication of the sound film of the future, for it is far from that. Although in places the sound is employed with imagination, such as the satire of voices by musical instruments at the unveiling of the statue, *City Lights* is ostensibly a silent film with music and titles. And, in passing, I would suggest that at least half of the latter are badly written and the remainder superfluous, a fact which is rather surprising if the film received the production care which it is reputed to have done.

I have remarked before on the tendency towards naturalness that has characterised the Chaplin pictures as one by one they have come before the public, and I have pointed out that he has gradually eliminated the caricaturish element from them. Moreover, with this transition of his characters from the grotesque to the natural, the plots of the films have become more logical, until in *The Circus* and *City Lights* they are almost commonplace. The background and supporting cast in the latter picture possess all the outward appearances of everyday places and persons, and only on occasion are used as symbols of satirical comment, as in the opening. Miss Virginia Cherrill as the blind flowergirl behaves perfectly normally and does things that a flowergirl would do; but Miss Edna Purviance, you will remember, quite often comported herself according to slapstick conventions. The crowds that shoulder Chaplin aside as he wanders along the street are similar to those employed in any American picture, very different from the extras engaged for *A Dog's Life* and *Shoulder Arms*. Even Mr Harry Myers, whose playing as the double-minded millionaire adds much to the humour, is only eccentric in his behaviour and not unnatural in character. Such naturalness may be deplored by the fervent admirers of the old Keystone slapstick, but I feel that it does much to help widen the appeal of *City Lights*.

Chaplin is always the same likeable character. Wandering on to the screen to join a bunch of idlers, he passes through a whirlwind of adventures in which he suddenly and quite against his will becomes involved, until he leaves again a wanderer. It is three years since he was seen sitting on an upturned box in the middle of a field, gazing disconsolately at the star on a fragment of paper torn from the hoop through which the girl jumped, all that remained of the circus ring and his loved one. He shrugged his shoulders as only Chaplin can, flicked his cane, and cheerfully walked away into the distance in his inimitable manner as the screen darkened. From that empty field he has come to a great city and, homeless as usual, found shelter for the night in an about-to-be unveiled statue. Yet again he falls in love, this time it would seem with more success. In fact, the suspense of the ending of *City Lights* gives many people reason to believe that this film is his swan song, the end of all things, which I do not believe.

If *City Lights* be regarded from a detached point of view, and if for a moment we are indifferent to Chaplin's engaging personality, we shall see that it is quite different in texture from any other current picture of American origin, and in particular from the comedies of Harold Lloyd and Buster Keaton. There is no quality in it to suggest that it was produced in the neighbourhood of Hollywood. It does not bear the American studio imprint as do most American films, especially the comedies of Lloyd and Keaton. It might, for instance, have been made in England, with the exception of one or two minor points such as the policemen's uniforms and scavengers' clothes. It might be a film of any city or a synthesis of all cities.

This international quality which distinguishes all Chaplin's films is, I think, worth considerable attention. It is not unconnected with the relation between Chaplin, as an independent producer-director of films, and other directors whose creative ability is held in check by the production-committee of the ordinary studios. A more significant example of the difference that exists between the two distinct types of film production—the individual creative picture and the mass production product—could hardly be found than a comparison between either Harold Lloyd's *Feet First* or Buster Keaton's *Parlour, Bedroom and Bath* and Chaplin's *City Lights*. All three are tremendously amusing, but what widely divergent methods lie behind their construction. And although the three films in question happen to be representative of the comedy element in cinema, the object lesson provided by their comparison—they were all to be seen in London about the same time—applies equally to other types of theatrical pictures.

While not wishing to be accused of invidious intent, I do not think that either Harold Lloyd or Buster Keaton are ever likely to be reckoned as serious creative artists, or even comedians who resort to any great lengths of imagination or inventiveness in order to provoke laughter. They are content to rely on a series of clever and compromising situations thought out with great labour by a well-paid staff of 'gag-men,' amplified these days by an occasional wise-crack. To all intents and purposes both *Feet First* and *Parlour, Bedroom and Bath* are mechanically constructed articles from two of the most skilled firms of movie-makers, Paramount and Metro-Goldwyn-Mayer respectively, products of that one-hundred-per-cent efficiency of organisation which is the foundation of the American film industry. These pictures are calculated to make people in their millions rock with laughter, and there is little doubt that they succeed in this aim. They are played for a week or a month according to their worth, and then are forgotten, for they contain precious little to justify remembrance.

City Lights, on the other hand, is the work of three years' spasmodic but concentrated imaginative effort by a sensitive and exceptionally brilliant creative artist. Its humour is perfected by a hundred small touches that have taken many months to find their correct expression. Below its surface lies an age-old theme retold with fresh beauty and sentiment, a theme that has perhaps lain dormant in Chaplin's mind for many years and has now found its fulfilment. Into this film the man has put his last ounce of mental energy and probably the greater part of his financial earnings. It is the outcome of a single mind.

We all know which of these films deserves our unstinted admiration, but because we have paid to see each of them they are reduced to the same level. The laughter-making machines and the genius are both dependent for their existence upon a public of millions, a public which cannot differentiate between the superficiality of the one and the depth of the other while it laughs at them both. And yet it is beyond question that when in fifty years to come students make research into the development of the cinema, they will discover Chaplin in every reference, predominant then as he is now, whilst Keaton and Lloyd will have faded into oblivion.

Contemplation of Chaplin's position as an independent producer may well be made, and we can applaud his achievement of such a status, for had he not been at liberty to follow his own course when the rest of the screen talked, we should have seen him destroy all that *City Lights* means to-day with the lugubrious banality of speech. If only more directors were able to achieve this enviable position, we should have many more worth-while films instead of so many patently committee-made products. Fairbanks, it is true, has reached the stage of independent production, but amongst his many gifts he has not that of creative ability. But there are directors in America who have that power, and I would that they could aim to strike free from the trammels of studio routine. I wish that it were possible for more independent pictures to be produced, along certain commercial lines but without the tyranny of the studio executive-committees.

There are scarcely any directors in the cinema to-day who can make films as they wish, and who are allowed to rely on their own experience of what the public desires in the way of entertainment. Chaplin is not by any means the only director who is capable of independent production, but he is the only one who has broken free from the herd. King Vidor, Erich von Stroheim, John Cromwell, George Hill and Josef von Sternberg, to mention but a few, would each probably make infinitely more interesting films if it were made possible for them to do so. The stranglehold of the big companies and the difficulties presented by distribution, however, prevent this from becoming a reality.

And so, after years of hard work and shrewd foresight, as well as the development of an individual and rare instinct for the fundamentals of the cinema, Chaplin triumphs. He has defied commercialism in the interests of natural cinematic progress, and he will most probably win. At the moment, it is impossible to forecast the influence that *City Lights* will have, but it is possibly significant that speech is being severely curtailed in forthcoming American pictures, a tendency that can be directly traced to *City Lights*, and to a lesser extent to René Clair's post-synchronised *Sous les toits de Paris*.

I am conscious that these remarks on the genius of Chaplin and the greatness of *City Lights* do not altogether reach to the root of the matter. But words are hopelessly inadequate to express emotions brought about by a constantly moving succession of images which rely for their appeal on pictorial value, and which are the product of a deep-thinking, amazingly creative mentality that has as its breath and life the fundamental essence of the cinema. In truth, Chaplin has reached nearer to the heart of real cinema than them all.

Earth (1931)

(From *Celluloid*)

Since the films produced in the Soviet Union have become the play-things of the boys and girls of London's smart set, to say nothing of the denizens of Bloomsbury, Chelsea and Hampstead, it is fashionable to argue both for and against the Russian cinema. When, on the one hand, a hoary-minded critic denounces the films of Russia as one and all hysterical subversive propaganda which incite ordinary men and women to raze the Houses of Parliament to the ground; and when, on the other, a youthful enthusiast, carried away by his emotions, claims every Soviet film to be a masterpiece of cinematic art, we may well conceal a smile and go to see for ourselves what all the trouble is about.

By now it is generally recognised, I think, that the film industry of Russia is entirely State-controlled, and that any production launched in the studios or on location in the Soviet Union has as its primary object the dissemination of Communist propaganda. Whether it is made for home consumption by the peasants and workers or whether it is intended for export in the hope of attracting fresh converts to the red banner, the Soviet film has propaganda as its life and breath. Once this is grasped and assessed according to our personal attitude, we can proceed to acknowledge that the Russian cinema as a whole is one of the most, if not the most important contribution to world cinema. I have explained elsewhere at some length just how much the technical achievements of such cinematographers as Pudovkin, Eisenstein, Kuleshov and their colleagues have meant, how the scientific principles of the Soviet con-structivist cinema have arisen, and how certain of the better films have succeeded in approaching nearer to the ideal film than any produced in Western Europe and America.

If the position were as simple as I have described all would be well and there would be no reason for clashes of opinion. But unfortunately the complications attending the presentation of Soviet films outside their country of origin are various, and nowhere have they reached a more preposterous stage than in England.

The factors contributing to this tangled situation are many. In the first place, Russian pictures are generally considered by the film trade to have no commercial value, and hence bookings for them at ordinary cinemas are few and far between, more especially since the advent of the talking film. Secondly, a certain section of movie writers has been at pains to praise all the products of the Soviet cinema without any discrimination between the good and the bad, with the result that many students of the cinema, who have been unable to judge for themselves, have placed a much greater value on the general methods of Russian production than was necessary. Thirdly, owing to this legend of the unvarying greatness of Soviet films, the growing film society movement throughout the country has demanded to see the so-called masterpieces, and has as a consequence met with opposition from local watch-committees, magistrates or council authorities, who on their side have been guided by staunch ideas of Victorian patriotism and a reasonable distaste for Communist beliefs. Fourthly, the Russians themselves, not slow to turn the position to their own advantage, have by devious methods introduced many of their films into London, and have indirectly encouraged the setting up of film societies in big industrial centres where these pictures, under the guise of artistry, were likely to have the most effect on working-class audiences. Were the circumstances to be examined, it would probably be found that the rental cost of Russian pictures to societies in such fruitful neighbourhoods is much lower than it is to the more select societies which profess a serious interest in cinematic art. This, briefly, is the state of affairs that is encountered every time we, who are serious, may wish to see a new Soviet film. To add to the conflagration, the lay Press considers that the matter has quite a notable news value, and it is common to find voluminous correspondence on the pros and cons of Russian films in our daily newspaper.

Under such conditions it is inevitable that the sheep should suffer with the goats, and that to see such a remarkable piece of work as Dovzhenko's *Earth*, one must either join a film society or journey to some remote part of London, where a cinema exhibitor has possibly booked the picture at random or has been influenced by the chance of a little free publicity. To convey my point, I would mention that of the several times which I have seen *Earth*, certainly the most curious was at a small theatre in the east of London, in a district that can hardly be described as attractive, and where at least two-thirds of the audience was composed of people who had come from the West End to see this film by Dovzhenko, about which they had read.

I have been at pains to stress the difficulties surrounding the presentation of Soviet films in England in general, and the difficulty of seeing *Earth* in particular, because without having seen portions of Dovzhenko's film it is impossible for anyone to come to a full realisation of what contemporary cinema can mean. If it were as easily possible for the vast general public to see *Earth* as it is for it to waste hard-gotten money on *Whoopee*, *Resurrection* and *Kismet*, there would be no cause for discontent. But the position remains that whereas *Whoopee*s and *Charley's Aunt*s are as thick as the pebbles on the beach, such a film as *Earth* happens only on the rarest occasions and then is hidden away out of all reasonable reach.

With Room's *Ghost That Never Returns*, and Trauberg's *The Blue Express*, Dovzhenko's *Earth* is presumably one of the last of Russia's contributions to the silent cinema before the Soviets turn their attention to the problems of the sound film. It is all the more interesting, moreover, because Dovzhenko's method of working provides a sharp contrast to those of the more exhibitionist directors of the left-wing. *Earth* affords an excellent comparison between the violent, feverish styles of Pudovkin and Eisenstein and the peaceful, slow, yet strongly dramatic style of Dovzhenko.

Not only this but *Earth*, as well as the earlier work of the same director, marks a fresh outlook in Soviet production, for it attempts the philosophical rather than the sociological or political thematic content. Whilst the subject-matter deals to a certain extent with the contemporary Soviet problem of the adoption of collective farming, as did *The General Line*, the real intent of *Earth* is the cinematic representation of nature and the expression of a new attitude towards birth, life and death, set in an environment of extreme natural beauty. The age-old theme of the supremacy of the new over the old, the Soviet methods overthrowing the ancient privileges of the Kulaki (the rich farmers), and the superiority of the machine over the animal, these are all present, but they are subservient to Dovzhenko's beautiful rendering of nature and ingenuousness of the peasant mind. A crude form of propaganda is overcome by a visionistic outlook—an outlook that seeks to express the richness and materialism of life. There is nothing glorifying in the coming of the tractor in *Earth*, rather does Dovzhenko evoke our sympathy and love for the graceful horses and milk-white oxen whose tasks are now at an end. *Earth* gives us something new in cinema, something which—although slightly similar in technical methods of approach—is a thousand removes distant from the revolutions of an Eisenstein and a Pudovkin, or the shuttlecock activities of a Dziga Vertov.

The slight narrative interest which Dovzhenko has written for the theme of *Earth* is remarkable for its simplicity, since any complexity of plot would have impaired the main purpose of the interpretation of nature. In a small village in the Ukraine, the peasants and Kulaki are quarrelling. The youth of the peasants seek to further the setting up of communal farms while the youth of the Kulaki seek to protect the land which is theirs by ancient privilege and right to possession. The fathers of both, rich in experience of toil, watch on, mistrusting the new inventions and at the same time jealous of each other. A tractor is sent by the Government, and Vassily, a young peasant, brings it in triumph into the village. In his joy he drives it across the lands of a Kulak, as the result of which he is shot by Thomas, a Kulak's son, as he returns to his home in the quiet of the night. At the urge of his father, Vassily is buried by his friends, not with the customary ceremonies of religion, but with the spirit of the new faith, with fruit and songs and joyous belief in this new philosophy; whilst Thomas, his murderer, admits his guilt, but is ignored by the singing peasants. That is all.

A calm, slow, measured development distinguishes the opening sequence as Dovzhenko gradually absorbs us into his mood. Great expanses of corn and wheat ripple in the wind. There is fruit on the trees, great clusters of apples and pears. We are aware of the luxuriant fertility of the soil, of the sun that ripens and the rain that softens. There are smiling faces, sunflowers, and happiness. Amid banks of fruit, surrounded by his son and grandson and great-grandson, an old man lies dying. For many years he has toiled and lived on the fruits of his toil. Death does not mean much to these men of the land. Life takes its natural course. This death is but an incident in the life of something greater. The old man eats an apple, and as he does so his eyes wander to a child eating an apple also. The beginning and the end, all is the same with the fruit of the soil. All his life this old man has worked, and he has received no medal for it. Medals are only given by the new collective farm, and he is too late for that. An interchange of words brings out the primitive beliefs of these peasants. 'Send me word, Peter, what heaven or hell is like.' The old man smiles with happiness and quietly sinks back into death. The whole sequence has been peaceful, marked out by shots held on the screen for a considerable length of time, leisurely and with little movement.

Suddenly we come to the heads of laughing women, to uproarious mirth, blatant and ugly. The cutting quickens with the rise in mood. The women are jeering at the rich Kulak. He is the laughing stock of the village. He resents the overtures of the communal farm. Then we shift to the peasant's house, where the son, Vassily, is trying to convince his father of the need for the communal farm, of which the father is both suspicious and resentful.

Down a long dusty track stretching over the fields, we await the coming of the tractor. The young men have gone out to bring it into the village. The whole landscape seems to be waiting. Grouped in positions of vantage are the peasants, waiting to see for the first time this marvellous machine of which they have heard so much. Even the horses and the cattle are assembled, curious to see their successor make its triumphal entry into the village. The grouping of these shots, each related to the next, is magnificent. A single white cow, two great oxen, a man between two horses; one man, two men, three men, standing quite motionless against a sky that is almost black; photographed from below in dramatic perspective. A row of horses' heads, three Kulaks, a single white sleek-flanked mare. Shots arranged in deliberate progression, compositions of superb beauty, expressing anticipation of the sight of the tractor.

Far along the road, the machine has broken down, the radiator is empty. At the headquarters of the communal farm they do not believe it. A tractor cannot break down. Backwards and forwards we flash from head to head, split up with titles, 'It's coming!' 'It's stopped!' By their own resource, the peasants refill the radiator and Vassily drives into the village, followed by a cheering crowd. Men look at the tractor and exclaim with surprise, 'It's real!'

We follow to a swift sequence of harvesting. Vassily, delighted with the efficiency of his new love, waves to his father, who is scything away as he has done season after season. 'Throw away that old broomstick of yours, Dad.' The cutting quickens as we watch the girls binding and stacking, until the whole screen is vibrating with movement. Corn, grain, flour; moving here, there, everywhere. A frenzy of speed and achievement.

Then quietness again as evening draws on. Rest and peace descend after the labour of the day. Shadows grow long across the screen. It becomes difficult to see. Layers of creeping mist circle over a pool of water. Groups of men and women stand together, holding hands in the cool of the evening. Supreme in safety, a girl leans her head against her lover's breast. Fingers are entwined with fingers, rough with the touch of corn-stalks. There is perfect stillness in the dusk. Away in the distance, the Kulak's son is reeling home, dancing drunkenly from side to side of the road. A neighbour follows and tells him that the tractor has been driven across his fields. Elsewhere, Vassily is returning to the village, his heart filled with joy at the success of his day. It is now almost dark and deathly silent. A horse grazes in the dew-strewn grass. Vassily stops and wonders as his soul is filled with the greatness of life. Gradually he begins to dance, gently at first and then quickly, movements of joy and happiness. Faster and faster he twirls in the dusty cloud at his feet, advancing step by step up the winding white road. The camera retreats before him as he throws his whole heart into this dance of passionate joy, until he comes near the lights in the village. Suddenly, at the height of his movement, he drops flat in the dust. The startled horse lifts its head. Vassily lies dead.

The father is stricken with grief. He shouts to the four winds across the expanse of the fields, 'Who has killed my Vassily?' A priest comes to his house but is refused admittance. Instead, the father goes to the communal farm and asks that his son may be buried in a manner befitting the new spirit, with songs and hymns to the future instead of with the mockeries of religious pomp. The funeral takes place and Vassily's friend addresses the crowd. A branch of leaves sweeps across the calm face of the dead boy. Thomas can keep his secret no longer, and running across the fields, looks down on the people. He clutches at the ground, buries his hands in the earth—his earth by hereditary possession. He shrieks to the crowd that he killed their Vassily—in the night—but they take no notice. He is puzzled and angry, and he shouts. But the peasants are too occupied with their singing to listen to him. He screams with dismay, dances the dance of a madman, buries his face in the bare soil. Until finally the film closes with a beautiful series of shots of fruit splashed with rain, and the gradual breaking through of the sun. A cluster of apples, three apples, two apples, one apple filling the screen.

So moved am I by Dovzhenko's film that I find it difficult to express in words the full meaning of the moving images that are at once lovely in themselves, lovely in sequence, and lovely as a unified work of art. So well has Dovzhenko welded his separate images into a single, vibrating, immensely powerful whole, that it is almost sacrilegious to probe and dissect its construction. The images sweeping from cloud to earth, from fruit to sunflower, from graceful steeds to sturdy oxen, from small figures of men on the distant horizon to great close ups of heads, are so beautifully arranged that they defy literary description. The gradual changing of mood from silent calm to noisy excitement, from sun to wind and rain, is so skilfully effected that we are unconscious of the means employed. The touches of mysticism, the deep feeling of soil, the sensitivity to all that is lovely, are so new to the art of the cinema that for the moment we are dumbfounded. We are left with our minds satiated with pleasure, with a curious wonderment as to the birth and origin of what we have just seen.

Alexander Dovzhenko is, or was, a painter, and his arrangement of pictorial composition and extremely delicate sense of beauty is apparent not only in *Earth* but in his earlier work. Both *Zvenigora* and *Arsenal*, the former a queer mystical fantasy of the changing ideas and strong belief in folk-lore in an Ukrainian village, and the latter an account of revolution in the Ukraine, revealed Dovzhenko as one of the most interesting of the Soviet directors. In these two films his technical ability was not sufficiently developed to do justice to his breadth of vision, and, although fascinating by reason of their unique conception and use of contrasted static and moving images, they did not reach the high level attained by *Earth*. But despite their uneven qualities, they sufficed to show that Dovzhenko would very soon develop into a cinematographer of exceptional genius, an expectation that has now been more than fulfilled in *Earth*.

An intense interest in the life and customs of the Ukrainian people is strongly indicated in all these three films, so much so that portions of *Zvenigora* which dealt with local poetic legend and traditional customs were quite incomprehensible, not only to Western audiences, but to people in other parts of Russia. In *Earth* we see this characteristic brought out in the old man listening at the grave of Peter for word of what heaven and hell are like, and in the particular stress laid on dancing—the drunken dance of Thomas, the wonderful death-dance of Vassily, and the final frenzied dance of Thomas when he refuses to part with his lands. Moreover, throughout the film we can perceive Dovzhenko's peculiar understanding of local types, mentalities and superstitions, a quality that is not to be found in the work of other Soviet directors, but which is linked up with René Clair's appreciation of human weaknesses, Chaplin's sensitivity to pathos, Griffith's feeling for intimate sentiments, and Seaström's tendency towards poetical lyricism.

Projecting through the beauty of the theme, the new spirit of Russian youth is thrown into relief against the traditions of the older generation. In the Soviet Union to-day, it is the young rising generation which is being systematically schooled into a new form of life as laid down by Lenin. The elders are being left to finish their days in comparative peace so long as they outwardly conform to Soviet doctrines, but the young men and women are being rigorously trained to their tractors and collective farms. This new attitude is expressed throughout *Earth*, in the gaiety and enthusiasm of Vassily and his friends, in their delight for the tractor and in their ruthless devotion to the interests of the communal farm. Set against this, we have the older generation typified by Vassily's father, at first dubious of his son's keenness for the new methods, but converted to the new way of thinking by Vassily's death, and the still older generation in Vassily's grandfather, who dies at the opening of the picture. Dovzhenko has chosen these types as being representative of the transition that is taking place to-day, together with the tractor as symbol of the machine that is the god of modern Russia. These are the bones to carry the main drive of the film.

I have already made clear the wonderful poetic quality of Dovzhenko's work, so implicit in the grassy hillside slopes of *Zvenigora*, and even greater in the many magnificent shots of fruit and foliage, animals and landscape in *Earth*, and I repeat that as far as I am aware nothing quite like it has been achieved before on the screen. In my experience, there are few directors who are capable of taking such a fundamental and universal theme as *Earth*, expressing it in terms of visual images on the screen, and translating the poetry of fruit and flowers into cinematic images, as Dovzhenko has done, without becoming sentimental. Such a work demands delicacy and restraint of direction, qualities that are most characteristic of Dovzhenko's style. In every portion of the film, whether the mood is one of excitement or one of sadness, this admirable restraint carries the theme across with a high degree of emotion. Added to which, Dovzhenko maintains a very firm hold over all his material—scenario, photography and editing. This is evidenced in the exactitude with which each shot and each sequence plays its part in the make up of the whole. Had he relaxed control for one moment, the intimacy with nature that dominates the film would have been lost. Moreover, the restrained key in which so much of the picture is played greatly amplifies the more exciting moods. This is especially noticeable during the first reel, when, after the long, leisured sequence in which old Peter lies dying, Dovzhenko abruptly switches to the heads of the laughing women. It is such modulation of mood that goes to the making of a great film.

The artist's mind of Dovzhenko, thinking in terms of lovely pictorial compositions with the material on the screen at rest, is apparent in the entire length of *Earth*. He has a strong tendency towards building up mood with a series of static shots—approaching the crescendo of a sequence by increasing the grouping value of the screen material—that establishes his painter's outlook. I have referred earlier to the powerful effect of this method of assembling, in the scene in which the peasants and the animals are awaiting the arrival of the tractor, and we find it employed again in other parts of the picture. In the same manner, the beautiful sequence of the falling of dusk and the gradual creation of the peace and quiet of the hot evening in the village is achieved almost entirely by a slow procession of static shots, each matched perfectly with the other in grouping and intensity of light. From this description, it may perhaps seem that the artist's outlook of Dovzhenko would tend to isolate the images, as in Dreyer's *La Passion de Jeanne d'Arc*. But happily Dovzhenko is able to think also in terms of cinema, that is to say, in terms of constant movement of the celluloid as well as movement of the material being photographed, with the consequence that his work is doubly effective. As I think correct, his shots rely equally on their compositional value and their time-length for the full expression of their content. This question of the artist's static outlook and its relationship to the cinematic outlook of the film director is worthy of considerable thought, and should produce interesting revelations.

By this emphasis on Dovzhenko's use of the static image, I do not imply that he eliminates movement of the screen material altogether, for that would be absurd. On the contrary, when desirous of employing movement other than that of the celluloid and of the camera, Dovzhenko's matching up and intermixing of rhythms is admirable. No better example of screen movement could be instanced than that of the gradually increasing tempo of the gathering of the harvest, the binding, the stacking, the sifting, the dough-kneading, and finally the baking of the bread, the movement being so speeded up that at the finale the whole screen is rocking with energy.

If fault be found with *Earth* at all, I think it lies in the funeral scenes of the last reel. To me these do not reach the beauty or the power of the preceding reels, firstly because they are not conceived in such measured terms of relationship between images and editing as the rest of the film, and secondly because their photographic value does not achieve the same standard as that of the earlier scenes. To make a comparison, I prefer the famous religious procession in *The General Line*, an episode which admittedly marks the height of Eisenstein's work to date, but which nevertheless has a certain affinity to the procession in *Earth*. Whereas in the former film, Eisenstein collected a hundred small movements of both intellectual and physiological significance into one magnificent whole for the expression of the futility of religious belief in the face of nature, Dovzhenko in *Earth* conflicts a simple moving mass of people with the isolated figure of Thomas running against the horizon. Eisenstein gathered every thread of his argument and so cleverly interplaited them that, with the aid of brilliant rhythmic cutting, the emotional effect of the scene was tremendous. But in my opinion, Dovzhenko loses the threads of his theme, as well as his photographic excellence, and were it not for the sudden compelling madness of the Kulak's son and his remarkable dance, this sequence of Vassily's funeral would be a blemish on the film.

Despite the simplicity of the story, I found that the continuity and consequential development of the incidents—especially in the earlier portions—is a little difficult to follow. Whether this is because the film is primarily intended for Russian audiences, or whether it is due to my lack of knowledge of Ukrainian legend, I am not sure, but there are certain points of narrative interest which were not clear until I had seen the picture for a second time. I would add, also, that the priest's visit to Vassily's home seemed poor in dramatic quality and might well have been eliminated except, of course, that it served as anti-religious propaganda.

Some comment should be made on Dozhjenko's selection of acting material, for like other of the Soviet naturalistic directors, he disapproves of the use of professional actors and actresses. He is consistent in his employment of actors chosen for their type from the ordinary people, and I am given to understand that he believes every person is capable of playing at least one part for the screen—that of his or her individual character. To contradict this, however, I note that the actor Nicolas Nademski plays both in *Earth* and in *Zvenigora*, his performance in the latter being distinguished by his clever make-up as an old man, an artificiality that surely opposes the creed of naturalism?

These remarks on Dovzhenko as a film director would be incomplete if I neglected to stress his wonderful ability to create mood by the relationship of visual images. No words of mine can describe the amazing spirit of youth and vigour with which he contrives to imbue the scenes of

Vassily and the tractor. I am unable to express the gaiety with which he surrounds the girls as they bind the corn, any more than I can capture the magic of the fruit scenes with their sun and rain or the rising mists from the river. Perhaps it is because Dovzhenko is seeing with an artist's mind and setting down the truth of what he sees aloof from any false ideas of entertainment value. Perhaps it is because of his passionate love for the soil, for the fertility and for the beauty of his native Ukraine. Perhaps it is because his marvellous rhythm of emotions runs through man, beast, and land alike. Perhaps because he combines the inspiration of a poet with a rare genius for photography. Whatever hidden quality it may be, there can be no question that Dovzhenko takes his place beside the creative geniuses of the film. Even in such a prolific medium as the cinema it is seldom we see such an emotional and well-made film as *Earth*, especially one with such a perfect blending of creative impulse, technical accomplishment and rich pictorial value. From this point of view *Earth* is unique.

In the Soviet cinema as we can regard it from England, Dovzhenko projects as an isolated figure quite alien to the main flow of cinematography headed by Eisenstein and Pudovkin. His poetic outlook and his love of mysticism set him apart from the formalist school, with its sole interest in technical problems. The simple technique employed by Dovzhenko—and it is remarkably simple when compared with the complex montage principles of Eisenstein—is merely a means to an end and not an end in itself. It is perhaps possible that Dovzhenko is an indication of a new type of film mentality in Russia, a development from the new peasant classes that are in the process of formation to-day.

It would be unfair, perhaps, to compare Dovzhenko's film with other pictures being shown in London about the same time, and yet we are so accustomed to indifferent films that when something worthwhile is seen the reaction is remarkable. If we compare *Earth* with such films as *Scandal Sheet*, *Body and Soul* and *The Criminal Code*, we will learn just how negligible the ordinary run of movies is, and how great true vision and feeling in the cinema can be. In addition to which, *Earth* probably cost about a quarter of the sum expended on any of these American programme pictures. To this there is the obvious reply, of course, that *Earth* was not made for financial reasons, whereas such a film as *Body and Soul* was mainly produced on account of its money-making capacity. But to the believer in real cinema, Dovzhenko's film offers an immensity of feeling, a sensitivity to the progress of life, a susceptibility to heaven and earth and nature, an expression of the building of a new country, in place of an artificial story performed within the limits of a cast-iron studio by made-up actors and actresses who by their ill-assumed sophistication merely succeed in being vulgar. *Earth* is one of the few films in the cinema up till now which means something.

Pabst (1967)

(From *Films and Filming*, February 1967)

I appreciate the reader who wrote suggesting that this back page of mine should be put at the front of the paper, but I always thought that the stop-press was what you read first, if not for the racing results then for news of the rat-race, which is what so much of film-making is and mostly has been. The same reader asks for more about the 'Golden Period' (my original phrase) of the German silent cinema but I suggest to him that this is amply covered by such authors and experts as Dr Kracauer and Lotte Eisner in their books; and there is always the old *Film Till Now* to fall back on.

At the same time I am moved this month to write about one of the great directors of all cinema, the Bohemian born Georg Wilhelm Pabst, now in his 80s. Last year I tried to call him in Vienna but, alas, he was not well enough to come to the telephone. But I am always proud that as a young film-maker I was once closely associated with him and gratefully record how much his films and way of working influenced me when later I came humbly to direct films myself. To have known and talked with Pabst is like saying you knew and talked with Leonardo.

Also partly responsible for this piece is the fact that the other night I was playing a record of the original Brecht and Weill's *Die Dreigroschenoper*, made in 1928, given to me by the East German TV Organisation a couple of years back, of which operetta Pabst made a memorable film in 1930 in German and French versions. For years its distribution outside Germany was held up because Warner Bros bought the rights for an American remake which was never made.

What are the outstanding facts that stand out today from Pabst's major films? First, I emphasise that *Westfront 1918* (1930) and *Kamerad-schaft* (1931) were made when the Third Reich was no longer a beer hall dream and when the Wermacht tradition was as strong as ever as an evil force in German national life. The novel from which *Westfront* was taken, *Four of the Infantry*, by Ernst Johannsen, was a success in Germany but it did not achieve the world success of Remarque's *All Quiet on the Western Front*, also made into a film by Milestone. But in adapting Johannsen's book to the screen, Pabst was directly attacking war as bestial, useless and humanly degrading. It exposed the futility, barbarism and senselessness of war. It struck at the heart of the national-istic militarism beloved of so many German people and of which we may be seeing a resurgence now. (How the German people would have applauded the recent TV documentary on the Guards Regiments!) Although the film as a whole remains in my mind (I have not seen it for many years), no moment lives deeper than the German soldiers covering with earth the exposed hand of a soldier, the rest of whom is already buried in mud. And again when the French girl is left spread-eagled after a German has tried to rape her. The Nazis demonstrated against the film and later it was withdrawn from German circulation. It remains one of the greatest anti-war films ever made, with no concessions to mock heroism or sentiment.

Kameradschaft, made the next year, was one of the strongest appeals in cinema for international understanding. As is well known, it was based on an actual event, when an explosion occurred in a French coalmine that extended beneath the Franco-German frontier and how the German miners voluntarily went to the rescue of the trapped French miners in spite of all national barriers. The film's ending when the bars are put up again down the pit to mark the frontier division is the ironical comment so typical of Pabst's social and political outlook. It was cut off from some versions of the film. The wonderfully built studio-reconstruction of the mine (using real mining equipment and materials) and the gas explosion in the gallery were the work of Erno Metzner, the very talented art-director of so many German films, whose work later was to be wasted in British and American studios. *Kameradschaft* is a remarkable demonstration of the filmic blending of fact and fiction, of documentary and fiction, predating by many years the efforts of neo-realism and the *nouvelle vague*. (An analysis of this is in my *Documentary Film* book.) The crowd scenes at the barred gates of the French mine where the disaster has taken place, the terrible anguish of the waiting mothers and relatives of the trapped miners remain indelible. Its sound-track was more imaginative and experimental than anything that had been done up to that date.

Apart from what films went before or came after, these two pictures give Pabst a place among the highest talents and thinkers of world cinema, films with a social purpose that was naked and strong in a world already heralding another world war.

If you will put aside for a moment the slap-happy gimmicks and coggeries which hardly distinguish so many critically admired current pictures by the Carnaby Street/Kings Road trick-slippery school of movie-merchants, there is much to learn about the real craft of film-making from these films of Pabst. In London he once said to me on a memorable evening, 'The camera has only one eye—the lens—and that is all revealing. All film is movement either in action or by the camera or by cutting. Seen through the lens, and not the human eye, everyone—actor or non-actor—becomes a new personality.' When the whole studio was opposed to Pabst's casting of Garbo in *The Joyless Street* (1925), he said, 'You have not seen her *through* the lens of the camera. I have.' History proved how right he was! The majority of directors in recent years have not learned to use one camera properly, let alone two or three simultaneously. How many directors know how to take a shot so that its beginning and ending action can be cut on movement? Pabst's *Loves of Jeanne Ney* (1927) contained sequences which brilliantly revealed this dynamic, cinematic, inherent quality of cutting on movement. Similarly, Pabst never used a movie-camera shot that began or ended static. Always there was movement, not of the camera only but of what was being shot. There were interminable examples of this in *Westfront* and *Kameradschaft*.

Pabst was—as I have always been—a deep believer in the fact that psychoanalysis is of great help when getting a performance out of an actor. The camera can only reproduce the outward expressions of the inner mind and that expression cannot be left only to the skill of the actor, however gifted he may be. Pabst knew better than almost any other director the intense revealing power of the camera angle, or set-up. The Russians also knew this in their silent films. Murnau, too, knew it. The other night I was watching for the third time Stanley Kubrick's *Paths of Glory* on TV. How much it owes to *Westfront 1918*. And Kubrick's film is very good indeed. There may be some who say why look back to films and film-makers of the past—cinema is ephemeral, of the present. But just as in the other parts, the contemporary artist studies and learns from the work of, say, (my own choice) Mozart, El Greco and Swift, so the film-maker of today can learn from his master. Did not Orson Welles sit through weeks, if not months, of projecting famous films from the past *before* he made *Citizen Kane*?

I note the meant reverence paid, quite understandably, to Sternberg. Is it not time that even greater reverence should be paid to Pabst, whose mastery of film Sternberg never approached? Some readers will perhaps write to remind me of what happened to Pabst, the socialist and internationalist, during the last war. I have all the answers. Pabst in Vienna today, an old man, can rest content; his work for humanitarianism, for peace among mankind, and his immense artistry in the cinema is not forgotten, nor I hope will it be in the film schools of the future.

Some Principles of Documentary (1935)

(From *Documentary Film*)

Every tendency in cinema reflects the social and political characteristics of its period, which in turn may, or may not, according to your reasoning, be a reflection of the obtaining economic conditions. The documentary method, as a distinct kind of film, as an interpretation of social feeling and philosophic thought quite different in purpose and form from the entertainment motives of the story-film, has materialised largely as the result of sociological, political and educational requirements.

In the foregoing estimate of documentary traditions, we have tried to show that documentary is a genuine independent kind of cinema, as distinct from the story-film or photoplay as is the biography from the novel. Further, we have tried to define the main characteristics that exist between the plain descriptive pictures of everyday life (travel pictures, nature films, educationals and newsreels) that fall short of documentary requirements and the creative dramatisation of actuality and the expression of social analysis that are the first demand of the documentary method.

At any rate, it is clear, I think, that in purposeful documentary we enter a range of perception wider than has so far been attempted in descriptive films, for propaganda needs persuasive statements and implications that furrow deeply into the surface of modern experience. In the use of documentary for dialectical purpose, for example, we can conceive whole periods of time, symbolised by their existing heritages today, being arranged in dramatic shape to express a variety of outlooks. We can imagine how the fundamental sentiments of the human mind can be analysed and dissected to suit a multitude of purposes. The immense range of discursive power made possible by film technique suggests the documentary method as an admirable instrument for clarifying and co-ordinating all aspects of modern thought, in the hope of achieving a fuller analysis that may in turn lead to more definite conclusions. But how does this interpretation of the documentary method evolve from the traditions which we have just described? Before we can arrive at even first definitions, the existing tendencies require further analysis to discover if they are progressing on the most suitable lines.

Flaherty serves us well to demonstrate the elementary demands of documentary. He asks an observation of natural material on its actual location, from which the theme may arise. Further, he asks an interpretation of that material, to bring it alive as a reality on the screen, which can be attained only by a complete understanding 'from the inside' of such material and its relationships. For his own method, he prefers the inclusion of a slight narrative, not fictional incident or interpolated 'cameos', but the daily routine of his native people. For his themes and locations he goes to those parts of the world where, supposedly, Man has still to fight Nature for his existence, although in most cases Flaherty reconstructs native life of a past or dying generation. The heroes of both *Nanook* and *Man of Aran*, for example, were waxwork figures acting the lives of their grandfathers. And it is precisely this choice which leads us to explore the validity of his approach in relation to documentary's social purpose.

In the modern world in which most of us live, it is doubtful if we are primarily interested in Man's primitive relationship with Nature. Pushing back the sea to build a quay wall, or damming a river to harness its energy, admittedly present great achievements of scientific and engineering skill. But does not their importance, from a social aspect, lie less in the actual feat itself than in its resultant effect upon the geography of the landscape and ultimately the benefit to the economic life of the people concerned? The idyllic documentalist, it is true, is chiefly interested in Man's conquering of natural objects to bend them to his ends. Admittedly, the sea was an obstacle to communication until Man built ships to cross it. The air was useless to Man's economic life, except as wind-power, until he learnt to fly through it. The minerals of the earth were valueless until Man discovered how to mine. And, in the same way, production today is generally acknowledged to be more than sufficient to meet the needs of the community. But the success of science and machine-controlled industry has resulted in an unequal distribution of the amenities of existence under the relationships of the present economic system. Side by side with leisure and well-being there is also unemployment, poverty and wide social unrest. Our essential problem today is to equate the needs of the individual with production, to discuss the most satisfactory economic system and to present the social relationships of mankind in their most logical and modern ordering. Despite their braveries, Man's fight against the fury of the Sea, Man's creation of unnatural pain to prove his manhood, Man's battle against snow and ice and animals are of secondary interest in a world where so many urgent and larger problems demand our attention.

Granted that we may not expect the sentimentalist director to grapple with the materialist problems of our age, but at least we may expect from him an acknowledgement of their existence. Surely we have the right to believe that the documentary method, the most virile of all kinds of film, should not ignore the vital social issues of this year of grace, should not avoid the economic relationships which govern the present productive system and, consequently, determine the cultural, social and aesthetic attitudes of society?

Let Flaherty's fine feeling for photography stand, accept his unique sensibility to natural movements and his grand poetic vision of Man against the Sky, confess (in passing) that *Man of Aran* avoided all the important issues raised by sound, but let us realise, in the face of all the gilt of Venice, that the Flaherty method is an evasion of the issues that matter most in the modern world, is devoid of any attempt at serious social analysis. Give to Flaherty his credits; and they are many. Acknowledge our deep obligation to his pioneer spirit, his fierce battles to break down commercial stupidity and the bravery of his struggle against the despicable methods of exploitation from which he has suffered. But realise, at the same time, and within the sphere of documentary, that his understanding of actuality is a sentimental reaction towards the past, an escape into a world that has little contemporary significance, a placing of sentimentalism above the more urgent claims of materialism.

No slums or factories, no employment exchanges or income tax bureaus, no weekly rents or tithes exist in this fairy world of make-believe created by the romantic tradition of documentary. Only Man against Nature; cruel, bitter, savage and heroic but unrelated to modern society. Industry and commerce are as remote as their craven symbols which flank the Albert Memorial, or as the muscular stalwarts that lean nonchalantly on slender sledge-hammers and the bronzed workers who flourish torches of servility under the nose of good Victoria. True, Flaherty observed in his own way the craftsmanship of the potter and the glass-blower when in the Midlands for *Industrial Britain*, but is it not significant that those very trades are fading before the advance of mass-production and machinery? And did not the filming of coal and steel and other heavy industry in that film fall to other hands?

In every location which he has chosen there have existed social problems that demanded expression. Exploitation of native labour, the practices of the white man against the native, the landlords of Aran, these have been the vital stories, but from them Flaherty has turned away. Probably he realised that their exposure would have clashed with the interests controlling the production and distribution of his films. It was not, we may grant, in his power to expose. Instead he was content to present the 'braveries of all time'. Certainly he retreated into an acceptance of the irrelevance which is the fate of all escapists. Idyllic documentary is documentary without significant purpose. It takes romanticism as its banner. It ignores social analysis. It takes ideas instead of facts. It marks a reactionary return to the worship of the heroic, to an admiration of the barbaric, to a setting up of 'The Leader'.

The symphonic approach of the Continental Realists, on the other hand, goes at first appearance to realism. But for the most part the French and German directors see the documentary film as a work of art in itself, as a symphony of tempos and movements, rather than that the art should be an offshoot of the larger issue of a job well done to meet a special purpose.

Thus the symphonic conception of *Berlin* provides a pleasant enough pyrotechnical exercise, skimming over the many tantalising rhythms of modern life in street and factory and countryside, without thought of the 'how' and 'wherefore' underlying the social scene. Yet, despite their exciting tempos, despite their bustle and thronging of modern city life, these big and little symphonies of big and little cities create nothing more valuable to civilisation than a shower of rain. All the outward signs of a busy metropolis are there. People work and eat: a suicide and a wedding: but not one single implication underlies it all.

Again there is evasion, a deliberate self-satisfaction in the surface rhythms of a printing-press or the processions of a milk bottling machine, but nothing of inflated circulations or wages paid, nothing to suggest that the social and economic relations contained in the subject are the real material of documentary. The manufacture of steel is visually exciting. Ruttmann, Dr Kaufmann and Basse have shown us that. But they did not think to show us that steel builds bridges, builds ships to cross the seas, radio masts to throw a girdle of communication round the earth, pylons to carry a new power up the length and breadth of the land, knives to cut with and needles to sew with. They did not tell us that steel is a State ceremony, that its foundrymen and smiths are in a sense national figures: nor that its labour might be underpaid, its risks horrifying and its markets cut across by private speculation.

Based on the same method of approach, but lacking the technical trickery that made *Berlin* of interest, Basse's film *Deutschland von Gestern und Heute* admirably epitomises the realist tradition of the Continental school. Cross-sectioning in painful detail almost every aspect of German life, it is typical of the method in that it observes the pictorial surface of the scene but refuses to penetrate beneath the skin. It is said for Basse that he intended to show how the style of living in former times is still affecting modern life, that from the prehistoric forms of a primitive economic system the film leads historically over the Gothic style to Renaissance, from baroque to rococo, from the *Biedermeierzeit* to the complacency of present middle-class society, the provincial character of which makes possible the crescendo of a modern city's activity.[i] But I do not find Basse doing anything of the sort.

Instead, we have all the ingredients of the photographer's album, towns people and countryfolk, pastimes and processions, customs and conventions, industry and agriculture, mediaeval city and modern metropolis. They are all neatly shuffled and labelled, arranged in order like a good picture-book, with the camera roving here and there and round about. But as with Ruttmann, so with Basse. Nothing is related socially. Nothing is said creatively. Nothing lives. The long-winded procession of images, some of them not too well photographed, meanders along without drive or purpose. Running to story-feature length, this film more than any other exposes the weakness of a purpose-less theme. It is as if Basse just did not care how and why his images came to be. Unrelated geographically, they are put together in some form of contrast from which a mild implication might be drawn, but there is no essential aim behind it all. A few fleeting comments on the childish-ness of official parades, passing observations on the idiotic behaviourism of the *petite bourgeoisie*, but that is all. Had it been political, had it been sociological, had it been a compromise of respective description, it might have had point.

The visual arabesques of plunging pistons, the endless streams of trams and trains, the ballet movements of spinning bobbins, the belching issue of a steel furnace, the plough team and the harvest and the tractor, these as beautiful, exciting, poetic things in themselves are the main delights of the pseudo-realist approach. More difficult, perhaps, than the noble savage hero, who in himself is a curious being, but even more escapist for its delight in surface values; more subtle because of its treating with familiar scenes but more dangerous because of its artistic avoidance of vital issues. Its virtue lies in the surface beauties of techniques and tempos; its value is craftsmanship with no end in view except its own virtuosity. It may have poetry, lyricism, beauty of movement, sensibility, but these are minor virtues. The point is well made in Grierson's criticism of Elton's *Voice of the World*, a documentary of radio-gramophone production.

> Concentration on movement and rhythmic good looks obscures *importance* of the instrument. The building and *delivery of* the instrument, the key to the situation, not dramatised sufficiently. The result powerful but less than heroic. Elton possibly unappreciative of radio's social significance and therefore lacking in proper (aesthetic) affection for subject. This point important, as affecting almost all the types of documentary. Too damned arty and post-war to get their noses into public issues. Miss accordingly the larger dramatic themes possible to the medium.[ii]

The Continental Realists and their many imitators, then, are occupied principally by their interpretation of surface rhythms. They fail to appreciate the significance of their images or tempos. They give us a concerto of rotating wheels as a visual rhythm but do not realise that these stand as images of an epoch, symbols of an era of economic industrialism; and that only by relating these images to the human society which has given them existence can they become of real interest on the contemporary screen.

Analysis of all the tendencies of documentary, in fact, gives rise to the criticism that one of the real issues of modern society is being almost wholly avoided. In this age of social realism, surely one of the first aims of documentary should be to examine the problem of Man's place in society? Surely it is pointless, if not impossible, to bring alive the realities of the modern world unless we do so in such a manner as to base our themes on the relationship of Man to the world in which he lives? Machinery, agriculture, craftsmanship, culture and the rest cannot be divorced from their human fulfilments. Yet this is the very mistake into which some of our documentarists seem to have fallen. Apparently they fail to realise that the basis of the documentary method is a materialistic basis; that it is the material circumstances of civilisation which create and condition the present cultural, sociological, political, religious and aesthetic ideas of society.

On almost every side, moreover, documentary has deliberately been allowed to avoid the existence of the human being as the main factor in civilisation. Certainly people of many types have appeared in documentary but they have rarely been treated as anything but impersonal puppets. In following a path opposite to that of the story-film, documentary has been permitted to prefer the mass to the individual, or, in some cases, simply an impersonal statement of facts. Not only have the documentarists failed to relate the mass to the individual, but, despite the fact that their material and subjects are naturalistic, they have also failed to relate their themes to current social consciousness.

It is interesting, at this point, to note that this problem of setting the human being against a naturalistic environment is the main subject of discussion in the present Soviet kino. Practically the whole of the preliminary closed conference preceding the Moscow Film Festival of 1935 was given over to criticism of the Soviet cinema's inability to recognise and incorporate the individual in its films. That is why *Chapaev*, a dull film technically, was accorded such praise. That is why we have Dinamov making the plea that 'the theory of a film without a plot is a very dangerous theory', and Eisenstein stating that 'a film without emotional feeling is scarcely worth consideration'.

The fact is that since the Russians left their initial period of blood-and-thunder and strike, since the era of *Mother* and *Potemkin*, not one of them has succeeded in tackling the problems set by a new state of society, unless it will be Dovzhenko in his new film *Air-City*. It was one thing to evolve a set of rhythms which made the Odessa Steps massacre a scene of tremendous emotion, but quite another to relate the working of a milk separator to collective farming. So, in *The General Line*, we had a fine display of fireworks and slapstick by an expert showman; in *A Simple Case*, a set of artificial people with petty passions and a return to the Civil War for blood-and-thunder action, which all the splendid improvisations of a 'Birth and Regeneration' sequence failed to justify. From his insistence on the importance that the real struggle lay at one's own backdoor, we might suspect that Pudovkin saw the fault in *Deserter*, but, as Grierson pointed out, he still evaded the issue by retreating to the street riots of Hamburg (so like the *St Petersburg* location) and observed the working of his Russian factory with all the badness of a great artist.

Nor, when all was said and done, did the enthusiasms of a hundred thousand toilers in a Dziga Vertov cacophony do much to solve the task.

Nearer the mark was *Counterplan*, in which the ideas were better than their fulfilment; but most progressive of all, to my mind, was *Men and Jobs* which grappled with the problem of the untrained worker at the building of Dnieperstroi. Here, at least, was a bid to meet the issues of Russia going to school. The human being was, in a sense, related to the problems from which the theme arose. As persuasion for the shock brigader to learn from American efficiency, it was probably effective. But observe that the philosophy was still unsound. Enthusiasm, no matter how inspired, can never conquer science. Together they may achieve idealist aims but no engineer's science can be learnt as this film suggested. A crane is not worked by enthusiasm, although a film may have it so. A dam is not built by faith alone. A country cannot exist on a diet of ideology. And, in this measure also, *Men and Jobs* minimised its task.

Equally in their own sphere, the EMB films of Britain avoided the major issues provoked by their material. That was inevitable under their powers of production. The real economic issues underlying the North Sea herring catch, the social problems inherent in any film dealing seriously with the Industrial Midlands, lay outside the scope of a unit organised under a government department and having as its aim 'the bringing alive of the Empire'. The directors concerned knew this, and wisely, I think, avoided any economic or important social analysis. Instead they contented themselves with attempting a simple statement of facts, dramatising the action material of their themes, but leaving untouched the wider human fulfilments of the job.

It is strange that these many and varied efforts to realise and solve the problem of people in documentary are marked by an increasing, and perhaps dangerous, return to theatricalism. Having been freed from the banalities of the story-film, having been developed along fresh and stimulating lines, we may now be faced with the sad if faintly ironic spectacle of documentary returning, in spirit if not in material, to the studio. With the Russians arguing for a discontinuance of 'typage' and the resuscitation of the trained actor, with Ruttmann's linking of love with steel, and the GPO Unit romanticising their Savings Banks and making a melodrama out of the designing of a stamp, it looks as if we shall yet see the all-star documentary, if indeed we have not already done so in *BBC: The Voice of Britain*.

But the fact remains that this, one of documentary's most important problems, must be faced. Clearly a full and real expression of the modern scene and modern experience cannot be achieved unless people are observed in accurate relation to their surroundings. To do this, there must be establishment and development of character. There must be the growth of ideas, not only in theme, but in the minds of characters. Your individuals must be of the audience. They must be familiar in type and character. They themselves must think and convey their thoughts to the audience, because only in this way will documentary succeed in its sociological or other propagandist purpose. Documentary must be the voice of the people speaking from the homes and factories and fields of the people.

And it is these very requirements which will continue to distinguish documentary from the story-film. For in the latter, a character is seldom permitted to think other than trivial personal thoughts, or to have opinions in any way connected with the larger issues of existence. just as in documentary the facts of the theme must be important facts, so also must be the characterisation and outlook possessed by the individuals, for they are, in turn, conditioned by those same facts. In documentary this is possible, whereas in the story-film, at any rate under present conditions of manufacture, facts and ideas as well as characterisation are suppressed in the interests of the balance sheet and technique alone is left to the director.

The foregoing severe criticism of purpose and method in documentary today is, of course, necessarily arbitrary. Documentary is a type of film possessing certain well-defined characteristics. Each of the films included in our estimate falls within its scope. But because they do not all carry the social analysis which, in some opinions, is documentary's most important task, does not deny their often brilliant craftsmanship or our respect for their director's outlook. Rather does this signify that, quite reasonably, interpretations of the documentary method may differ; that there are different intentions underlying different observations; that whereas Flaherty, for example, can find his theme in the heroic braveries of all time expressed through some up-to-date 'primitive' tribe, others find their material on the home front, in the back streets and factories and locations closer to those actualities among which so many of us live; that, whereas some prefer the attitude of romanticism, others of us set ourselves the task of building from a materialistic basis. It is purely a question of personal character and inclination, of how strongly you feel about satisfying private artistic fancies or communal aims. No director makes documentary simply for the wages he is paid. That we leave to the panjandrums of the story-film. Your documentarist creates documentary and believes in the documentary method of cinema because he considers it the most powerful means of social expression available today.

Yet, despite my plea that the maker of documentary should be politically and socially conscious in his approach to everyday experience, he has no claim to the label of politician. His job is not upon a platform to harangue the mob but in a pulpit to persuade the mass to a wider consideration of human affairs. He is neither a fighter nor a barnstormer. Rather is he a prophet concerned with the broadest references of human associations. He is a propagandist making use of the most influential instrument of his time. He does not march with the crowd but goes just ahead, asking contemplation and discussion before action is taken on those problems with which he deals. In cinema, it is the documentary method which has proved the most suitable for these ends because it is a method of philosophic reasoning.

The immediate task of the documentarist is, I believe, to find the means whereby he can employ a mastery of his art of public persuasion to put the people and their problems, their labour and their service, before themselves. His is a job of presenting one half of the populace to the other; of bringing a deeper and more intelligent social analysis to bear upon the whole cross-section of modern society; exploring its weaknesses, reporting its events, dramatising its experiences and suggesting a wider and more sympathetic understanding among the prevailing class of society. He does not, I think, seek to draw conclusions but rather to make a statement of the case so that conclusions may be drawn. His world is in the streets, the homes, the factories and the workshops of the people, presenting this experience and that event to make his point. And if the documentary method today is being put to a double-headed use, if it is being employed to express a meaning within a meaning, then it is not the fault of the documentarist but of the time in which he lives.

Throughout this book I am laying emphasis on the documentary method rather than on documentary as a particular kind of film. For this reason, although documentary has been characterised by its creative use of the materials and apparatus of cinema, although it has made special use of actualities rather than of artificialities, it is the method which prompts this practice that is important and not the type of film produced. The documentary method will not, I believe, remain fixed in a world defined, on the one side, by *Drifters* and, on the other, by *Nanook*. Already the limits have been expanded to embrace such a poem as *Coal Face* and such a piece of journalistic reporting as *Housing Problems*. Story, characterisation and studio are likely to enter the documentary film but it will be the method and not the materials that will count. It will be the sociological, political or other purposes being served by the method which will continue to be of first importance.

In short, the documentary method is more complex than its traditions would have us believe. No longer is it the mere pictorial description of things and people and places of interest. Observation alone is not enough. Camera portrayal of movement, no matter how finely observed, is purely a matter of aesthetic good taste. The essential purposes of documentary lie in the ends applied to this observation. Conclusions must be indicated and the results of observation must be put across in a manner that demands high creative endeavour. Below the surface of the modern world lie the actuating economic issues of modern civilisation. These are the real materials of purposeful documentary. In Industry, Commerce, Civics and Nature the mere superficial portrayal of actuality is insufficient. Such surface description implies no intellectual ability. Rather are the implications and fulfilments of his material the concern of the documentarist. It is the meaning *behind* the thing and the significance *underlying* the person that are the inspirations for his approach. To the documentary method, every manufacture, every organisation, every function, every scheme of things represents at one point or another the fulfilment of a human interest.

In such circumstances, it seems improbable that your hero can still be the noble savage of Flaherty's choosing, or the centrifugal rhythms of a crankshaft which deceive the pseudo-realist's mind. No matter whether politics, culture, economics or religion, we are concerned with the impersonal forces that dictate this modern world. The puny individual must be refocused into his normal relationship to the general mass, must take his place alongside in the community's solid struggle for existence and forsake personal achievement. Daily jobs, no matter how well described by rhetoric of camera and intimacy of microphone, are not documentary material in themselves. They must be related to the wider purposes of the community.

Above all, documentary must reflect the problems and realities of the present. It cannot regret the past; it is dangerous to prophesy the future. It can, and does, draw on the past in its use of existing heritages but it only does so to give point to a modern argument. In no sense is documentary a historical reconstruction and attempts to make it so are destined to failure. Rather it is contemporary fact and event expressed in relation to human associations.

Frequently I hear it said that documentary aims at a true statement of theme and incident. This is a mistaken belief. No documentary can be completely truthful, for there can be no such thing as truth while the changing developments in society continue to contradict each other. Not only this, but technical reasons also preclude the expression of a completely accurate representation. It is often suggested that documentary has close similarity to the newsreel. By the Trade they are naturally confused because they both, in their respective ways, deal with natural material. But there the likeness ends. Their approach to and interpretation of that material are widely different. The essence of the documentary method lies in its dramatisation of actual material. The very act of dramatising causes a film statement to be false to actuality. We must remember that most documentary is only truthful in that it represents an attitude of mind. The aim of propaganda is persuasion and persuasion implies a particular attitude of mind towards this, that or the other subject. To be truthful within the technical limits of the camera and microphone demands description, which is the aim of the instructional film, and not dramatisation, which is the qualification of the documentary method. Thus even a plain statement of fact in documentary demands dramatic interpretation in order that it may be 'brought alive' on the screen.

We may assume, then, that documentary determines the approach to a subject but not necessarily the subject itself. Further, that this approach is defined by the aims behind production, by the director's intentions and by the forces making production a possibility. And because of the film camera's inherent capacity for reproducing a semblance of actuality and because the function of editing is believed to be the mainspring of film creation, it has so far been found that the best material for documentary purpose is naturally, and not artificially, contrived.

But it would be a grave mistake to assume that the documentary method differs from story-film merely in its preference for natural material. That would imply that natural material alone gives the distinction, which is untrue. To state that only documentary makes use of analytical editing methods is equally mistaken. At least one leading exponent of the documentary tradition (Flaherty) was creating the living scene in film before the scientific experiments of the Russians became common knowledge, while the latter have applied their methods of technique to many purely fictional films. To postulate that documentary is realistic as opposed to the romanticism of the story-film, with its theatrical associations, is again incorrect; for although documentary may be realistic in its concern with actuality, realism applies not only to the material but more especially to the method of approach to that material.

Such inspirations as I suggest are the essential aims of documentary demand a sense of social responsibility difficult to maintain in our world today. That, I am fully prepared to admit. But, at the same time, your documentary director dare not be neutral, or else he becomes merely descriptive and factual.

The function that the film performs within the present social and political sphere, as indicated in our first chapter, must be kept constantly in mind. Relative freedom of expression for the views of the documentarist will obviously vary with the production forces he serves and the political system in power. In countries still maintaining a parliamentary system, discussion and projection of his beliefs within certain limits will be permitted only so long as they do not seriously oppose powerful vested interests, which most often happen to be the forces controlling production. Under an authoritarian system, freedom is permissible provided his opinions are in accord with those of the State for social and political advance, until presumably such a time shall arrive when the foundations of the State are strong enough to withstand criticism. Ultimately, of course, you will appreciate that you can neither make films on themes of your own choice, nor apply treatments to accepted themes, unless they are in sympathy with the aims of the dominant system.

Notes

i See Rudolph Arnheim, *Cinema Quarterly*, vol. ii, no. 3.
ii *Cinema Quarterly*, vol. i, no. 2.

Films of Fact and Fiction (1938)

(From Theatre Arts Magazine, New York, March 1938; reprinted in Rotha on the Film)

It took a world depression to shake our belief that public affairs jog along smoothly enough without much worry by the ordinary citizen. It was the depression, with its personal as well as national tragedies, that brought a ripening of social conscience in country and city. Since that memorable year of 1929 there has been a growing public thirst for information about current affairs. The constant repetition of labour strife, of political corruption, of exposures of brigandage by industrialists, of undeclared but bloody wars all over the outside world, of the darkening menace of the dictator states, all these things have urged the citizen to ask what's happening beneath the surface, and why? Public affairs have at last become of public interest.

To meet this demand, new techniques have been developed in all modern mediums for communication of fact. From the straight-forward presentation of news to the dramatised expression of an editorial opinion, there have been experiments which might not have been made if aesthetic purpose had been the sole urge. The success of pictorial journalism in such American papers as *Life* and *Photo-History*, of dramatic rendition of current events over the air by the *March of Time*, and of such sociologically important productions in the American theatre as *The Living Newspapers*, *Pins and Needles* and *The Cradle Will Rock* is proof of the existence of an alert public interest in public affairs. The film industry, usually slow to catch on to new movements, has played a leading and influential part in this dramatisation of fact. The camera-work of newsreel and documentary films has been mainly responsible for the great strides made in photo-journalism. Today, the movie as a medium for presenting fact, as a reflection of reality, offers more stimulating chances for creative experiment than the socially-constricted fiction film.

Regular moviegoers know what is being done to bring reality to the screen. The *March of Time* swings along with its pendulum beat. The newsreel, still shy of public reaction to screen controversy, scores an occasional success by a cameraman who has the luck and toughness to be on the spot, as at the Chicago steel riots and the *Hindenburg* airship disaster. The documentary film grows out of its infant stage of romantic impressionism and gets down to using human beings as well as machines. But at each step forward the makers of factual films are met by the same problem—the representation of the individual and the relating of that individual to his social and economic background.

The closer the movie gets to a dramatised expression of reality, and I mean current reality, the more acute becomes this problem of the portrayal of the individual. In the newsreel, facts are represented simply in terms of their physical appearance in time. While current they are news, but they soon become history. The drama lies in the vitality and authenticity of the material and not in the method of presentation. *The March of Time* monthly film issue made its appearance in America in 1935. The reel adapts from the newspaper a reporting purpose which claims to give the inside story behind current events and borrows from the fiction film a dramatic method of presentation. Using partly the same naturally-shot material which is the stuff of newsreel and partly staged dramatic scenes with both real people and actors, it tries to present a selective picture of an event which implies a comment, often ironic, upon the event itself. Like the newsreel, it uses also the method of the personal interview but bends the individual to fit its editorial purpose, as with the junk-merchant in the Scrap-Iron item recently issued. Its narration is written in a highly descriptive, provocative style and delivered with a breathless emotion which does not always coincide with the subject of its visuals. But its journalistic insistence on speed leaves little time for treating individuals; the reel lacks human quality almost as much as the newsreel from which it stems.

In the Soviet Union the dramatisation of fact has been a first aim since the cinema was nationalised in 1919. Many of the earlier Soviet films dealt with what was to their sponsors and creators the greatest event of modern history—The Workers' Revolution of 1917 and the historic events that led up to its success. Pudovkin's *Mother* was based on Gorky's novel of the 1905 revolution; Eisenstein's *Potemkin* on the Black Sea mutiny of the same year. It is worth noting that both films, along with others, departed freely from actual fact.

The physical effects made possible by rhythmic arrangements of shots, as had been first used by D.W. Griffith in *Birth of a Nation* and *Intolerance*, were exploited to put across in a semi-sensational, semi-hysterical manner this blood-and-fire material. Analysis of their editing methods showed Eisenstein and Pudovkin a way in which the film medium could conform to the fundamental principles of Marxist dialectic reasoning. Their films of mutiny and uprising were largely based on the clash of class against class, or the mob versus the military. Their drama was conflict. And so long as their subject material was the stuff of revolution, their methods were successful.

In many of the early films, natural actors were used. While they were running around in the mass, they ran as well as any trained actors could have run. But when individual characterisation was required, new and serious problems arose. People as individuals in relation to their social and economic background demand psychological understanding and screen interpretation which cannot always be achieved by tricks of editing. Thus the Russians found themselves up against both a technical problem in film direction and a sociological problem of the place of the human being in society. In interpreting human beings in films, the Russians had also to interpret the individual's attitude towards the State and his economic and social relationships, a problem that had not before been seriously met in movies. In most American and European fiction films the subjects did not reflect the social conditions of the period, except in such rare cases as the modern story in Griffith's *Intolerance* and in Von Stroheim's *Greed*. But once the Soviet directors, like the British documentary film-makers later, decided that their films should deal with real life, they were inevitably involved in the bigger sociological issue.

Recent events have shown that the solution to this problem depends largely upon the development of social and economic problems in the Soviet State itself. The enthusiastic self-criticism so popular in the Russian arts has continually expressed dissatisfaction with these efforts, and at the Moscow Film Festival in 1935 it was stated that the films of Pudovkin and Eisenstein were 'undramatic' and 'coldly intellectual'. The crowd must no longer be the hero; it must be represented through the character development of its leader. The theory and practice of montage which had worked so well with non-actors and mass movement must be reconsidered in the light of the emotional powers of the professional actor. 'We need actors with great passions,' proclaimed Dinamov; and

Chapaev, with its actor-hero Boris Babotchkin, was the film of the year, although technically it was inferior to the work of the better-known directors. The subsequent development of this trend produced films like *The Youth of Maxim* in which story and acting illustrated the developing intellectual and emotional experiences of the chief protagonists as they reacted to changing social occurrences.

Pudovkin attempted to meet the difficulty by going straight to the individual himself, studying his behaviour, trying to understand his reactions and then building the character filmically by editing methods. He got his actors to externalise their feelings before the camera by using various trick stimuli. Eisenstein, on his return from Mexico and the US, did not resume production but assumed the role of professor and developed a series of methods (the 'internal monologue', the creation of a class character who will act as *pars pro toto* for the mass) by which he hoped to emotionalise and humanise the ideological film. Thus actors and acting returned in full force to the Soviet film studio. Stories and plots were invented. With this sudden swing from one use of the medium to another there has inevitably resulted a technical and aesthetic setback. The recent Russian films have had more human qualities than those of ten years ago but they have not equalled the technical brilliance that made *Potemkin* and *Storm Over Asia* world-famous.

In Britain, the documentary film-makers are at present faced with this same problem of the individual. Technically and aesthetically, the documentary film includes most of the innovations of the past ten years but it is important to remember that, as in the Soviet cinema, aesthetic purpose has come second to sociological aim. Through historical research, social reference and economic understanding, they try to bring the ordinary citizen closer to the world which is intimately his own. Like the Russians, they aim to interpret the modern scene but their basis of production is different.

Although subsidised, these documentary films should not be confused with commercial advertising pictures such as are produced in Britain and America. The documentary film is an outcome of a public relations movement and results from a conscious desire on the part of government departments, industrial firms and various public bodies to create a deeper understanding between their activities and public awareness. Their makers take subjects which are only of acknowledged public interest and pursue the line that their films provide a basis for discussion on some of the more vital social issues of current living. By creating on the screen a dramatic picture of how people live and how public services work and what status the ordinary citizen can have in everyday life, these films have achieved a certain civic value. During the last six years films have been made on such divergent subjects as airways, shipping, unemployment, slum-clearance, radio and postal communication, electricity, gas, education, book-publishing, railroads, nutrition, and city administration. Thus while such social problems as unemployment and slum-clearance had been discussed in Parliament and the Press, the living fact of each as it affects the people has been brought to the screen, making audiences conscious of their vital concern in current public affairs.

Most of the early British documentary films, like *Industrial Britain* and *Contact*, treated the individual simply as an uncharacterised type. He may have been given a name and a place by the commentator but he was invested with no human feelings and related to no background beyond his immediate job. In many cases, the interest of the film director lay in the job and not in the man who was doing it, unless it was to make him the romantic figure of a craftsman as did Flaherty with his glass-blowers and pottery-makers in the Black Country. Most often the documentary film-makers were embarrassed at the thought of handling their people *as people* and took the easiest way out by treating them as symbols ('the man behind the machine'). In addition, most of the directors were young and lacked familiarity with the materials of the medium. When Grierson made *Drifters* in 1928, he confesses that he did it 'without knowing one lens from another'. Again, the romantic style most nearly approached the 'interest' pictures and travelogues to which audiences were accustomed and thus the films made in this style, like *Contact* and *O'er Hill and Dale*, were at first the most popular. It was not long, however, before simple lyric films like *The Country Comes to Town* were developed into such an aesthetically satisfying film as Basil Wright's *The Song of Ceylon*, and the striving after social analysis made something more of *Shipyard* than just a descriptive film of shipbuilding. This trend continues to be developed, using new techniques of sound and speech, and has resulted in such emotionally exciting and sometimes romantic films as *Night Mail* and *The Future's in the Air*, although the place of the individual is still largely ignored.

The personal interview with camera and microphone, first used in Elton's *Workers and Jobs* and Anstey's *Housing Problems* in 1935, cut right across this impressionist style. Here were real human beings spontaneously speaking and gesturing right into the lens and microphone. This was not acting but normal behaviour far as the presence of the camera would permit. Sociologically, this was important; but the method deprived the documentary film of much of its cinematic quality. It became an illustrated lecture studded with personal interviews which provided 'documentary' evidence that the unseen commentator was speaking the truth. To set up camera and microphone and to record what is placed before them, occasionally cutting away from the portrait of the speaker to visuals of what he is talking about, is nobody's creative fun except that of the newsreel cameraman. *The Nutrition Film (Enough to Eat?)*, *Smoke Menace* and *Children at School* followed the same method although the latter staged small scenes in which professional actors were used. Valuable as sociological documents, and it is important that they are being made, these films contribute little to the fundamental problem of the dramatic presentation of human beings. Aesthetically, they mark a conscious effort to break with the romantic approach of *Coal Face* and *Night Mail*.

This danger of journalistic reporting and the snapshot influence of the *March of Time* were recognised by Cavalcanti. In *We Live in Two Worlds* he tried to combine both the interview and the impressionistic style in an intimate globe-side chat with Mr J.B. Priestley. But even this was not using the individual as actor. The Swiss peasants were as uncharacterised as the glass-blowers in *Industrial Britain*. The attempt to humanise the postal-workers, especially the nervous trainee in *Night Mail*, was more successful. So far only two British documentaries have got down to the real problem.

The Saving of Bill Blewitt, a story of fisher-people in a small Cornish village, is perhaps the best example of the handling of natural actors in documentary. But the plugged publicity angle of the Savings Bank was so incongruous beside the honesty of the people themselves that despite its subtle introduction, the audience was resentful at being fooled. For all the natural quality of the acting and the technical skill of Cavalcanti and Harry Watt's production, the film never got beyond being a publicity film as did *Night Mail* and *The Song of Ceylon*. *Today We Live*, a film of social service activities, carried a slight story based on fact and alternated between two locations—a town in a depressed mining area in South Wales and a country village in the Cotswolds. The characters were played by unemployed miners and country villagers. None of them was required to do anything which he or she did not do in ordinary life, with the result that, although sincere, their 'acting' was without emotional appeal. By nature of its dual location, moreover, the film lacked the space to develop human characterisation in each sequence and would have succeeded better, I believe, had its sponsors agreed to tell one story instead of two. Despite this, *Today We Live* gave an authentic picture of life as it is lived in two widely differing parts of Britain and, for almost the first time in documentary, had intentional humour. The characters grew out of their surroundings and their economic circumstances determined their actions. It is doubtful if professional actors would have done the job better.

The few available American documentary films do not contribute much to this discussion. The Mexican-made *The Wave* used non-professional actors but either lack of direction or the superimposition of a philosophical argument on persons who did not fully understand its implications resulted in a picture of embarrassing awkwardness. Neither of Pare Lorentz's well known films, *The Plow that Broke the Plains* or *The River*, had any attempt at characterisation. Despite its difficult production circumstances, Joris Ivens' *The Spanish Earth* had considerable human feeling which arose, I suspect, from the very nature of the material and Ernest Hemingway's narration.

In retrospect, we must not overlook the films of Robert Flaherty. It is true that he is mainly interested in the re-enactment of fading customs and crafts among semi-primitive peoples, but Flaherty, more than any other documentary film-maker, has known how to handle his people in front of the camera. He is helped, of course, by the fact that most of us are unfamiliar with his people and it is only when he treads on the home front, as in *Industrial Britain* and *Man of Aran*, that we realise his shortcomings. But his habit of digging himself in, absorbing the background and letting the theme emerge gradually is, without doubt, a sensible method if the production budget permits.

As far as the individual in the studio-made fiction film is concerned, we shall find that few fiction films deal with subjects which have their roots in reality. While subjects have little in common with real life, this discrepancy does not matter. But when the movie touches social reality in the gangster film, Cagney cannot be just Cagney. No more can Muni be just Muni when the social background becomes real, or pretends to be real, in *Zola*. Here was a character who must needs be deep-rooted in his background. Relation of character to background is a familiar matter to the stage actor but it is more difficult on the screen. More difficult because the illusion of background on the stage is known and accepted as an illusion, whereas the screen can present a background that, for all its studio artifice and back-projection, is very close to the real thing, in fact, often is. A wide difference exists between Muni playing Zola with the aid of an elaborate make-up and weeks of historical research, and Cagney playing Tom Powers in *The Public Enemy*. The first was a deliberate fake; the second was real. I am not suggesting that Mr Cagney is, or was, a gangster but I am saying that he, like so many other born New Yorkers, knew what he was acting about. He knew the smell of the thing because it was contemporary and real. As a result, he was able to create a closer relationship between character and background than did Mr Muni, whose performance was nearer to that of a filmed photoplay than a film. I doubt if it is the screen's function to show dressed-up history. The medium is perhaps too real.

I have raised, I hope, a whole series of questions that go right to the heart of the movie. Can the studio-made fiction film with actors and sets come as close to presenting reality as the realist film? No matter how faithful the sets, how convincing the acting and how accurate the research, can a studio reconstruction achieve the dramatic intensity which is inherent in the real thing? Could the trick department restage the burning of the *Hindenburg* so as to give us that same sense of horror which we got from the newsreel? Shall we not always be aware of the fake? Then is it possible to bring about a blending of the two methods; or should the fact film and the fiction film pursue their divergent courses? Only on such rare occasions as Pabst's *Kameradschaft* have the two approaches been married with success. Pabst's mixing of actors with real people, or real exterior backgrounds with studio-built interiors, was so perfectly done that the audience was not aware that it was not seeing reality. It is surprising that so little has been done to develop Pabst's theories, theories which he himself has been unable to develop owing to the unsuitable subjects of his later films. But *Kameradschaft* does suggest a logical development of the realist film which takes the best from both the fiction and the fact film.

Neo-realism: *Bicycle Thieves* (1950)

(From *Public Opinion*, 6 January, 1950; reprinted in *Rotha on the Film*)

We start with New Year luck. A brilliant film is on view in London; in my opinion the most brilliant film for many years. It reaffirms all one's faith in the cinema. It fulfils hopes long held. It proves conclusively (if anyone doubted it) that a man with ideas and skill, with a simple story and a movie camera can still make a film which outshines all the gaudy expensive products of the film factories. This is the real art of cinematography.

Vittorio De Sica's *Bicycle Thieves* arrives here garlanded with international prizes and praise unstinted from critics both American and European. It deserves them all. His *Shoeshine* will be remembered. Here is a story of an out-of-work, gaunt-faced man in an industrial suburb of Rome—the sort of Rome you do not usually see on the screen. Here is his wife, patient yet desperate in her struggle to keep things going. And here is their young son, eager, puzzled, wanting to help and understand. Then comes the chance of a job, bill-posting, but only if the man has a bicycle. He has, in pawn. So in its place goes the bed-linen. The wonderful next day dawns with work to be done. But within the hour, the bicycle is stolen. With it goes all, save the faint hope that the thief can be found. The search begins and goes on all Sunday. The bicycle is not found, the thief is; but there are no witnesses. In utter despair, finally, the man himself steals a bicycle—one among the hundreds he sees around him. He is chased, caught but generously released. He walks home with his son through the crowds.

All my life I shall wonder what happened to Antonio, to his son and wife—and then I realise it was all a story. No bicycle; no sheets. It only happened for the camera. Antonio is really Lamberto Maggiorani, a metal-worker from Breda. Says De Sica, 'He left his own work for two months to lend his face to me'. The boy, Bruno, is Enzo Staiola, 'the most loveable child in the world . . . son of refugees whom I met by accident'. The rest of the characters, with only one exception, are also real people. The surroundings are not sets in the studio; they are the streets, the markets, the passages, the little rooms, the stark concrete blocks of flats, the very reality of workaday Rome.

They say this is a simple film because the basic story is simple. To me it is not a simple film; underneath the few events and the handful of characters is the profundity of a wealth of human experience and a wide range of cinematic skill. It is not easy to film real life except as raw newsreel record, It is fantastically difficult to film a drama of events taking place in real surroundings where the director seems to have control over the very crowds and traffic of Rome. To make things even harder, De Sica deliberately chose to set one of his incidents in a torrential downpour of rain, which meant that in the remaining sequences the streets and pavements had to be wet to preserve visual continuity. Throughout, the photography is magnificent. The American *Naked City* had a naive crime story superimposed on some real filming of New York. *Bicycle Thieves* has a deeply emotional, intensely human story arising from, and an inseparable part of, post-war Rome. I know of no other film that catches and dramatises everyday existence and shapes it to tell a story with such subtlety, observation and penetration. Comparisons are a waste of time. This is not a pioneer picture but a deeply-rooted milestone that will be looked back on for many years. It is a complete vindication of the man with the camera and a conscience.

From the opening scene on the steps of the Labour Exchange to the closing shot of the camera moving with Antonio and his weeping son along the thronged pavements at dusk, one wonderfully subtle sequence follows another to create the pattern of the whole. The covey of young priests sheltering from the rain, the cabaret rehearsal taking place alongside the political meeting, the piles of bed-linen reaching high up to the pawnshop ceiling, the chase among the outraged girls in the brothel out-of-hours, the epileptic fit of the thief in the sun-drenched back street and the crowd ganging in to protect him, the dumb little gathering of believers in the fortune-teller's bedroom, the meal in the restaurant when Antonio tries to restore his son's confidence in him, these are only a few of the thousand images which pursue me from this film. And the little moments within a scene: the expression on the fortune-teller's face when the boy tries to give the fee to her instead of to the maid, the police-superintendent more concerned with the armed jeeps getting to the labour meeting than with a workman's stolen bicycle, Maria venting her bitter anger on the zinc washtub—these moments reveal De Sica as a director to be placed on the level of Stroheim and Pudovkin at their very best.

Satire is there, deliberate barbed shafts that hurt where they are intended to hurt. I have no sympathy for the wounded in this battle against poverty and humiliation. I have no use for the hypocrisies of the well-off. I side with De Sica in his stinging comments on the care handed out to the poor herded into the soup-kitchen church.

The search for the stolen bicycle could easily have been just another search, but it is paralleled with an expression of the relationship between father and son that is moving in the extreme. Universal in its appeal, it cannot adequately be described. Frustrated and angry in their abortive search, Antonio abruptly and without cause strikes his son. The moments that follow leading up to the father's sudden thought that the boy has thrown himself into the river are handled with a psychological understanding and a skill of cinema that are unique in many years of films. It is no use talking of this child's 'acting'; it is behaviour, not acting. The look in this boy's eyes, his movements and reactions, are not acted. Between him and De Sica, between the others in this film and De Sica, lies a secret something to which only a great film director knows the answer. We cannot probe it; we can only admire it.

Nothing is irrelevant in this film. What speech there is relates only to essentials. The music of Alessandro Cicognini is beautifully unobtrusive, there when needed and then sparingly. Fundamentally it is a visual film. De Sica and his cameraman, Carlo Montuori, tell it all through the eye. 'To see,' says De Sica, 'is very useful to an artist. Most men do not want to see because often the pain of others troubles them. We, on the contrary, want to see.' And he sees not only tragedy, pain and pathos but humour, joy and laughter. The film, although tragic, is full of comedy. Some will call its ending inconclusive. How, in truth, could it be otherwise?

Let Mr Rank, balance sheet in hand, observe this film. Let Sir Alex stroke his leonine head in envy, for here is something that will live longer and give more pleasure than all the reconstructions of Tolstoy and Wilde. Let Mr James Lawrie (of the Film Finance Corporation) forget for a moment to be photographed with film stars and mark how a film can be made on a shoestring if the genius, the ideas and the purpose are there. Let the producers, directors and other makers of films in our academies and unions look humbly at a work which burns with sincerity and technical brilliance. *Bicycle Thieves* is a true work of cinema which, if exhibitors everywhere have an eye to good business, will satisfy audiences of every kind. But it is useless to play it between the Huggetts last week and Betty Grable next week. It offers a challenge to exhibitors, not to their audiences. It must be presented with a new kind of showmanship that must be learnt for other films as well as this if the industry is to survive.

Umberto D (1955)

(From *British Film Academy Journal*, Spring 1955; reprinted in *Rotha on the Film*)

To interpret the reality of living on the cinema screen has been a constant challenge to many directors and writers since the early days. On the one hand, the newsreel reporting what its cameras see and its editors select; on the other, the fictional story played by acted characters basing its events and situations on real life; in the middle, the documentary in all its many forms, drawing from reality like Flaherty and the early Eisenstein, or intermixing actors and non-actors as in the films of the Crown Film Unit. In the post-war years, due perhaps to documentary influence, many Hollywood and British films attempted stories set against real 'backgrounds' but few, if any, achieved an honest interpretation of reality. Occasionally the French succeeded, as in Renoir's often overlooked *Toni* and in Clément's *Les Jeux Interdits*.

The growth of what is called neo-realism in Italian cinema stems from Visconti's astonishing film *Ossessione* in 1942. Those who missed the single performance of this rare and forbidden film at the New London Film Society were unfortunate. Although Rossellini's *Rome—Open City* and *Paisan* hogged most of the limelight in the immediate post-war years, it soon became clear that Vittorio De Sica and the screenwriter Cesare Zavattini were the two most significant figures. De Sica had been busy as a charming, polished actor in cinema and theatre for many years, had directed his first film *Rose Scarlatte* in 1940, and had collaborated with Zavattini as far back as 1941. In *Sciuscià* (1947), *Ladri di Biciclette* (1948) and *Miracolo a Milano* (1950), the team of De Sica–Zavattini proved to be the most formidable in the dynamic Italian cinema that was too soon to fall under Hollywood influence and consequent glamorisation and decadence.

Zavattini has himself described how in each of these films he tried to get nearer to the unvarnished, unadulterated presentation of life, and seemed in 1950 to be thinking along lines that were reminiscent of Dziga Vertov's Kino-Eye theories of the early twenties. If he still holds this view, then he must quickly transfer his talents to the television outside-broadcast cameras with their capacity for immediacy and eavesdropping but with their very limited powers of selection. De Sica, perhaps because of his actor's training, has still maintained a use of characters to interpret the reality of living although he has used in the main real people or little-known actors for his purpose and has eschewed the artificialities of the studio wherever possible. So we come to the film *Umberto D* by these two distinguished film-makers, which has only recently had a public screening in London although made in 1951. And it is in England, oddly enough, that this picture has first had wide critical acclaim, a fact that has delighted De Sica and for which he has expressed his heartfelt gratitude.

It was ironic that while De Sica was being promoted by the Unitalia people as its most handsome, seductive actor during the Italian Film Festival in London, *Umberto D* was screened to the critics ex-Festival at the National Film Theatre (with De Sica present) and scooped the reviews of the week from all the critics who matter. It had languished two years in British Lion's vaults. They could not, it was said, find an exhibitor to book it, though no reason was ever offered why they did not themselves show it at their Rialto. However, we must be grateful to the Curzon for taking the icy plunge.

Umberto D, as is now well known, is a moving study of the loneliness of old age as experienced by a retired civil servant eking out an existence on a pension too meagre for the humblest living in post-war Rome. It is dedicated by De Sica to his father and is his own best-loved film. From its exciting opening sequence of the dispersal of a demonstration of old-age pensioners by the police to its almost unbearably moving ending when the old man is prevented from suicide by his beloved dog's fear, it is a masterpiece of human observation, of detail and of mood. It has warmth, satire, humour and pathos but is never sentimental as the wonderfully handled scenes between the old man and his terrier could so easily have been. The understanding shown by De Sica and Zavattini for the feelings of the unwanted, the aged who have served life faithfully, the penniless through no fault of their own, pitifully trying to keep up the semblance of respectability, makes this film into, in my opinion, one of the great films of all time, worthy to rank with the best of Chaplin, Stroheim, Griffith or the Russians.

The actors, to us unknown names and maybe some not actors are as real people in actual surroundings, with all the suffering and pathos and delight in small things that are true of our own lives if we have experienced life fully. How much they owe in their performances to De Sica's direction, how much to their own interpretation of a 'part', is and should remain a director's secret. The scene in which Maria, the little servant-girl, pregnant by one of two soldiers in the barracks opposite but she doesn't know or much care which, gets up from her mattress on the floor to clear up the kitchen in the morning, opening a cupboard door with her toes—this is a moment when collaboration between director and actor is sacred. In its sharp satire on the Roman Catholic Church, the hospital-ward scene with its handing out of the rosaries, its brusque medicos and smirking nuns is reminiscent of the church charity sequence in *Bicycle Thieves*. These are only two of dozens of scenes that each interpret the minor daily events in the lives of this small group of people—old Umberto himself, a figure of dignity and grandeur and tenderness beautifully expressed by Carlo Battisti (said to be a university professor), his tarty, calculating, cold-hearted landlady (Lina Gennari), Maria the servant-girl, wonderfully played by young Maria Pia Casilio, the unbelievably intelligent dog itself and dozens of small portraits each of which remains in the mind long after the picture has been seen. It is photographed in the casual, almost newsreel manner of the Italian neo-realists by G.R. Aldo, who also shot Visconti's *La Terra Trema*.

I can understand some people actively disliking this film, as at its time Stroheim's *Greed* was disliked, because it is too close to reality to be pleasant to those who refuse to face up to reality. It is a social protest made with tenderness and affection. And unlike so many such protests, it has no bitterness in it. It has a purity, an unswerving integrity of purpose, and an awareness of simple people that mark De Sica, once again, as a great artist of our time. Zavattini, too, must share the credit.

Gavin Lambert has given some of the reasons why *Umberto D*, and other examples of the neo-realist group, are disliked by the authorities in Italy. He quotes from an open letter by the Under-Secretary to the Prime Minister's office to De Sica, published in the Italian Press after the première of *Umberto D*. 'We ask the man of culture,' wrote the under-secretary, 'to feel his social responsibility, which should not be limited to description of the abuses and miseries of a system and a generation . . . If it is true that evil can be fought by harshly spotlighting its most miserable aspects, it is also true that De Sica has rendered bad service to his country if people throughout the world start thinking that Italy in the middle of the twentieth century is the same as in *Umberto D.* . . . We beg him never to forget this small duty of healthy and constructive optimism, which really encourages humanity to move forward and hope.[i]

Umberto D is, of course, a film of hope, of belief in people's inherent goodness, and any tourist who wouldn't visit Italy because of it had best stay at home. Driven to attempted suicide, Umberto nevertheless draws back when he sees that belief in him, even if held only by an animal, is to be broken. We do not know how he will continue his struggle but we do know he has restored a faith placed in him.

It is quoted by Zavattini as being said that 'Neo-realism does not offer solutions. The end of a neo-realist film is particularly inconclusive.'[ii] This he cannot accept. He counters: 'With regard to my own work, the characters and situations in films for which I have written the scenario, they remain unsolved from a practical point of view simply because "this is reality". But every moment of the film is, in itself, a continuous answer to some question. It is not the concern of an artist to propound solutions. It is enough, and quite a lot, I should say, to make an audience feel the need, the urgency, for them. In any case, what films *do* offer solutions? "Solutions" in this sense, if they are offered, are sentimental ones, resulting from the superficial way in which problems have been faced. At least, in my work I leave the solution to the audience.' These last are familiar words to those who understood the documentary movement in Britain twenty years ago or more.

But the present days are dark for the neo-realists in Italy, as indeed they are for many other film-makers who would interpret reality in terms of human respect and understanding. With a prosperous, glossified Italian film industry, its eyes set on the gold of foreign markets, with official pressures exercised against them, the neo-realists are hard put to it to realise their aims, relatively cheap though their films may be to make. Like von Stroheim before him, De Sica has recently spent much of his time exploiting his popularity as an actor; only in this way can he build up reserves which will allow him to direct again as he wishes. He and Zavattini have plans for another picture; that is the best news for a long time.

Notes

[i] *Sight and Sound*, vol. 24, no. 3, pp. 147–166.
[ii] Ibid. vol. 23, no. 2, pp. 64–69.

ROTHA'S WRITING

II

CINEMA AND BRITAIN
CULTURE AND INDUSTRY

Paul Rotha's commitment to the promotion of the art of the film in Britain informs a great deal of his writing. As part of a generation which was profoundly influenced by the emergence of an intellectual film culture in the 1920s, Rotha was interested in developing and extending that culture. The major achievement of the Film Society was the exposure it gave, albeit to a limited London audience, to a much broader range of cinema than that offered by commercial distributors and exhibitors. It was a showcase in particular for 'art' films from Continental Europe which collectively presented very different aesthetic approaches to the kind of Hollywood product which dominated British screens.

But the Film Society was not the only place where alternatives to the mainstream could be seen, and there were also the pioneering activities of a small number of enlightened exhibitors who are described by Rotha in 'The "unusual" film movement' (1940). Such activities, however, were necessarily limited and subject to commercial pressures. Consequently Rotha makes a case for a more firmly established approach to the promotion of an intellectual and informed film culture via the exhibition of a broad selection of the best of international production in 'Repertory film movement' (1931). This essay effectively makes the case for a London-based national repertory film theatre, programmed by an expert advisory committee and connected to a regional network of film societies. Rotha also identifies the pressing need for the achievements of international cinema to be documented and for the publication of a magazine or journal dealing with the development of the medium in a comprehensive and intelligent manner. This agenda is broadened and complemented by 'A museum for the cinema' (1930) which advocates the setting up of a museum of film technology, a library of films, and accessible collections of books, posters and stills. Much of what is proposed in the latter two articles was ultimately incorporated into the activities of the British Film Institute, which was established in 1933. In due course the BFI came to incorporate a National Film Theatre linked to a network of Regional Film Theatres; an extensive film (and subsequently television) archive, including a stills, posters and designs department; a library and information department; an education department; and the publication of two intelligent magazines, *Sight and Sound* and *Monthly Film Bulletin* (which merged in 1991). It is significant that at the time of writing, the future of the institute as a distinct body is once again under debate and proposals have been made to incorporate its activities in a larger publicly-funded film council.

Rotha believed that a greater and more sophisticated appreciation of the art of the film would have a positive impact on indigenous film-making in Britain. 'The British film' (1930), from *The Film Till Now*, is a scathing indictment of wasted opportunity and lack of imagination and vision on the part of British producers more interested in emulating their American counterparts than exploring the artistic potential of the medium. Such an unsympathetic environment hampered the efforts of talented Continental film-makers like E.A. Dupont who had begun making films in Britain in the late 1920s, and even the best work they produced rarely matched the achievements of their earlier films. However, Rotha retained a certain fondness for the Continental émigré. He became a close friend of the German screenwriter Carl Mayer, who had worked on some of what were, for Rotha, landmarks in the development of the art of the film including *The Cabinet of Dr Caligari* and *The Last Laugh*. The three short pieces on Alexander Korda can be read in this context, with Rotha praising the Hungarian impresario not for his creative brilliance but for recognising potential and seizing opportunities to which British producers were blind, resulting in major critical and commercial successes such as *The Private Life of Henry VIII* (1933). Such warmth demonstrates a more nuanced appreciation of a figure who in every other respect fitted the image of the kind of commercially oriented producer Rotha despised.

Being a practising film-maker as well as a critic and theorist, Rotha was well positioned to consider the relationship between artistic and industrial factors in the promotion of creative film-making. By the end of World War II the quality of British films had risen considerably and some were even beginning to achieve levels of popularity comparable with the slick Hollywood product that continued to make up the lion's share of British exhibition. But this was also a time of great debate around what kind of cinema Britain wanted and needed. The major indigenous player in the film industry at the time was the Rank Organisation which owned the two largest studios, the largest British distribution company and two of the three major cinema chains. The concern this raised formed the major thrust of the Palache Report of 1944 which cautioned against tendencies towards monopoly in the film industry. The 1940s was also a period of major government intervention with programmes of nationalisation in industry and the initiation of the welfare state. Similar thinking was being applied to the film industry, and in 1945 Rotha submitted his own report 'The government and the film industry' which argues the case for a Government Film Corporation to finance and produce independent British features and documentaries. Such a move would result in the production of more British films which could in turn help combat American dominance; such a body would work against monopoly by providing an alternative force in British production, and it would provide a stable environment for the pursuit of excellence. Rotha also takes the opportunity to make the case for the documentary, which had a 16-year history of public support but which was particularly vulnerable outside a protected subsidised sector.

The kind of body eventually established by the government to aid the film industry, the National Film Finance Corporation, fell far short of Rotha's ambitions as is demonstrated in 'A plan for British films' (1949), which makes certain pointed suggestions for improvement in accordance with his original vision. The question of government intervention in the film industry remains a central one today. Since the disbandonment of the NFFC in 1985 and the Eady Levy (a subsidy on admissions which was used to support production) there have been frequent calls for various kinds of measures to promote film-making in Britain from tax breaks to subsidies. The recent creation of the National Lottery has led to a substantial new source of funding for production but questions remain as to how money is awarded and the kinds of films subsequently made with lottery support.

The final essay in this section, 'The problem of the short film' (1966), raises important questions about the cultural value and necessity of this form as a means for new film-makers to learn their craft and reach an audience, and the problems of securing adequate and appropriate distribution for such work. Recent collaborative schemes like 'New Directors' and 'Tartan Shorts' initiated by the BFI and Scottish Screen in association with broadcasters such as Channel 4 and the BBC respectively, testify to the continuing importance of the short film as a cultural form.

The 'Unusual' Film Movement (1940)

(From *Documentary News Letter*, June 1940; reprinted in *Rotha on the Film*)

To see good films in London today is simple: you go to the Odeon or the Empire or the Academy; the Polytechnic, the Paris, the Everyman, the Cinephone or Studio One; maybe to the Curzon or the Embassy. Few good foreign films fail sooner or later to get to London.

Twenty years ago it was not so easy. Big American films had their premières at West End theatres, at the Scala, Drury Lane, Covent Garden, the Palace or the London Pavilion. But Continental films, except for the spectacular Ufa product, crept in sideways, lay about in Wardour Street vaults, got maybe (after 1925) a London Film Society showing.

The Davis brothers were really the first showmen to present Continental films of a 'different' kind in London. They owned the Marble Arch Pavilion, then London's premier cinema, and showed *Caligari* there in 1920 and followed it later by other famous Ufa films—*Metropolis* and *The Spy*. The Polytechnic, managed then, as now, by Mr Leslie, ran *Destiny* in 1924. *Anne Boleyn* (*Deception*) and *The Golem* got Scala showings and that was about all. But none of these cinemas adopted a policy of regularly running 'different' Continental films.

If memory is reliable (curse the evacuation!), the first London cinema to announce a Continental policy was the Embassy near the Holborn Restaurant. It ran Grune's *The Street* and Volkoff's *Kean* before closing. That was in 1924. Like the handsomely produced monthly, *The Silver Screen*, the Embassy was before its time. No one else tried the experiment. Occasional Ufa pictures like *The Last Laugh*, *Manon Lescaut*, *Vaudeville* and *Berlin* went to the Capitol (now the Gaumont) or the New Gallery. *Siegfried* was given a spectacular setting at the Albert Hall, where Mr Charles Cochran later presented *Faust*, complete with Sir Landon Ronald and a symphony orchestra. London had no equivalent of the Paris 'little cinemas', no Vieux Colombier, Studio des Ursulines, or Studio 28.

Again the story switches to the Davis brothers. Their theatres were now (1927) included in the Gaumont circuit, but the brothers retained the right to book pictures and act as managers. They owned, among others, the small Shaftesbury Avenue Pavilion which showed pictures on their second London run. But it had become dwarfed by the big new theatres and second-runs were being well looked after by the new suburban houses. Now part of a chain, it was an awkward house to book for. Thus when Stuart Davis went to Reginald Bromhead, managing director of the circuit, and suggested a new policy, Bromhead agreed. The new policy was to show Continental films, new and old, an idea which Stuart had seen working the year before at the Cameo in New York.

Davis was lucky. Wardour (now ABPC) had long had a Ufa contract and the newest German picture was *The Loves of Jeanne Ney* which the censor slashed and Wardour retitled *The Lusts of the Flesh*. Davis took over the Avenue Pavilion, hung out a banner inviting the Shaftesbury Avenue passers-by to see *The Lusts of the Flesh*, but was shrewd enough to do dual publicity with Pabst's name and for his own new policy. The 'Unusual' Film Movement and 'The Home of International Film Art' had begun. Stuart did good business with two publics. The one that mattered to him was the 'intelligent' audience which was rowing as a result of the London Film Society's private shows, the little highbrow paper *Close-Up*, the columns of one or two progressive film critics like C.A. Lejeune first in the *Manchester Guardian* and later *The Observer*, and Walter Mycroft in the *Evening Standard*. Iris Barry's book, *Let's Go to the Pictures*, must also have helped.

Stuart got, kept and enlarged that audience in the two years he ran the Avenue Pavilion. He revived all the old German classics (not so old then), *Caligari*, *The Last Laugh*, *The Street*, *Manon Lescaut*, *Warning Shadows*, *The Student of Prague*, *Tartuffe*, *Two Brothers*, *Vaudeville*, *Faust*, *Danton*, and the rest. He paid £200 to an ex-W&F salesman for a four-week run of *Waxworks* and took £1,800. He revived the famous Hollywood classics, *Woman of Paris*, *Greed*, *Foolish Wives* and *He Who Gets Slapped*. He dug up the Swedish *Gosta Berling*, the Russian *Marriage of the Bear* and *The Postmaster*. He wrote intelligent hand-outs for the press. Above all, he made his theatre a place where many people for the first time saw The Film at its best. His tiny office became a meeting-place for the most ardent film followers. Stuart himself was always the charming host.

After a while the film supply gave out so Stuart Davis went off to Paris. Here was a new field, the films of Clair, Cavalcanti, Feyder, Epstein, and the *avant-garde* shorts of Deslav, Lacombe, Man Ray and the others. He bought the English rights of the lot, started a French season with a white-tie opening and the French ambassador. He introduced London to *Finis Terrae*, *The Italian Straw Hat*, *Les Deux Timides*, *En Rade*, *Rien que les heures*, *The Fall of the House of Usher*, and many others. But his greatest success was with Feyder's *Thérèse Raquin*. First National had a copy sent over from Germany, where it had been made with a Franco-German cast for quota requirements. They were about to send it back unbooked but happened to mention it to Stuart Davis who promptly booked it. Unluckily his press show coincided with an M-G-M show. Only one critic turned up—Walter Mycroft of the *Evening Standard*. He gave it the review it deserved. The rest of the press bombarded Stuart to see the film but he refused. Next day they lined up in the public queue. The film did big business, got many provincial bookings and certainly helped to obtain Feyder his M-G-M contract in Hollywood.

Summer, 1929, saw Stuart Davis's contract with Gaumont expire. The latter decided not to carry on the policy and, at Stuart's suggestion, opened the theatre as London's first newsreel cinema. Stuart Davis took over managing the Davis Theatre, Croydon, which he still does.

It looked as if London would no longer have a 'Home of International Film Art'. But down the street was the Windmill Theatre which Elsie Cohen was managing as best she could with second-run pictures. Miss Cohen had for a long time been interested in the Continental film and had worked in Holland and Germany on production. Now at the Windmill she started an 'Unusual' Film movement and was able to get several Soviet films past the censors, her biggest success being *Turksib*. She also revived some of Stuart's successes. This lasted until the autumn when the owner of the theatre discontinued showing films and Vivian Van Damm began his famous Revudeville.

Meanwhile a few of the old regulars at the Avenue Pavilion—among them Margery Locket, J.B. Holmes, and F. Gordon Roe—started the Film Group. Stuart Davis gave us his mailing list. We circularised 12,500 people in the London area to see if they would support a successor to the Avenue Pavilion. Eighty per cent said they would. But no suitable theatre could be found except the Academy, run by Eric Hakim, who used to be a violinist at the Davis theatres. Stuart himself had tried Hakim with the idea but Hakim wanted too big a rent. A week or two later he let Elsie Cohen take over the house and announced a 'new' policy of Continental films, old and new. Hakim himself had little faith in the project and thought Miss Cohen crazy when she opened with Dovzhenko's *Earth*. But what could not be foreseen was the talking film. When it did come, it was generally predicted that the French and German film would disappear from London. Yet next April, the Academy will celebrate a decade of its policy for Continental films.

Repertory Film Movement (1931)

(From *Celluloid*)

Remarkable though it may seem in consideration of the large public interest in the serious side of the cinema, there has not as yet been established a repertory theatre of the film. Most filmgoers will admit, I think, that there are certain films of the past which, because of their achievement at their time of making and because of their influence on later production, should be available to the student and the filmgoer for reference as well as reminiscence. There are many pictures of the silent period which for emotional value and sincerity of purpose remain unsurpassed, and in my opinion it is a matter of grave importance that these films should be preserved, not only for the benefit of students today but for the pleasure of future generations.

The extraordinary growth of the private film society movement in England during the last few years—there are now, I believe, some fifteen or more active groups—clearly indicates that serious interest in the cinema is increasing. The film is first and foremost the art of the people, for of all the arts it comes nearer—or shall I say it has the capacity for coming nearer—to presenting ideas of common interest than any of the lesser means of expression. Year by year, film by film, more and more people discover that the cinema is the natural medium of the twentieth century, a synthesis of art and science that has long been the aim of intellectual activity, until to-day there must be thousands of persons who wish to see its attributes employed as they properly demand.

There are two ways in which this desire to see good films, both current and repertory, can be met—either by the private film society or by a permanent repertory cinema. But both of these solutions possess their obvious drawbacks. A film society is limited in its programmes by expense and by the increasing difficulty of procuring desirable films. A repertory cinema, if made available to the general public, which I deem essential, is open to restriction of its programmes through censorship. Yet whilst neither of these movements fully meets the requirements of the enthusiastic film student, they nevertheless deserve the warmest encouragement from anyone who cares for the future of the cinema.

Although in many ways the film society movement is admirable, there is always an inclination amongst restricted membership groups towards precocity, which in the case of the cinema is fatal to a proper under-standing of the medium as a whole. There is a prevailing tendency at the moment for film society members to favour vague phrasings of a distinctly 'arty' nature, attributing a variety of meanings to films and their directors of which the latter are quite innocent. It is fashionable to talk airily of subject-value and attach too great an importance to irrelevant theories of technique, which not only defeats the aim of societies but brings general disfavour upon the works of perfectly com-petent and simple-minded directors. Too few of these enthusiastic amateurs penetrate to the heart and meaning of cinema; they are happy to bandy slick phrases one with another and avoid the real significance of the film medium.

This effeminate dilettantism would, I think, be largely eliminated if a permanent specialist cinema could be established, possibly on the lines indicated, but not as yet realised, by the Film Group. It is essential that this movement for better cinema should originate from the public itself and not from the wishes of an elite few. The successful but brief career of the Avenue Pavilion, London, to some extent met the wishes of this more discriminating public, and the popularity which that cinema attained may be taken as part evidence of the need for a more up-to-date scheme. In recent months, several enterprising exhibitors, having scented the way of the wind, have played seasons of silent revivals. The indiscriminate selection of their programmes, however, and their obvious ignorance of what films deserve showing has limited their appeal to the student. Mention, also, must be made of the excellent work during the last five years of the London Film Society, who have done much to encourage the serious appreciation of the cinema among a certain restricted public.

What is desperately needed, what I have tried many months to achieve, and what eventually must be established despite all obstacles is a central cinema in London, where will be shown films selected as the best of their particular type by an appointed advisory committee of competent specialists. These programmes should be composed wherever possible of new foreign sound films in their original versions, revivals of silent pictures to meet the demand of the new filmgoer, with the plentiful addition of comedies, sound cartoons and a properly edited newsreel. No film exhibited at this cinema would be presented without a definite reason for its choice by the advisory committee, who would amplify their reasons in the cinema's printed programmes, which would also include interesting data concerning the film in question. Attached to the cinema should be a Clubroom and Library, for the use of those members of the general public who desired to become intimately associated with the policy of the scheme. Lectures, demonstrations and exhibitions could be arranged to meet the wishes of these more serious filmgoers; and for reference in the future, an information bureau and file of still photographs should be begun under proper supervision.

Affiliated to this central cinema, the various provincial film societies would be certain of a regular supply of interesting programmes (which is their present difficulty) as well as the advantages of interchange of opinions and lectures. In this way—which is, of course, the policy originally laid down for the Film Group but not at the moment of writing fulfilled—a definite cultural centre of cinematography such as exists nowhere in the world would be begun in England which, moreover, would secure for the future much intensely valuable information which is difficult to obtain even to-day.

The widespread lack of knowledge with regard to films of the past, their hire, history, condition and whereabouts, tempts me here to stress the immediate importance of taking stock of what the cinema has already accomplished in its comparatively short span of life. The time is at hand when the achievements of cinema should be recorded whilst they are still fresh in our minds. It is surely a matter of much urgency that we should document this great medium which is developing so rapidly before it has passed altogether from its primitive stage. In this respect but little help is forthcoming from the Press, for all but a scanty few writers are uninterested in the development of the cinema, being content to describe with vague lightness the pictures of the week. Neither does the industry itself in this country display any inclination to extend facilities to this outstanding need, for big profit-reaping concerns and theatre chains booking films on block have little concern for the welfare of the cinema. Furthermore, there is not any British paper or magazine that deals in a comprehensive and at the same time intelligent manner with the gradual development of cinematography. It is, then, the duty of this organisation which I visualise to fulfil this want and to make a start with this vast business of selecting and appraising the major works of the film.

The task will be difficult even now, for films made but a few years ago are frequently untraceable to-day, and not until accurate information is sought will it be appreciated how hard is the work to be done. When it is realised that only two positive copies exist of such a celebrated film as Robison's *Warning Shadows*, and that those are both privately owned; that there is only one copy each of *Destiny* and *The Golem*, both held by Ufa; and that copies of such instructive films as *The Loves of Jeanne Ney*, *Moana*, *Thérèse Raquin*, and *Forbidden Paradise* are unobtainable in England until someone shall step forward to pay the cost of a fresh copy, the importance of the work is merely suggested. This is the position which has to be met if any move is to be made—and in the interests of the film both as an art and as an industry it must be made—to put the cinema on the basis that it deserves as the predominant medium for expression of culture, philosophy and propaganda of the century.

A Museum for the Cinema (1930)

(From *The Connoisseur*, July 1930; reprinted in *Rotha on the Film*)

No more suitable time than the present could be found for the formation of a museum to meet the requirements of the student of the cinema and to create interest in films as objects of collectable value. The cinema has been in existence for roughly thirty-five years, during which period it has suffered shifts and divergences in natural accordance with the rapidity of its scientific, commercial and technical developments. But only in the last few years, up till the opening of the second cycle of its career marked by the introduction of mechanically-reproduced sound, has the film itself shown any qualifications that cause it to be considered as a potential work of art. The early days, however, were distinguished by innumerable although crude experiments in both America and Europe, and these, such as they are, now assume definite value as primitive examples of cinematic art.

The problem of collecting such objects may be regarded from two points of view. Firstly, there are articles of purely scientific interest relating to the evolution of the instrument itself, including early examples of cinematograph cameras and projectors, as well as various types of lighting apparatus, used by the pioneers, Edison, the Lumière brothers, Friese-Greene, Robert Paul and Thomas Armat. Secondly, and of more general interest than the mechanical side, there is at present the opportunity for the collection of actual films themselves, beginning with the 'primitives', now somewhat rare, and proceeding down the years to the scarce remaining copies of films of comparatively recent make, the rarity of which is due to the destruction of the original master negative, either by fire or by copyright laws. Few copies remain, for instance, of the short freak films with 'magic' effects made and shown by Georges

Méliès at the *Théâtre Robert Houdin* in Paris during the late '90s; whilst little product of the old London Film Company, which was making films up till the time of the outbreak of the Great War, still exists, most having been burnt under copyright agreements and still more destroyed accidentally by fire. Early films made in America, by such men as D.W. Griffith and Sydney Olcott, during the first and second decades of this century, are also difficult to obtain.

Apart from the obvious necessity that these early efforts should be gathered together, it is important also that some source of reference should be accessible to the student and the collector in order to keep check on the course of the development of the film as an art. What actually is needed is a library of films, representative of all countries, each exhibit marking a new phase in the growing aesthetic significance of the art, being examples of the ever-increasing schools of intellectual cinematography. Almost unknown to any but close observers of the cinema, there exist today several groups of film thought in Europe and America, each having its own theories and following of directors and writers. Upon investigation, it is clear that the work of such groups must be considered as being quite distinct from the usual forms of commercial cinema to which we are generally accustomed. It is not as yet widely recognised that the Russian cinematographers aim at the development of the film into a new intellectual form, a vast synthesis of art and science which is 'the purpose of all intellectual activity'.

It is essential that the progressive and in some cases valuable work of such artists, for thus they may well be termed, should be put on permanent record for educational and referential purposes. Added to which, there are other supplementary objects in connection with the cinema worthy of preservation. Such as the best film posters (those in circulation on the Continent are infinitely superior in artistic merit to the lurid scenes usually displayed in England); critical books on the film written by authoritative writers; designs for settings and costumes by well-known film architects; as well as a large number of still photographs from various distinguished productions. In this way, with the main body of the collection composed of outstanding examples of cinematic art, could an interesting and informative museum, of great value in the future, be inaugurated.

The basis for such an institution is housed at the moment in the Science Museum at South Kensington. This is the collection of films and cinematograph equipment belonging to Mr Will Day, which has been on loan, and which there is every reason to believe is unique. Over a period of thirty years, Mr Day has gathered together any exhibit that is connected with the evolution of the cinema, from ancient wax figures used in Chinese shadow-shows, all manners of colour tops, kaleido-scopes, devices for optical illusions and panorama peep-shows, from Paris, London, New York and other parts of the world, to Edison's original Kinetoscope and projector, Paul's animatograph camera and a Lumière combined projector and camera used for the first public exhibition of films in France in 1896. There are also scraps of early films of historic interest: of King Edward VII's Coronation, of the Delhi Durbar, a copy of Georges Méliès's *Trip to the Moon* (1897), as well as a series of photographic plates taken in Pennsylvania by Edward Muybridge for his famous work, *Animals in Motion*. Although Mr Day's collection is more of scientific than aesthetic interest, nevertheless it would form an admirable nucleus around which a museum of wider conception could be built. There have, I believe, already been some attempts to found an institution such as that indicated above, but so far as I know, they have failed to materialise.

There are, of course, several other collections of old films in existence, such as that of Mr Pearl Cross, who has from time to time loaned examples for exhibition at the performances of the London Film Society. Three instances of this have been episodes from one of the first serial films, *What Happened to Mary* (1912); *The City of Westminster from an Argyll Car*, made by Hepworth, providing some amusing views of Edwardian London; and *Athalia, Queen of Judah*, an old French Pathécolor picture. Various producing companies, also, possess rare copies of celebrated films, such as *The Cabinet of Dr Caligari*, the famous 'expressionist' film made by Robert Wiene in 1919, which created a revolution in cinema circles; *Destiny*, made by Fritz Lang in 1921; and *The Golem*, made by Paul Wegener and Henrik Galeen about 1920. Rare versions of these and other notable pictures, several of them the only complete copies in existence, are in the guarded possession of the Ufa Company in Berlin, and are seldom to be seen. The Gaumont-British Company in England recently edited a number of old 'topical' newsreels into one picture, *Royal Remembrances*, which included scenes taken at the funeral of Queen Victoria, the coronation of King Edward and other famous occasions of historic interest. The original film version of *Dracula* is now extremely rare. This was made in Germany by F.W. Murnau in 1922, without permission having been secured from the copyright owners of Bram Stoker's novel. In consequence, a court ruling was obtained and all copies of the picture were ordered to be destroyed. One, however, escaped the flames and when shown two years ago at the London Film Society, proved to be of remarkable artistic value. Yet another challenging aspect for the collector is the possibility of acquiring, probably for a small sum, portions of films that have been removed by the censor, owing to historical, political or even religious reasons!

Thus it will be seen from the few instances cited that not only have films as well as cinematograph equipment assumed a collectable value but that there is a definite and urgent need for the establishing of a permanent collection, to be constantly brought up-to-date by examples of each new movement, either technical or aesthetic. For only in this way will it be possible to follow the rapid evolution of the cinema both as an art and as a scientific achievement.

The British Film (1930)

(From *The Film Till Now*)

The British film is established upon a hollow foundation. Perhaps it would be more significant to write that it rests upon a structure of false prestige, supported by the flatulent flapdoodle of newspaper writers and by the indifferent goodwill of the British people; inasmuch that a film emanating from the studios of this country to-day is at once enshrouded in a blaze of patriotic glamour by the public, who actually feel that the product (with one or two notable exceptions) is unworthy of its esteem.

The whole morale of the modern British cinema is extravagantly artificial. It has been built up by favoured criticism and tolerance of attitude. If a few critics had consistently written the bitter truth about the British film, if they had criticised it ruthlessly and stringently according to its desserts, I am convinced that this country would have revealed at least half-a-dozen thoroughly capable, intelligent film directors and a group of perspicacious, courageous producers. Well-merited castigation would have laid bare, and therefore more easily remedied, the root of the evil. Instead, there have been British Film Weeks and National Film Campaigns which have nourished the cancer in the industry. As it is, the British film is spoon-fed by deceptive praise and quota regulations, with the unhappy result that it has not yet discovered its nationality.

The British film has never been self-sufficient, in that it has never achieved its independence. Leon Moussinac writes: *'L'Angleterre n'a jamais produit un vrai film anglais'*,[1] a remark that is miserably true. The British film lacks honest conception. It has no other aim than that of the imitation of the cinema of other countries. For its obscure source it goes first to the American, and secondly, but more difficult to discern, to the German film. Of one thing I am confident, that the British film will never prosper, save as the child of the American cinema, until our producers bring themselves to recognise the value of experiment. Only on exceedingly rare occasions does a producing firm in this country countenance a new form of technique, a development of outlook, or anything that is alien to their conservative methods of working. British studios are filled with persons of third-rate intelligence who are inclined to condemn anything that is beyond their range. Producers, directors, scenarists, cameramen, art-directors, and their *confrères* are afraid of any new process, in case their feeble mentality is not sufficiently clever to grasp its significance. We are slow to learn from other film-producing countries, but we are always quick to imitate. But the danger lies in the disastrous fact that we generally imitate without understanding, without probing to the base of the ideas that we adopt (as for example, the mixed technique of Asquith's *Cottage on Dartmoor* and the ill-designed *décor* of Elvey's *High Treason*). For this reason there has never been any school of *avant-garde* in Britain. I do not suggest that an advanced school of cinematic experimentalism is essential, but I believe that it would stimulate the directors of the commercial cinema. There is, moreover, no school of thought for the furtherance of filmic theory, such as is found in other countries. There is none of the *enthusiasm* for the progress of the cinema which is so prevalent in France, Germany, Soviet Russia, and even America.

On occasions, our studios burst into a flare of latent modernism that is usually deplorable. In such a vein was the already mentioned Gaumont-British film, *High Treason*, which was made by a director with over fifty productions to his credit. It is not, moreover, as if British studios were insufficiently equipped or inadequately staffed. On the contrary, the technical resources of Elstree, Welwyn, Islington, and Walthamstow are as good as, if not better than, those of almost any other country in Europe, a point upon which every foreign visitor will agree. The trouble lies in the way in which these excellent resources are employed. A good film and a bad film pass through the same technical process. The amount of good and the amount of bad in each depends upon the minds which control the instruments.

It need scarcely be reiterated that Britain is the most fertile country imaginable for pure filmic material. Our railways, our industries, our towns, and our countryside are waiting for incorporation into narrative films. The wealth of material is immense. When recently visiting this country, S.M. Eisenstein expressed his astonishment at the almost complete neglect by British film directors of the wonderful material that lay untouched. Why advantage had not been taken of these natural resources was exceptionally difficult to explain to a visitor. Oxford, Cambridge, Liverpool, Shrewsbury, Exeter, the mountains of Wales and the high-lands of Scotland are all admirable for filmic environment. Nothing of any value has yet been made of London, probably the richest city in the world for cinematic treatment. Grierson alone has produced the fine documentary film of the herring fleet, the epic *Drifters*. This film, good as it was, is but a suggestion of that which waits to be accomplished. But what British company is willing to realise these things? British Inter-national Pictures, it is true, have made *The Flying Scotsman* under the direction of Castleton Knight, but what of it? Anthony Asquith made *Underground*, but became lost in the Victorian conception of a lift-boy, in place of the soul of London's greatest organisation. Instead, our studios give forth *Variety*, *Splinters*, *The Co-optimists*, *Elstree Calling*, *A Sister to Assist 'er*, and *The American Prisoner*.

What has been done with the Empire? It is well, first, to recall Epstein's *Finis Terrae*, Flaherty's *Moana*, Turin's *Turksib*, and Pudovkin's *Storm Over Asia*. The material lying unused in all parts of India, Kenya, Nigeria, Malta, Cyprus, is vast. There have been made *A Throw of the Dice*, *Stampede*, and *Palaver*, but what did they tell of those rich countries, save a superficial rendering? Without proper methods of film construction, without a knowledge of the capabilities of the cinema, it were best for this wonderful material to be left untouched.

The root of the trouble in this country lies in the conservative and narrow-minded outlook of the producing executives. There are not the men of broad vision, receptive to new theories and progressive ideas. (I do not here refer to the general adoption of the dialogue cinema, for that was a position forced upon British companies by American domination.) When the industry underwent a revival some years ago, after a decline period of inactivity, British producers seriously considered that it was more necessary to erect studio-cities than to train the young men who were to work in them. Every effort at that time was concentrated on making the public believe that Elstree was the new Hollywood; but the public shrewdly reserved its judgement until it should see the product of this studio-city.

Not only this, but producers lack the courage of their own convictions. When the dialogue film swept into Britain by way of the American-owned theatres in London, several directors in British studios were just beginning to grasp the rudimentary principles of film construction. They were groping and slowly developing for themselves some ideas on the theory of the cinema. But the whole studio organisation of this country was thrown into chaos by the American revolution of the dialogue film. If only one firm had remained level-headed when the tidal wave came, I am convinced that the best intelligences in British studios would have stood with it and would have acted independently of the dialogue innovation. If one company had been content with small profits and a gradual increase of its output, developing its knowledge of the silent film, there would have been some tendency, some initiative, some independence in the British cinema of which to write. As it was, the studios tried to transform their inadequate knowledge of film-making into 'the new technique', and continued with their slavish imitation of the American cinema.

The importation of foreign talent did not have the same influence in British studios as it did at an earlier date in Hollywood. It will be remembered that the work of Lubitsch, Murnau, Pommer, and Seastrom had serious effect on the minds of the younger school of American directors. But in Britain, Arthur Robison, E.A. Dupont, and Henrik Galeen, three directors of talent, have had no effect on the Elstree school. On the contrary, their ideas were totally misunderstood and unappreciated in our studios. Foreign directors failed to discover in Britain the collectivism and team-work so vital to film production. They were unable to understand our idea of picture-sense and we were at a loss to interpret their filmic outlook. (E.g. Robison's *The Informer* and Galeen's *After the Verdict*; yet these directors had earlier been responsible for *Warning Shadows*, *Manon Lescaut* and *The Student of Prague*. The conclusion to be drawn is obvious.) Dupont alone attained to some measure of success in *Piccadilly*, but only because he employed a German cameraman and architect. The importation of foreign talent was due to the eternal craze for a picture of *international* appeal. Producers were convinced that the inclusion of a foreign star would give a film an instant attraction in other countries. For this reason, Lya de Putti, Lars Hanson, Hans von Schlettow, Anna May Wong, Olga Tschechowa, Gilda Gray, and others have played in this country, but the advantage is somewhat obscure, save that it has been successful in the suppression of natural British talent.

Analysis of the output of British studios since the war is impossible in the same way as has been done with that of other countries. Nor, on the other hand, is it proposed to give even a brief survey of the commercial development, for that has been lightly touched upon at an earlier stage. I am unable to discern a realistic, expressionistic, naturalistic, decorative, or any other phase in the development of the British cinema. Added to which, there are no tendencies to be traced, for British films do not have tendencies, unless allusion is made to the prevalence of cabaret scenes and war themes. I propose, therefore, to examine several isolated productions and the work of a few individual directors, who demand some notice.

Without hesitation, there is one production that is pre-eminent in the British cinema, Grierson's film of the herring fleet. As far as I am aware, *Drifters* is the only film produced in this country that reveals any real evidence of construction, montage of material, or sense of cinema as understood in these pages. Admittedly, Grierson was influenced in his work by the rhythmic construction of Eisenstein's *Battleship Potemkin*, but, as has been pointed out elsewhere, he gave to *Drifters* something that was lacking in the celebrated Soviet film. As is now well known, Grierson was connected with the preparation of the American version of the Soviet picture, and had, therefore, every opportunity to analyse the work of Eisenstein at close contact. Although Grierson failed to understand completely the construction of *Battleship Potemkin*, he nevertheless contrived to build a film of great strength and beauty in *Drifters*. Like Epstein's *Finis Terrae* and Ford's *Iron Horse*, the theme of *Drifters* was pure in filmic texture. The ships that sailed out at night, the casting of the drifting nets, and the climactic race home to give their haul to the markets of the nation was splendid film material. The film was filled with the beauty of labour and a sense of ships. It lacked, possibly, a universal idea of the sea by its concentration on detail, but it was so far in advance of normal British productions that to write unfavourably of it would be ungenerous.

There are several directors in and around British studios who, in my belief, would realise interesting films were they afforded the means. There are also, on the other hand, many directors who have failed to make use of ample opportunities when they have had them. And again, there is a large number of second- and third-rate directors on whose spasmodic work it is impossible to comment in a book of this nature.

Although Miles Mander has been connected principally with acting, he has made one film that provided evidence of his wit and intelligence in filmic expression. *The Firstborn*, made at Elstree two years ago, was almost entirely the product of Mander's creative mentality; the story, scenario, direction and principal role being his individual work, supported by Madeleine Carroll. In the copy of *The Firstborn* shown to the public, however, the merits of the direction and the continuity were rendered almost negligible by the poor assembling of the material by the distributing firm. It is understood that the film was edited without the control of the director by a professional cutter, and hence much of Miles Mander's original conception was destroyed. As a light commentary on married life, flavoured with an environment of semi-political domestication, *The Firstborn* was conceived with a nice subtlety of wit. The treatment, especially of the eternal arguments and the dinner party, was sophisticated and clever. Mander has obviously a shrewd knowledge of feminine mentality and succeeded in transferring this into his handling of Madeleine Carroll. Had the film been well assembled, according to the original manuscript, I believe that *The Firstborn* would have been a unique instance of an English domestic tragicomedy in the cinema.

Probably Anthony Asquith is the most fortunately situated of British directors. He has certain ideas on cinematic representation, and he is happily able to put them into realisation. He has been concerned with four productions till now, *Shooting Stars, Underground, Princess Priscilla's Fortnight,* and *A Cottage on Dartmoor.* That he possesses a feeling for cinema was proved by all these films, but that he is still groping and undecided in his mind as to how to find expression for his ideas is equally plain. He has learnt varied forms of treatment from abroad, but has not as yet fully understood the logical reason for using them. He has studied the Soviet and German cinema, but has failed to search deep enough. His technique still remains, after four productions, primitively on the surface. In his last picture, for example, there were several instances of quick cutting and symbolic reference, but they were employed because of themselves and not as a contributory factor to the film composition. For this reason, Asquith's work appears that of a virtuoso, whilst in reality he is undecided in his mind as to what to do next. He is legitimate in borrowing from superior directors only if he comprehends that which he borrows and why he has borrowed it. His films seem principally to lack centralisation of purpose. This was exemplified in *Underground*, which, instead of being a direct exposition of the spirit of an inanimate organisation (and what superb material) degenerated into a movie of London 'types'. All his work has been unbalanced and erratic, and it is essential for him to lose his Victorian sense of humour before he can favourably progress. He has, on the other hand, some feeling for the use of dramatic camera angle, some ideas on dissolve shots, but an uneven sense of pictorial composition. He needs to receive a course in architectural construction in order to appreciate proportion; and to realise the relation that lies between the visual images and the expression of the theme.

The accredited pre-eminent director of the British school is, I suppose, Alfred Hitchcock, whose first dialogue film, *Blackmail*, has been generally accepted as the best of its kind. I believe, however, that Hitchcock's most sincere work was seen in *The Lodger*, produced in 1926 for Gainsborough. In this thriller melodrama, he displayed a flair for clever photographic angles and succeeded in creating an atmosphere of a London fog with some conviction. He continued with a series of unpretentious pictures, *Downhill*, *Easy Virtue*, *The Ring*, *The Farmer's Wife*, and *The Manxman*, but did not develop along the lines indicated by *The Lodger*. The production of *Blackmail*, although handicapped by poor narrative interest and the inevitable restrictions of dialogue, nevertheless showed Hitchcock in a progressive mood. His much commented-upon use of sound as an emphasis to the drama of the visual image was well conceived, but inclined to be over-obvious. Incidentally, the silent version was infinitely better than the dialogue, the action being allowed its proper freedom.

Although not strictly the work of British technicians, Dupont's *Piccadilly* was undoubtedly the best film of its type to be made in this country. It was moderately well constructed and expensively finished as such pictures should be, but was chiefly notable for the wonderful camerawork of Werner Brandes and the delightful settings of Alfred Jünge. The action was slow where it should have been fast, and fast where it should have been slow, but taking it as a whole, *Piccadilly* was the best film to be made by British International Pictures. Dupont's first dialogue film, however, was an unprecedented example of wasted material. The theme was one of the most dramatic that it is possible to imagine, the sinking of a great liner. The film was based on a play called *The Berg*, which in turn was founded on the *Titanic* disaster of 1912. The facts available to the director were these: the maiden voyage of the largest liner in the world, supposed to be unsinkable; the striking of a low-lying iceberg; the sinking of the ship in less than three hours, with the loss of one thousand five hundred and thirteen persons. It was a tremendous situation, calling for an intense psychological representation of the reactions of the passengers and crew. It could have been one of the most powerful films ever made. It was one of the stupidest. First, the bathos of the dialogue was incredible; secondly, the acting was stage-like, stiff and unconvincing; thirdly, the actual shock of the collision was completely ineffectual. Technically, the photography was flat and uninteresting; the (unnecessary) model shots were crude and toy-like; and the mass of nautical errors was inexcusable; added to which there was a complete discrepancy of the water levels as the vessel sank. I can think of no other example where so fine a theme has received such inadequate treatment.

Comparison can be made with point between *Atlantic* and Pudovkin's *Storm Over Asia*. Both had great themes; each contained errors of detail. But whereas in the former, discrepancies were brought into prominence by the weak direction, in *Storm Over Asia*, the treatment of the film as a whole was so impressive that mistakes (in military detail, etc.) tended to be overlooked.

There are three groups of films that merit inclusion. The series of reconstructed war events made for New Era and British Instructional Films under the producership of Bruce Woolfe, by Messrs Geoffrey Barkas, Walter Summers, Michael Barringer, etc., including *Armageddon*, *Zeebrugge*, *Mons*, *The Somme*, *The Battles of Coronel and Falkland Islands* and *'Q' Ships*. All these were excellent examples of the documentary film. Three extremely amusing comedies directed by Ivor Montagu, *The Cure*, *Day Dreams*, and *Bluebottles*, from stories by H.G. Wells, with the ever-delightful Elsa Lanchester, were the best instances of comedy burlesque that I have seen. And the numerous *Secrets of Nature* films, made by British Instructional under Bruce Woolfe's producership, have always been admirable in conception and execution. They are, in fact, the sheet-anchor of the British Film Industry.

Notes

[i] *Panoramique du Cinéma*, Leon Moussinac, 1929.

Korda

1933 Interview
(From the *Philadelphia Public Ledger* and the *New York Post*;
reprinted in *Rotha on the Film*)

London, October 31, 1933
Alexander Korda walked quickly up and down his office while I asked
him several pertinent questions. He has just finished work on a second
costume picture, *Catherine the Great*, in which we are to see the intelligent and attractive Elisabeth Bergner playing with Douglas Fairbanks Jr.
In his mind Korda is planning yet a further costume picture, this time of
the Elizabethan era, but although the Virgin Queen will appear in the
film I gather that she will not be the central figure of interest. Korda
promises more of a national theme than the flimsy *Henry VIII*, more of
Tudor England's position in the sixteenth-century affairs of the world
than we had in Henry's matrimonial experiences. The questions I posed
him were admittedly difficult when we take stock of his responsible
status as the head of a small and young company, London Film Productions, slowly steering its way to success. There are many demands to be
met, the constant problem of entertainment values, the idiosyncrasies of
distributors, before such a man as Korda can satisfy his own conscience.

He has, it transpired, little use for the social theme in movies, or
indeed for any purpose other than the telling of good stories for entertainment with a high degree of craftsmanship. He has no time to spare
for theory. He dislikes the academic approach to film; which is his
dismissal of the modernists. For example, we discussed the social issues
of *Kameradschaft*, and while he has the highest admiration for Pabst's
craftsmanship, he ridiculed the social issues arising from the mining
picture as being 'sentimental'.

Documentary, he agreed, was the most difficult of all approaches to cinema and one which demanded the most cautious handling. He would like to make documentary but he seemed to hesitate when I asked how he would reconcile this ambition with his previous disparagement of the social theme.

Presently we descended to technicalities and naturally found common ground where the delicacy and finesse of craftsmanship were concerned. Nothing irritates Korda so much as a camera movement which is not quite correct—perhaps too fast or too slow—or a timing of action which is not perfectly in accord with the motion of the camera. He appeared peculiarly sensitive towards the relation of his actors to the camera and the environment of both in the set. Where he differs from most views on film construction, however, is in the value he places on editing. Naturally, editing is uppermost in his mind when directing on the studio floor and he supervises the assembly of his material by two cutting-assistants. Yet he does not seem to share the belief that all celluloid material is just so much dead stuff until it is given life and breath and meaning by the correlation of the film strips by editing.

Thus we find that he places primary importance on the writing of the script and its fulfilment on the floor; and really secondary importance on the assemblage, which when regarded in this light becomes a mere business of correcting floor mistakes as distinct from the vital function which the Russians and we documentary-makers claim it to be.

As we parted, Korda let fall a few words which epitomised his feelings towards the movie position today. He spoke of the deplorable conditions which govern most film production, the constant compromising which a director must raise as a barrage against the demands of the money-barons, and the hampering restrictions of absurd censorial views. And I felt that within the space of a second his mind was making a lightning survey of his career since those early pictures in Budapest and Vienna after the War up till this moment when he is perhaps the most discussed director of story-films in England with a company of his own and several creditable pictures to his name.

1956 Interview

(From *British Academy Film Journal*, Memorial Issue to Sir Alexander Korda, Spring 1955; reprinted in *Rotha on the Film*)

Some nine years ago, several informal meetings were held among senior British film-makers out of which finally came the British Film Academy.

One such meeting took place late one evening in Korda's apartment at Claridges. We broke up about one in the morning but as I was about to take my leave, Korda murmured to me to remain behind. Generous as usual, he gave me one of those little cedarwood boxes stamped with his initials and holding two cigars, put the brandy nearby and stretched himself out on the sofa in his cardigan.

'You are,' he said, in that inimitable (except by Ustinov) voice, 'as well as being a film-maker whose work I admire (although you do not give me that credit), you are also a historian of the cinema in your books. When I die one of these days, tell me, which of my films shall I be remembered by?' Thinking I knew him a little, I let a minute pass and then said:

'*The Private Life of Henry VIII*, Alex.'

'That is what you think I think. Tell me your own honest opinion.'

'The best film that you personally ever made was *Rembrandt*.'

'My biggest flop!' And he laughed.

A long silence. Then he said:

'Paul, I should like to be remembered by a little short film that I didn't make myself but helped to get finished—*The Private Life of the Gannets*. That was a beautiful and worthwhile picture. I used it as a curtain-raiser to *Catherine*. It is still playing in many places in the world after fourteen years. When Huxley showed me the rough material, I at once responded and found the money with which to complete the film. I am very proud of that now.'

He seemed very lonely that night, I remember thinking as I walked home.

The Private Life of Henry VIII (1933)
(From the *Philadelphia Public Ledger* and the *New York Post*, 21 November 1933; reprinted in *Rotha on the Film*)

The sensation caused by the first public showing of *The Private Life of Henry VIII* is the main gossip topic of the British movie-world. Generally speaking, the picture has received an unprecedented ovation from the Press here as the dual result of its undoubted excellence and a carefully-planned long-range publicity campaign. By our more responsible critics it has variously been described as a 'good film', a 'great film', a 'Rabelaisian show', and funniest of all, 'a documentary'.

It has been praised as being 'more likely to bring prestige to the British film industry, both at home and abroad, than anything we have done in the whole history of film-making'. It has been attacked as 'defying history and enshrining entertainment, libelling a great period and caricaturing a great King, and being calculated to please any alien element concerned to poke fun at British institutions and ideals'. This last from a dramatic critic.

In the midst of all these superlatives for and against, it is perhaps important to retain a cool head and investigate not the film, but precisely its achievement and what its influence is likely to be in the near future.

The real truth of the matter is this: that it is to the everlasting disgrace of our producers here that it has been left to a charming Hungarian, schooled first in Vienna and Berlin and then in Hollywood, to come to London, form a small company and with discrimination select a bouquet of talented technicians and actors to appear in a picture about British history and traditions.

Quite apart from Alexander Korda's individual ability as a director (and he is no Pabst) there is little in *The Private Life of Henry VIII* which could not have been produced by any intelligent producer. After all, the skilful photographic craftsmanship of Georges Périnal, one of the outstanding features of the picture, was available to any other producer who cared to employ him. We had already seen his ability in Clair's *A Nous la Liberté*. Similarly, much comment has been made on John Armstrong's costumes. Well, Mr Armstrong has been designing costumes for several years and would have been delighted, I am sure, to design costumes for any film during that time if any producer had had the sense to ask him. And the same goes for the sundry good-looking girls in the picture. Most of them were extra-players a year or two back. As to Laughton's Henry himself, well he has always been there for the using.

In making this film, Korda has shown up the ossified sterility of British producers and has clearly demonstrated that the stumbling block in the way of progress for British films is not the lack of technical knowledge, or histrionic ability, or good-looking women, or equipment, or the British climate but simply the sheer inability of our producers to recognise and employ good talent.

Recently I was talking with a well-known Hollywood writer/producer, a man of wide movie experience and intelligence, who has been visiting the studios in and around London.[i] He remarked in particular upon the absence of young directors. He seemed puzzled that almost every picture which goes on the floor is assigned either to a veteran or to a stage producer. He contrasted the directors now working on a certain Hollywood lot with the directors of a British studio. Whereas the American company included several directors in their mid-twenties with only one or two pictures to their banner, the British studio boasted little save greybeards. British producers have always been frightened of youth, alibi-ing themselves on the grounds of the lack of money for experiment. This attitude is, of course, sheer idiocy and reveals all the more plainly how easy it has been for a man like Korda to sail in and produce the first significant 'British' film.

This is not suggesting that Korda's task was easy. It was far from that. He risked a great deal in making a costume picture. He risked more in being unable to secure a release for his picture in advance. He threw all his resources into this picture and he has pulled it off. But no matter how great its success, it would be foolish to imagine that this single film will change the attitude of our Methuselah executives. For Korda it will mean, I hope, an assured future. For British films it will mean just one picture of which we may be proud. But it offers no hope of changed attitudes in the general studio kingdom.

As an example of courage and confidence, Korda's film will receive tremendous praise but this must not blind us to its real meaning as a film. For British audiences it is brilliant entertainment. It is polished, hugely amusing in a smutty way and luxurious in production value. But it is not, I suggest, the ideal of a good film and Korda would be the first to admit it. In his position it was the ideal picture to have made. But a picture in itself is not enough. It must serve a purpose beyond itself if it is to live and have meaning.

Notes

i B.P. Schulberg, of Paramount, died 1957.

The Government and the Film Industry (1945)

(Reprinted in *Rotha on the Film*)

I. Background

Since the end of World War I, the British film industry has been in constant trouble. Two Acts of Parliament and a Cinematograph Films Council have been unable to solve its major problem—the organisation of a healthy, creative and economically sound production of films in regular supply. The three sides of the industry—producers, distributors and exhibitors—have seldom found common agreement, unless the three have been merged into one vertically-integrated group. Thus, on the one hand, there has been a continuous dependence on imported Hollywood films with which the British exhibitor has occupied his screen up to 80 per cent of its showing time; while, on the other hand, British production has boomed and slumped in the manner described in the Lord Moyne Committee's Report (1937) and the Board of Trade's *Tendencies to Monopoly in the Cinematograph Film Industry* (1944).

During the recent War, however, a new monopoly controlled by Mr J.A. Rank has virtually dominated all British film interests except those held by the Associated British Picture Corporation group. Under this control some good and important British films have been made. At the same time, disquiet is felt in many quarters that so much power vested in one group is an unhealthy and precarious state for an industry which can so widely reflect the characteristics and opinions of a country's people.

In these twenty-five years of haphazard existence, the production of British films has done less than justice to the reflection of British ideas and thought to people overseas. In most markets, including the Commonwealth, the Hollywood film has had precedence. The qualities of the cinema as a great instrument of public education have been ignored by the industry's exponents. Small attempt, except in the field of documentary films, has been made to use this powerful medium as a British contribution to world thought. It has been a characteristic of the industry always to produce its films supposedly for the largest possible number of people and hence gain the biggest returns. Seldom have the social responsibilities attached to such an influential medium been accepted by the controllers of the industry. If the same disregard for social responsibility were to obtain in the publishing and broadcasting fields, Parliamentary and public concern would at once be expressed.

The cinema has grown up as a cheap and convenient form of community amusement, and until now the interest of various governments has been confined to its commodity value and its yield in entertainment tax. There is, therefore, an urgent need, accumulated over twenty-five years, for a new Government to adopt a fresh attitude to the film industry, not only in regard to its economic and trade aspects but also in respect of its national and international importance in the public service.

II. Independent Production in Britain

The national need is recognised for the increased production of feature films in Britain on an independent basis. This need exists for the following reasons:

(i) More British films are wanted to decrease the number of American films now imported to fill screen space in British cinemas, and so to reduce the export of British money to the United States.

(ii) British film production is at present dominated by two vertically-integrated cinema-owning groups, and by American-financed production, required in the United Kingdom to meet the legislation of the Act of 1938. This is an unhealthy position in a creative industry.

(iii) The export of more British films overseas would aid our monetary position and help to make understood more widely the British viewpoint in world relations—economic, political, cultural and sociological.

In recognition of the above needs, it is understood that a proposal is now being considered by which a Government Film Corporation might be set up to provide finance and studio facilities to makers of independent feature and documentary films, and to secure proper distribution for such films to cinemas in the United Kingdom.

This proposal very rightly implies an acknowledgement of the fact that a healthy, creative film production industry does not necessarily spring from a few big companies owning studios, machinery for film distribution and circuits of cinemas. It recognises that a steady flow of good films can result from a number of small independent units, without ownership of studios, provided that finance and studio facilities, together with fair access to cinema screen space, is guaranteed by Government action.

The success of such a Corporation would depend upon various factors, of which the main would appear to be:

(i) The terms of selection by which production projects will be considered for acceptance for manufacture by the Corporation. Corporation officers will require to be selected according to their knowledge of public taste, of film production methods and of adult education, as well as their ability to see the information policy of the Government interpreted in a dramatised feature production. It should be in the Corporation's power, moreover, not only to consider and approve production projects submitted to it, but also to initiate production according to the needs of the Government information service. It should have the authority to commission scripts from writers for feature films and to put these scripts into production through reputable independent Corporation facilities.

(ii) The Corporation's films must be as good as, or better than, films produced by ordinary commercial practice. To achieve this end, the services will be required of first-class producers, directors, writers, actors and technicians. The Corporation must offer greater freedom of subject-matter and more opportunity for technical experiment than exists under normal commercial production. Although there is reason to believe that some of this personnel might welcome and avail itself of the proposed Corporation's facilities, some arrangement may have to be made for part-release from contractual commitments.

(iii) The proposed Corporation should bear in mind that one of the most important essentials of good production is continuity. Film production is dependent on efficient teamwork between creative talent, experienced technicians and skilled operatives. Continuity of production is a necessary security on which to base teamwork. This can have effect in three of the Corporation's activities: in the full-time employment of the technical floor staff at any Government-controlled or owned studio; in the security offered to small units of creative film-makers working together from film to film; and in the steady flow of product to the screen so that audiences become familiar with, and desirous for, a better type of film.

(iv) It is fundamental that films produced through the Corporation should be regarded from the start as potential financial successes. It would be most regrettable if the Corporation were to be considered merely as a subsidy to production or if its films were not meeting a consumer demand. This policy should not, however, deter the Corporation from facilitating experimental production from time to time. A major brake on commercial British production has always been the lack of opportunity for creative experiment, whereas Hollywood has sometimes fostered experiment, even at the risk of financial loss, knowing that successful experiment can influence trends in film-making for several years ahead.

(v) An important part of the Corporation's production plans should be the institution of a carefully worked out Training and Apprenticeship scheme, which the industry has always lacked. The Association of Cine-Technicians union should be consulted in this matter and would no doubt welcome such a proposal.

(vi) Costs of production should be geared in relation to *receipts obtainable from the home market*. It might be possible to reduce actual production cost by instituting a method whereby key film-makers and actors could be paid on a working salary basis and receive a royalty on takings after the production and distribution costs of a film had been recovered. Any such method would have to be the result of agreement with the Screenwriters' Association and the Association of Cine-Technicians. Advance production costs might again be lowered by allowing studio running costs to be reckoned as indirect charges and divided proportionately among a year's productions. The Finance Officers attached to the Ministry of Information Films Division could no doubt make useful recommendations in this direction.

(vii) If it is assumed that the Corporation can get independent films produced in this way, there remains the problem of securing adequate screen space for exhibiting such films. It is understood that the three big British cinema circuits have offered to book the proposed Corporation's films in place of a proportion of imported

American films. This offer is to be welcomed. It should not be regarded, however, as anything but a temporary and partial solution to the problem. Acceptance of such an offer and its terms of agreement should be subject to scrutiny. A Corporation film could be rented out with another film produced by one of the organisations making this offer, with the result that it might be difficult to assess the relative allocation of percentage takings on the two films. It would not be to the trade's interest, presumably, to allow a Corporation film to gross more than, or even perhaps as much as, a normal commercially-made film.

The question of publicity would also need careful safeguarding. It should be remembered that the Corporation's films could represent a powerful competitor to the monopoly companies, not only in cinema receipts but in utilising the services of technicians. For these reasons, it is urged that other and more long-term methods of distribution be investigated by the Corporation. It has been suggested, for example, that as from a specified date exhibitors should allot a minimum amount of screen space (to be adjusted every year to the volume of Corporation production) to the showing of Corporation films. Exhibitors' programmes would thus be governed by two quotas: the quota of imported films and the Corporation quota. The balance would be filled by independently-financed British or British-American films. Another method, based on less compulsory action, is proposed in an Appendix attached to this memorandum.

III. American Films in the United Kingdom

While the production of more good quality British films is the most desirable way of lessening the number of imported American films, it is recognised that it will take years of intense British production before American films will be reduced to occupying even 50 per cent of British screen-time. One immediate way, however, to reduce the import of American films would be to legislate so that cinemas reverted to a single-feature programme, supported by short films, thus lessening the number of feature films required by the cinemas in the United Kingdom. Evidence from exhibitors suggests that such action would not result in decreasing attendances, but that it would mean more full houses per day and less public time wasted in queuing. Reversion to a single-feature programme would also abolish the current trade practice of distributors splitting their share of cinema takings between two feature films shown in the same programme; the independent producer invariably suffers if the other film is made by a company with which the distributor is associated. A single-feature programme would, moreover, be of great help to British producers of short films, not only documentary films but short-story films which would provide excellent opportunity for training new talent.

It is widely agreed that American 'B' films, which usually make up the second feature in programmes, are an undesirable element in British cinemas. If the present renters' quota under the 1938 Act were to be substantially raised, and if a single feature programme were to be introduced, it would aid in reducing the import of such 'B' films which, it is understood, do not represent a large revenue from British cinemas. American distributors in Britain would tend to import only their films which have the highest potential earning capacity and to cease importing those with the lowest.

A further way by which the production of films in Britain could be increased has been suggested in some quarters. American renters should be compelled to spend a high proportion of their earnings from American films in this country in the financing of films made in Britain to meet their renters' quota needs, which may be raised. It should be recalled in this connection, however, that American interests have never had the desire to participate in the making of films in Britain except under legal compulsion. Where such participation has occurred in the past, it has been undertaken either with a deliberate intention of discrediting British-made films, as in the 'quota quickie' films under the 1927 Act, or with the idea of making American films 'on location' which, after fulfilling their legal purpose for renters' quota in Britain, can be distributed overseas as products of American and not British skill (e.g., M-G-M's *Yank at Oxford, Good-bye, Mr Chips* and *The Citadel*).

IV. British Films Overseas

The recommendations under this head made in the Palache Report are to be supported. It is hoped that the proposed Corporation would be empowered to implement them.

At the same time, it is felt that the problem of securing adequate screening for British films in the United States is long-term, unless some reciprocal trade agreement can be negotiated between the two Governments.

It is believed, however, that the present policy adopted by the Rank Organisation of spending a larger sum on the cost of production than can be recovered from the British market, in the belief that this extra expenditure will help to gain access to American screens, is unsound. There is no evidence whatsoever available that an expensively-made British film will secure distribution in the cinemas of the United States more readily than a reasonable cost production. Provided the desire should be held by American cinema owners to play British films because of public demand, it is the subject and character of the film which would decide its selection and appeal, not its extravagant method of production.

Lacking any reciprocal agreement, it might be considered that legislation could be brought about whereby an American renter in the United Kingdom is compelled to guarantee distribution for a British film in the United States and the Dominions in return for being permitted to distribute a specified number of imported American films in the United Kingdom. An elaborate system of checking bookings and takings overseas would need to be introduced to prevent such an agreement from being abused.

V. Conditional Booking and Film Rentals

The Palache Report dealt frankly with the problems of Conditional Booking (page 17, para. 5.5 *et seq.*), by which is meant 'block-booking', or the renter's insistence that an exhibitor should book one or more films he does not want in order that he may have a film he does want. This was made illegal by the 1927 Act, but nevertheless the practice is believed to be still in operation. It is extremely harmful to British film production.

While recognising that it is very difficult to abolish this practice, except by actual control of cinemas by the Government or by municipalities, because it is more than an exhibitor's business is worth to disclose any attempt on the part of a major renter to impose 'conditional booking' upon him, nevertheless it is felt that the Board of Trade should look more closely into this matter with a view to taking effective action.

Film rentals are another feature of distribution and exhibition that demand inspection. The Palache Report is also outspoken on this matter. It should perhaps be considered that a fixed maximum percentage should be permitted as the renter's share of an exhibitor's takings. This matter will obviously arise in connection with distribution arrangements to be made for the Corporation's films.

VI. Documentary Films

Apart from the considerations set out below, it is assumed that the Government will continue its sponsorship of factual films, at present directed through the Ministry of Information Films Division and the British Council's Films Department, and that there will be a Films Division of the proposed Central Office of Information to commission films from the independent documentary units and to administer the Crown and Colonial Film Units.

The production needs of the proposed Central Office of Information may not, however, fully utilise the production capacity of the documentary units, nor may the terms of authority of the Central Office of Information embrace the whole scope of documentary and educational films.

Any proposed Government Film Corporation, therefore, must take into consideration the special needs of the British documentary film movement.

For sixteen years, and especially during the war, the majority of the financial sponsorship of the independent documentary units has come from the Government, originally through the Empire Marketing Board and the GPO and later through the Ministry of Information and the British Council.

This sponsorship has been maintained spasmodically and only the Governments own units at Crown and Colonial have had continuous security.

It should, therefore, be a first step of the Government Film Corporation to safeguard and develop the economic security of the independent documentary units, which have so far preserved their immunity from the monopolistic control that grips the feature film side of the industry.

Under Government sponsorship, documentary film-makers require a measure of protection from officials and 'subject experts' who know little of the actual conditions governing the making of films. The status and confidence of documentary producers are being progressively undermined by this official ignorance.

The documentary group of units derives a proportion of its finance from local government and quasi-official bodies and from large corporations. The Government Film Corporation could help greatly in developing this field of sponsorship in an articulate manner, in particular by establishing a planned system of production and a planned system of distribution supplementary to the planned policy for independent feature production and distribution.

Few documentary film units have established access to distribution in the public cinemas except during the war by Ministry of Information arrangement. A large number of short films shown on British screens are supplied by the major American companies, being either their own Hollywood product or cheaply-made British shorts acquired from the less-reputable, 'quickie' producers. In many cases, it is attempted to make these short films a condition of feature film booking, especially with the three main circuits.

The Government Film Corporation in securing a guarantee of distribution for its independent feature films should also take steps to achieve a similar security for suitable documentary short films.

The Government Film Corporation should plan a number of feature-length documentary films, say twelve a year, through the appropriate members of the Federation of Documentary Film Units and the Crown Film Unit, and guaranteed circulation should be secured at circuit theatre prices. These films should be considered apart from commissions which may be placed by the Central Office of Information.

The Corporation could be of great service to the documentary group of units by encouraging still further the expansion of specialised distribution, e.g. through the Trade Unions, Co-operative Societies, etc., and by aiding the activities of such bodies as the Scientific Films Association and the Film Societies.

The Corporation could aid greatly the development of the documentary group by instituting a public relations and intelligence service devoted to documentary films. The methods of presentation, press-relations and publicity used by the Ministry of Information Films Division during the war left much to be desired. Ministry of Information films were successful more often in spite of the Films Division's presentation methods than because of them.

The Corporation should be active in introducing a Training and Apprenticeship Scheme into documentary production in conjunction with the Association of Cine-Technicians and the Federation of Documentary Film Units.

In consultation with the proposed Films Department of UNESCO, the Corporation should initiate travelling scholarships for documentary technicians to other countries and vice versa.

The Corporation should keep in review the progress of educational, cultural and scientific films.

The Corporation should further draw up a plan for production and distribution in which the requirements and responsibilities of the Central Office of Information, the Ministry of Education and the Foreign Office are specifically blue-printed and the productive capacity of the commercial production companies is allowed for.

The Corporation should use the proposed UNESCO Films Department and a *properly reconstituted* British Film Institute as agencies for relationships with foreign educational groups.

The Corporation should maintain the closest contact with any Films Office set up by the United Nations and facilitate the theatrical and non-theatrical distribution of UN films within the United Kingdom and the Commonwealth.

Appendix

Proposal for a Distribution Plan for a Government Film Corporation

1. It is assumed that independent good quality British feature films will be made through the proposed Film Corporation, and that, in the first year of production, some ten films might be produced. Immediate screen space could presumably be found for such films by acceptance of the trade offer described in the preceding memorandum (see page 9.65). It is felt, however, that the Corporation must work out a long-term and more permanent method of distribution.

2. Various proposals to solve this problem of distribution which is fundamental to the whole concept of a Government Film Corporation, have been made. They range from nationalisation of the cinemas, or placing cinemas under municipal management, to control over a proportion of the space required by law for British films in each cinema. Most of such proposals, however, depend on the use of compulsory methods which, in the field of leisure and public education, are the least desirable.

3. The situation should be recognised, moreover, that poor as is the quality of some feature films offered today to the public, audience attendances still remain higher than at the outbreak of the war, although the restrictions on other ways of spending money should be borne in mind. This suggests that at least many people are satisfied with the films offered to them, although there may be many others who would pay to see a better type of film if it was available,

among them possibly many people who do not go to the cinema at all, or only occasionally.

4. It is characteristic of the film industry that production companies aim to make their products appeal to the largest number of people. Few, if any, attempts have been made to appeal only to a section of the public, as is the case in publishing, broadcasting and the theatre, and to gear production costs accordingly, mainly because the industry has never troubled about specialised forms of distribution.

5. There is considerable evidence today, however, derived from the increasing formation of film societies, from the experience of the Ministry of Information's Regional Films Officers, from the wide success of non-theatrical distribution, from the Press and from discussion groups and public meetings in all parts of the country, that a certain section of the national public would support a better quality type of film, both long and short, if there were the cinemas in which they could be exhibited. The film trade presumably does not reckon this section of the public profitable enough to cater to, and even if it were, methods of salesmanship and advertising would require drastic overhaul.

6. It is to this section of the public, which it is suspected is much larger than the trade supposes, that the Corporation might well look for the initial return on its cost of production on both feature and short films.

7. If this principle is accepted, the following proposal is made:

   (i) In every city or town in the United Kingdom, which has a population of approximately 50,000 inhabitants or more, there are four or more cinemas.

   (ii) The Corporation should acquire, either by outright purchase or by renting for five years, the use of one cinema in each such city or town, increasing the number of such cinemas in proportion to the population. In Manchester, for example, three might be the appropriate number; in London, twenty.

   (iii) A minimum of 500 such Corporation-controlled cinemas should be the aim. Choice of cinema should be governed by suitability of site and seating capacity. The latter should average 750 seats. The cinemas thus selected would range over both circuit and independently-owned halls.

   (iv) These cinemas should be placed either under the direct control of the Corporation, or under the management of the municipality (for which statutory powers would be needed), but in either case their programme booking would be controlled by the Corporation.

(v) Existing advance bookings in every case would be taken over so that Corporation films could be gradually introduced as and when their production was completed. As and when existing bookings allow, programmes should be changed to a single-feature plus shorts make-up. First priority of feature booking should, of course, be given to Corporation-produced films, but for some long time there may be insufficient of these to supply a regular programme. Second priority on booking, therefore, should be given to European and occasionally to American films not considered by the trade to be of wide appeal. Programmes need not necessarily be restricted to a week's booking, but be permitted to run as long as economically justified.

(vi) These cinemas should charge normal admission prices, but the entertainments tax should be payable into the Corporation's fund for production, to be earmarked perhaps for experiment. All box-office takings would be remitted direct to the Corporation, which would establish its own machinery for meeting the running costs of the cinemas.

(vii) In addition to observing the normal opening hours of the locality, these cinemas should be made available at appropriate hire rates in the mornings and on Sundays for specialised performances to meet the increasing projection demands of municipalities, educational bodies, universities, schools, cultural and scientific societies and specialised groups of all kinds that are using films more and more as part of their activities.

(viii) Care should be taken in the staffing of such cinemas to see that managers are of the right personality and possess the necessary local knowledge to build the cinemas into centres quite different from the ordinary commercial cinemas in the city. The public should be led gradually to expect a higher quality of entertainment combined with public education than the ordinary cinemas provide. At the same time, every city and town of any size would be assured of good projection facilities for any educational or cultural use of the screen, over and above those made available on 16 mm by any Government Information Service.

8. In this way, it is suggested, the Corporation would have an assured market for its independently-produced films which would ensure at

least a recoupment of production cost. If, however, the Corporation's films reach the quality and desirability believed possible, their market is not limited to the Corporation-controlled cinemas. They would be available to independent exhibitors for normal booking, but only after the programme needs had been met of the Corporation's cinemas. Bookings obtained in this way, both at home and overseas, would represent a surplus over production cost and would be utilised in the way proposed above.

9. This proposal, it is suggested, would cause the trade less dislocation than any proposals to nationalise cinemas or control a proportion of screen-time. It would represent the least interference with the industry on all sides, but at the same time it would both stimulate creative film-makers on the production side and supply the growing demand among the public, both at home and overseas, for a better quality film without asking the trade to take the financial risk.

A Plan for British Films (1949)

(From *The Leader*, November 1949; reprinted in *Rotha on the Film*)

This present two-year 'crisis' in British film-making is not a national one. Cinema everywhere is faced with a struggle for survival. Star-spangled products are no longer certain successes. Ask Hollywood! With television round the corner as a competitive entertainment, the cinema has got to be stripped to the buff to rediscover its universal appeal.

Film is art plus industry. Neither can survive without the other. The industry can commit suicide: cinema will exist so long as there is a camera and a piece of negative. The crisis has been reached because the basic attractions of the film have been forgotten by its exploiters. Britain can seize this chance for revitalising the cinema as can no other nation. As in the war years, we are in the unique position of coming to the rescue of cinema. But it cannot be done without Government action and aid. The complete nationalisation of the industry as in Czechoslovakia will not help us. The jungle cutthroat rivalry of Hollywood is no answer. Only a sane, balanced, intelligent relationship between State finance and control, individual creative contribution and the best efficiency of private enterprise can crack the crisis. Britain alone can do this with harmony.

One of the disappointments of the Labour Government has been its failure to grasp the basic problems of the British film industry; its promising initial interest was not pursued. Despite a new Films Act to safeguard British screen-time, a Film Finance Corporation with £5 million to spend in production, and a limitation on the export of earnings of American films in the United Kingdom, the Labour Government has ignored the fact that making films is a creative act first and an industrial process second.

Seeking to encourage British production, the Government has already spent a lot of public money putting on the screen mainly what the distributor—the middleman—wants. It has bolstered up trembling concerns and given out a handful here and a handful there to 'keep things going'. It has not touched the roots of the problem. Money alone is not enough. Money plus encouragement of new ideas and talent is what is wanted. To give distributors such control over ideas and talent is a deplorably reactionary step for a so-called progressive government.

The great weakness of the Film Finance Corporation is that there are no creative people in it; no one with any first-hand knowledge of film-making. Can it not see that pumping money into the industry, even with guarantees of this and that, only encourages the old mistakes to be made over again?

A major difference between the film industry and other industries is that when film executives make ghastly blunders, they seldom get fired. They always get 'another chance'. One permanent result is that the confidence of technicians and workers remains impaired. I am convinced that the operative manpower in the film industry will work hard and loyally to make more good British pictures if—and only if—there is absolute confidence that employers are capable of creating a healthy and progressive production industry that will give continuity of employment. Unhappily, there are few producer/employers today who command that confidence.

It is too late to cry 'We told you so'. But the fact remains that the fate which has overtaken so much of our production today was foreseen and stated at least three years ago. Nobody at the helm listened and they are not today's sufferers. That is the recurring tragedy of the film industry.

Drastic methods are needed to stop collapse. Nothing positive for the future can be done by patching. Direct action by the Government is inevitable. That means participation. How can it be done with immediate effect but with least upset?

1. *Production*: Leave to their own devices those studios whose personnel is fully occupied. Let them go full steam ahead with their schedules, without Government aid if possible. Of the remaining studio space, divide off ruthlessly the efficient and up-to-date from the war-worn and not-so-good. Divorce the running of these worthwhile studios from the actual producing companies. Put them under a Government Studio Corporation with experienced management. Make them available at reasonable rentals calculated on a non-profit-making basis to visiting production units. The latter should pay rent and overheads only when they are actually using the studio services. Make these studios simply into

well-run servicing plants not in any way connected with the success or failure of the films made in them. Their job is to provide the material industrial facilities needed to make films.

How are the films to be made? We must be quite cold-blooded about this. A film is basically made by three people—the producer, the director and the writer. *Crossfire*, a favourite example of a good film which was good box-office, was made by producer Adrian Scott, director Eddie Dmytryk and writer John Paxton. Stars, cameramen, grips and carpenters—they all contribute but, stripped down, a film is the conception and creation of a three-man team, occasionally a two-man team when the producer is also the writer or the director. How many such teams or units exist in Britain capable of making top quality pictures? Fifteen, perhaps? How many could be formed tomorrow by creative people who are either 'resting' or browned-off on work about which they couldn't care less? Another twelve at most. Some twenty-seven unit-teams in all. For our purpose, less, because some of these teams are already under obligations for some time ahead. Say fifteen teams could be found, each a small, self-contained unit with its own policy and control. It is these teams who will determine how many good British films can reach the screen next year. I suggest not more than thirty. Not the money nor the studio space nor the quota—but these key film-makers will decide our output.

2. *Subjects*: Once and for all let us get away from the fetish for adapting West End stage plays. Adapt good novels if you like, but don't make pre-publication a prerequisite of a script. Get the young writers out and about. Give them a fair weekly wage and give them subjects to explore and write up. With careful briefing and intelligent producer guidance, some first-class stuff will come in. Free the writer from distributor dominance, and subjects will flow in.

3. *Finance*: If ordinary capital remains shy as at present, then the Film Finance Corporation must operate further. I imagine that there's not much left of the original £5 million, but Mr Wilson suggested that he might get more. But, and again this is fundamental, this public finance for production must go direct to the people who make pictures and not, as has largely been the case to date, to the middleman who advances it to the producers. This practice has meant that the distributors have virtually decided what subjects are made, by whom and with what actors. The Finance Corporation must face up to the position that if it aims to save the industry, it cannot avoid financing projects put to it direct. To do this, it needs expert help. There must be found, I suggest, three or four

persons with between them a first-hand knowledge of film-making and a sense of public taste who will serve as a Production Committee to the Corporation. They should be selected and appointed by the President of the Board of Trade. One member should sit three years, the others changing every two years by rotation to assure variety of viewpoint and continuity of policy. There are such people, both in the film trade or closely associated with it. Their sense of public duty could be appealed to, for them to relinquish their present posts and put their ability and experience at the service of the public, the Government and the industry. This small committee could in actuality plan a great part of the future of the British film industry, that part which does not go ahead under existing arrangements.

The tastes of this committee must be wide. All kinds of films are wanted from slapstick to Shakespeare, the criterion being that they must be the good of their type. The aim should be to encourage talent, foster new ideas, create the conditions for creative film-making which at present do not exist. These few people must carry the confidence of all who make pictures and have the future of the industry at heart. It is not impossible.

4. *Distribution*: The Film Finance Corporation has insisted it backs no project unless it has a guarantee of release. But it overlooks the existence of the Films Act 1948. If films produced and financed along the lines indicated above do not get a release through normal channels (and remember exhibitors need to fill a 40 per cent quota), then surely release must be obtained through the clause in the Act that lays down that each of the three big circuits must distribute a minimum of six films per year from independent sources? In fact, if the Corporation finances a subject direct, this should guarantee its acceptance as one of the eighteen stipulated by the Act. The Corporation must appoint reputable accountants to see that the producer (and the Corporation!) gets a proper share of the film's earnings. It might even be necessary to set up a Government-controlled distribution agency, operating on a non-profit making basis, to ensure that as much money as possible flows back into production.

5. *Costs*: Obviously the home-market and the Commonwealth should be the first aim. Budgets should not exceed £125,000. Producers, writers, directors and actors should be asked to take a proportion of their salaries in deferments, that is to say, from takings after actual costs plus loans have been repaid. If they were assured of a fair deal from distributors, I think these key people would accept this, especially if the distribution

concern was under Government control. They might have to wait for their money, but they would get it.

None of the above proposals, practicable though they are, solves Mr Rank's or Sir Alexander Korda's problems. They are not meant to. But they are a bare outline of a plan that, if worked out carefully by the right people, could give new hope and encouragement to the hundreds of film-makers of all grades who are desperately anxious not only to have jobs but to put British films where they belong—at the top. It must be done before more skilled labour and brains dissipate into other industries or get thrown on the scrap-heap. It must be done, or something very like it, if the Government places any value at all on a healthy, progressive and hard-working film production industry. We have had lip-service enough; let us now have action.

The Problem of the Short Film (1966)

(From *Films and Filming*, November 1966)

While the Government in the near future is taking action, as it must do, to secure the future of British feature film production, the position of British short films—whether documentary, cartoons or short-story—must also be given utmost attention. As long ago as 1961, the National Film Finance Corporation's annual report stated: 'The plight . . . of the short film is lamentable. This country produces some of the best shorts in the world, many of them for official or industrial sponsors, but the commercial market provides no satisfactory outlet for high-class shorts unless they are made for a large organisation in their own programme (Rank and ABC) An attempt has been made to alleviate the problem by allowing shorts a larger percentage of the statutory levy but this has provided no real solution. Frequently the Corporation has to reject applications for short films which promise to be excellent entertainment precisely *because a loss both for the Corporation and the producer is a practical certainty.*'

We have heard it said so many times that the short film is the nursery of the feature film—that such widely disparate directors as Frank Capra, François Truffaut, Réné Clair, William Wyler and Tony Richardson, to name only a very few—all began their experience in short film-making. Yet little is done to encourage their making and exhibition in Britain, except when they have been sponsored by the Government or an industry, for information or public relations. In its heyday winning a world reputation, the British documentary film came from the EMB, GPO and Crown Film Units and a handful of independent units such as Strand, Realist and Films of Fact.

I am glad to hear that the Association of Cinematograph, Television and Allied Technicians is having prepared a full report into the whole current situation by two people who have experience in both the making and distribution of short films. I hope this report when it appears will have a wide circulation among those both official and unofficial who are involved in this important matter.

I am not so much concerned here with such bodies as the Shell Film Unit, British Transport Films and the National Coal Board Film Section. They do excellent work in their prescribed fields and sometimes one of their films hits the cinemas, but only after pressure. The Coal Board's monthly *Mining Review* has a theatre distribution of several hundred cinemas. But these units are backed by public money. How many independently-run units specialising in making short films exist without relying on some kind of sponsorship? Almost none, if any, because short films very rarely, if ever, earn their production costs back from the exhibitors. There is no means of finding out what rental a distributor gets from an exhibitor, or a circuit of cinemas, for a short film, so as to pass a fair share back to the producer. The unfortunate producer must rely on the book-keeping honesty of the distributor. And who determines what proportion of the box-office take goes to the main feature, maybe a second feature, the newsreel and the Cinderella short?

In the last year or two the Short Film Service has struggled hard to get good quality British as well as foreign shorts an adequate showing in this country. It has acquired the rights of some really brilliant European and American films but under the methods outlined here, it is having a fight to get screen space and will continue to do so unless new legislation is introduced.

The cinema distribution of short film in Britain is dominated by the Rank *Look at Life* and ABC's *Pathé Pictorial*, both of doubtful quality when judged by true documentary standards, with their guaranteed release through the Rank and ABC circuits. They therefore receive a disproportionate share of the British Film Production Fund, which surely they do not need with two such giant organisations behind them? The success of what independent British short films do get made, by hook or by crook, in overseas markets shows that they do not lack quality. They are often a success at the ubiquitous festivals. It is ironic that some British short films which have not even been shown in this country can earn more money in, say, Germany than they could if they had been shown here! The whole problem, as with feature films, lies in the outdated and deadly unfair methods of the distributor and exhibitor. Short films should not be tied to feature films in a package deal. They should be subject to separate booking contracts. This is one of many things which I hope the Monopolies Commission (it is said to have finished its report) has recommended and the Board of Trade will act upon when new legislation comes to be framed.

In many countries in Europe, the short film is really looked upon as the nursery school for the feature film. In West Germany, for example, every film, short or feature is submitted before distribution to a jury which can award the film a special certificate, or *Prädikat*, if it is considered of sufficient merit. (*The Life of Adolf Hitler* was awarded such a *Prädikat*). If a film gets such an award, this carries a tax remission of approximately 5 per cent to cinemas who show it, naturally an inducement to do so. It is available to films from other countries. The appointment of the members of the committee which makes the award is governed by their ability to assess films on their quality. In Italy, another kind of system, recently revised, seems to work well, with cash awards being made to the makers of the best short films by a panel which is composed not of civil servants but by two representatives of the arts (one of whom, the Chairman, is appointed by the Minister responsible for the film world) two film critics (appointed by the Union of Journalists and Film Technicians), and two University professors, one in science and the other in sociology or psychology (appointed by the National Research Council). They will be able to distribute up to 30 prizes every three months making an annual total of approximately £425,000. The prizes will be annually divided: 90 per cent to the producer, 8 per cent to the director and 2 per cent to the cameraman. Apart from a film's revenue, this method is indeed an inducement to make quality short films in Italy. I have not space to detail systems working in other countries—France, Holland, Canada and Scandinavia—but they all provide encouragement to short film-makers, including animated cartoons, which is absent in our own backward country.

I have heard criticism levelled at the trade's Association of Specialised Film-makers for its lack of leadership and its failure to initiate policy. This may or may not be true but it certainly lacks a sense of public relations.

Included among short films must be the experimental film, which needs so much support in Britain. True, the British Film Institute has just had an increased grant for this purpose but it is in all a niggling amount. Why not impose a levy of 1 per cent on the production budgets of all feature films produced in England costing more than, say, £100,000? And why should not, say 21 per cent of the Production Fund be allocated to such a purpose? But the use of such money, if made available, must be administered by a group, or committee, fully experienced in professional production and the aesthetics of the film, and it need not necessarily operate under the aegis of the BFI.

Somebody may dream up the idea of reviving the Crown Film Unit but, if it should happen, let us hope that Crown's latter-day errors of overspending are not repeated. Better still, the old idea of the thwarted Group Three might be revived. The Group failed for several reasons, a major one of which was that its films were never given a fair distribution deal by the trade's distributors. It was, I am told on good authority, Harold Wilson's own conception at the time in 1951.

The setting-up of a National Film School is under consideration. Before bringing this into being, good idea as it may be, something should be done to utilise fully the existing creative talent that lies around the place, frustrated and often unemployed. The whole situation calls for a creative approach, not under bureaucratic control. If I have not discussed TV as an outlet for short films, it is because I regard it as a separate subject.

ROTHA'S WRITING

III

FILM PRACTICE

Paul Rotha's first experience of actual film-making occurred in 1928 when he began work in the art department of Elstree studios. This prompted him to write 'Technique of the art director' (1928), his first article to be published in *Film Weekly*, which examines the vital role played by the art director in the film-making process before proceeding to criticise the situation in British studios. For Rotha, the only creative art director working in the British industry of 1928 was the German émigré Alfred Jünge. Such criticism by a junior employee was considered intolerable and led to Rotha's immediate dismissal from Elstree. 'The art director and the film script' (1930) continues his meditation on the creative role of production design but this time is influenced by his developing theoretical conceptualisation of film art. The crux of this article is the transformation of the art director from a set decorator to a technician, and the role of the setting from being merely a backdrop to it becoming an integral part of the entire technical process of film creation, from the initial writing of the script to the editing. It therefore follows that the art director should become more involved in the scripting (the first act of montage in the construction of a film), incorporating visual images—in terms of a combination of architectural diagrams, floor plans incorporating camera placements, and the story-boarding of sequences—with words.

The above articles were written with studio-based film-making in mind. But Rotha's return to production in 1931 was to be in the field of documentary, where he was to work exclusively for the next twenty years. After a short spell at the Empire Marketing Board, Rotha received a commission to direct his first documentary for Shell-Mex and Imperial Airways. The experience of this first major production is recounted in detail in 'Making *Contact* 1932–33', an extensive extract from *Documentary Diary* published in 1973, the first volume of Rotha's planned two part autobiography (the second volume of which never materialised). The article complements Robert Kruger's consideration of Rotha's career as a film-maker in this book and recounts in detail the preparation, shooting, editing and release of the film. Rotha learned a great deal from the experience and various problems encountered both in the production process and in dealing with sponsors and a rather hostile film trade.

'Presenting the world to the world' (1956) deals with the avowedly internationalist project associated with a range of films made by Rotha in the 1940s and 1950s, beginning with *World of Plenty* (1943), which was already looking forward to the end of war and the challenges presented by peace, and proceeding with *The World is Rich* (1947), *World Without End* (1953) and the BBC series of programmes initiated by Rotha, *The World is Ours* (1954–56). Collectively, these films make the progressive case for the creation of a better world, in which the potential of all people is recognised and resources distributed more fairly, and consequently demonstrate Rotha's commitment to film as a powerful tool for informing, educating and stimulating political debate. The article also examines the techniques developed during this phase of Rotha's career, in particular the use of direct speech and multi-voice soundtracks to convey both analysis and debate which became synonymous with his work right up to the last documentary he made, *The Life of Adolf Hitler*, which appeared in 1961.

The Technique of the Art-Director (1928)

(From *The Film Weekly*, 19 November 1928; reprinted in *Rotha on the Film*)

Three men are required, all working in perfect harmony and rhythm with one another, to make a film that is of high artistic merit. The Director. The Cameraman. The Art-Director. Of these, the first in late years has had world-wide publicity: the second has assumed the cloak of a magician and is regarded as such; while the art-director remains the unknown quantity, taken for granted, unmentioned by all save the student of the cinema. And yet he is the vital figure in the composition of the picture. How many art-directors can the ordinary person name off-hand? How often does one see their names in the press? And yet it must be realised that those great sets with polished floors and marble columns are conceived, designed and built by an artist. He it is, too, working in an obscure corner of the studio, who arranges the model shots, the miniature work, the glass shots, and designs the accurate models for use in the Schüfftan Process. Nevertheless his work goes almost unnoticed by both the public and the critics. Save for an occasional credit title, often as not deleted from the film after its pre-release, he remains the unknown worker.

His work is as hard as that of anybody in the film business. The qualifications alone required by an artist to fill the post of a competent art-director for a motion picture are many, and impose a severe strain on the mentality of the artist. They may briefly be set out as follows:

He must possess—

(a) a deep appreciation of line, form, proportion and composition;
(b) a knowledge of architecture in all its branches;
(c) an expert understanding of camera angles and perspective;

(d) a knowledge of colours and their photographic values under pan-chromatic and ordinary film stock;

(e) a working knowledge of lighting, and the use of light and shade, and tone values;

(f) a definite knowledge of such side-lines as furniture, pictures, costume design, materials, etc., and he must be competent enough to design any of these if necessary;

(g) a practical experience of plaster-work, carpentry, painting, varnishing, stone-work, joinery, etc.

He must be able to work in complete unison with his director, fulfilling his ideas, anticipate the necessary action entailed so that the set is practical, and agree with the cameraman as to the most effective lighting for both set and players. He must study the make-up of the latter so that the photographic tone of the walls of his set provides a suitable background for their faces. His work is always ahead of time. His proposed sketches of the sets should be in the hands of the director before the picture is begun. Once these sketches are approved he settles down to make detailed working drawings, elevations and plans which can be read with ease by the carpenters, plasterers and painters. Where it is possible to incorporate the use of stock fireplaces and windows possessed by the studio in which he is working, he does so, for economy is a god to be served. The work is then put in hand, the set is built, allowance being made for lighting, the plasterers do their stuff, the painters succeed them, the sprayer dirties down the finger-plates on the door, and cobwebs are specially prepared for the ceiling. Finally it is dressed with carefully chosen furniture under his direct supervision.

The difficulties to overcome are innumerable. He has the eternal problem of finding sufficient floor space for his sets, fitting one in with another; of working to scheduled time so that shooting may not be held up; of estimating the cost of his sets and the amount of time needed by a number of workmen to build them; of matching up the exteriors of houses shot on location with the interiors he builds in the studio. He must be able to have access to books of reference, for he may be called upon to erect the most out-of-the-way scenes imaginable. He must be assured of being accurate in his facts for surely his critics number the largest in the world for the arts. Above all, his mind should be capable of superb creative work, for there are films that call for settings of a fantastic nature such as *Caligari* and *Waxworks*.

The true aim of the art-director is simplicity. In the same way as a great artist achieves his effect by as few lines as possible in a drawing, so should an art-director be able to create the impression he desires with as little material as is necessary. Paul Leni achieved this in *Waxworks*. Unless the script definitely calls for spectacular sets, there is no call for them. They are waste of good money and material. It is well to bear in mind that Manet once said that three people make a crowd—if used in the right way. In such cases as the *Nibelungen-Saga*, however, large sets were justified; in *The Student of Prague* they were not needed and were not used. The highest art of the film designer is the decorative motion picture, where traditional motives are employed with the additional individual creative work of the art-director. *Warning Shadows* exemplifies this. Here the costume designs were traditional *Directoire* with an added exaggeration on the part of the designer that lifted them from the rut of orthodox historical costume to the realm of fantasy.

Costume design in itself is a vast subject, as yet almost unexplored on the screen, as Romanticism is out of fashion. There has been little achieved successfully in what has been done in this manner. Even historical costume has been badly ill-treated. There have not been half a dozen costume films made that are satisfactory, despite millions of dollars spent on them by American producing companies. *The Man Who Laughs* is an example of this. Never have there been such bad period sets and costumes as in this film, and yet they were supervised by Paul Leni, who achieved excellence in this respect with *Manon Lescaut*. The costumes failed in *Casanova* because the skirts of the men's coats were cut too short, and thereby threw out the proportions of every figure. Too much attention cannot be paid to details such as these because they can so easily damn the whole. Walther Röhrig was most successful in his designs for *Tartuffe*; Rudolph Bamberger in *A Glass of Water* was adequate. *Federicus Rex* was as historically accurate as has yet been seen. One remembers Claude Autant-Lara's work in *Nana* as being charming.

In England there is little creative set-designing. The type of films produced in British studios does not demand this treatment. They require strict realistic detail in a conventional manner and such work is being admirably done by J. Elder Wills and Norman and Wilfred Arnold. The only creative work being executed in this country is by Alfred Jünge, for E.A. Dupont's *Piccadilly*, and is amongst the best yet done in any studio. Jünge's knowledge of modern design is superb, his method of utilising the camera as showman for his work subtly clever. He recently designed a set with the most delightful mural decorations that have been seen for a long time. Jünge is a brilliant artist who realises all the possibilities of the cinema.

There is, however, one thing that must be realised. Every film cannot be a *Caligari*, or the screen would become dull. But there is no reason why just as much design and composition cannot be used in a kitchen set for a slapstick comedy as in an expressionistic setting. Neppach realised this in *The Edge of The World* and Söhnle and Erdmann in *The Joyless Street*. The dressing-table in *Bed and Sofa* contained as much arrangement as the Feast of Belshazzar in *Intolerance*, and was a great deal more praiseworthy. This clever arrangement of detail is marked in Pabst's *The Loves of Jeanne Ney*. Henrik Galeen has been seen to arrange an inkpot and two brass ashtrays on a table as carefully as Cézanne arranged a still-life.

The time will undoubtedly come when the importance of the art-director will be appreciated as is that of the *metteur-en-scène* in the ballet. But how much greater is his scope! The film, the newest art that contains all the other arts, offers a vaster canvas to the artist than could ever have been found in the past. The limitations are practically nil. He loses indeed his colour, but gains in every other conceivable way. It is surprising that more artists have not turned to the motion picture as a means of self-expression. It is without question the greatest art form yet discovered for the pleasure of mankind.

The Art-Director and the Film Script
(1930)

(From *Close-Up*, May 1930; reprinted in
Rotha on the Film)

The era of the creative studio production may be said to have been at its
zenith during the best period of the German art film, from the eventful
years of 1920 to 1925, when the cinema was still closely allied to the
theatre and its painted decoration. We know that at that time
the decorative setting was the binding element of completeness to the
thematic narrative. The Germans were (as Mr Harry Alan Potamkin
has pointed out) essentially film craftsmen rather than film creators, and
it was only to be expected that painted scenery usually connected with
the theatre should have played a large part in their film development.
By their essential mysticism and fantasy, the German themes at that
period demanded the decorative setting. We can refer to the key films
of the time, viz.: Wiene's *Caligari*, Kobe's *Torgus*, Lang's *Siegfried*, the
same director's *Destiny*, Berger's *Cinderella*, Robison's *Warning Shadows*
and *Chronicle of the Grey House* and Leni's *Waxworks*. These were all
pictures in which the decorative environment was the binding element
of the realisation, against which the thematic narrative moved with a
slow, psychological deliberation. These films ended in themselves.
They were supreme instances of the painter's cinema. The names that
mattered were Walther Röhrig, Robert Herlth, Walther Reimann,
Rudolph Bamberger, Andrei Andreiev, Erich Kettlehut, Otto Hunte,
Paul Leni, Alfred Jünge, Albin Grau, and later Neppach and Werndorff.
 Since that time, the film has progressed to find its true realisation in
an environment of reality. Through the work of the neo-realists and
naturalists, Pabst, the Soviet left-wing directors, the stumbling methods

of Dziga Vertov, the open-airness of Epstein, Flaherty, etc., there has been achieved the true cinema. No longer is it possible to feel that we should like to take down each image from the screen and hang it on our wall as we should a painting. This was so damning in Dreyer's *La Passion de Jeanne d'Arc*. Instead, we have learned that each visual image is but a fragmentary contribution to the whole composition of the film's unity. It is the film in its entirety that we frame and hang in our minds, where it is linked by a universal idea with other films, to become emotions remembered in tranquillity.

There is no place for the painter in the film studio. He is accustomed to think in broad terms of pigment and sentimental decoration (viz.: *The Little Match Girl*, *Le Voyage Imaginaire*, etc.), a habit of mind which is useless in the detailed building of a film. We know that a filmic mind is essentially one that thinks in terms of building; I call it arithmetic architecture. We know that Eisenstein has admirably compared the construction of a film to playing with a child's box of tricks. We have only to contrast the analytic and synthetic methods of Pudovkin with the *Chauve-Souris* decorative direction of the late Paul Leni in order to realise the value of constructivism.

The art-director has developed from a decorator into a technician, whose main work entails a strictly organised structure of settings at the will of the director. The setting, instead of being the binding environment dictated by the creative imagination of the art-director (such as it is in the ballet or the expressionist theatre) has become a part in the whole concatenation of events, alongside the technical accomplishment of the camera and the three stages of the organisation of the film material. It follows, conclusively, that art-direction must take its place in the construction of the script as an integral part of the preconception of the ilm in literary terms before its realisation on the studio floor, on location, or in the cutting-room.

The process of script organisation, which is the first act of montage in the construction of a film, is familiar to all film-makers. It is divided into three sections: one, the selection of the theme, environment and rough action and characterisation of the protagonists; two, the filmic treatment in narrative form of this theme, indicating its future visual and aural possibilities; and three, the preparation of the detailed shooting script, which we may also call the script plan. This latter consists, as far as is possible, of a complete literary expression of the film *as it will appear* when realised, and is divided and sub-divided into sequences, scenes and shots with the appropriate sound images. Further, we know that the script is welded into a whole by the constructive editing of shots into scenes, scenes into sequences, sequences into the film composition as a unified whole; a living, pulsating, throbbing thing. We anticipate the script to be built out of a thousand or more separate shots that are dependent one on another for their effect. It is by means of this composition of shots, which is eventually achieved by editing (the final act of montage), that the film is made to come alive, thus giving rise to emotional and intellectual audience reaction.

We are aware, of course, that a scriptwriter selects his shots from an unlimited number available to him, and it is assumed for the purposes of argument that there is no angle or position from which an object, a person or a piece of action cannot be photographed, both terminals of the shot (the object and the camera) being either static or in motion. It is the obligation of the writer to select from the shots in his imagination those which are the most vividly dramatic in order that they may bring out the full significance of the content of the scene as required by the narrative. These selected shots he describes in his script by words, for want of better means, although obviously the words themselves are of little interest as compared with the visual images, as well as the sound images, that they represent. The procedure of the script plan is the preliminary representation on paper of the eventual visual images on the screen and the sound images on the film strip or on disc, as the case may be. In the hands of the scriptwriter, the camera and the microphone dig down deeply into the inner reality of everyday life, bringing consciousness of inanimate things to the spectator. The whole aim of the film lies in the representation of unnoticed things and motives for the living and the unliving, presenting them filmically for the pleasure or boredom of the spectator, according to his receptive interest.

The incorporation of draughtsmanship is of the greatest importance for the clarity and perfection of representing visual images in the shooting script. I believe that not only should the script be written, but it should also in part be drawn.

In the first place, purely architectural diagrams of the lay-out of sets, mobility of the camera (travelling shots, panning shots, etc.) should be included in order that a clear visualisation of the action of the characters in relation to the movement of the camera may be possible from the script. Added to this, the shooting angles and set-ups of the camera can be indicated, as conceived in the imagination of the writer, based, of course, on his *first-hand* filmic knowledge and studio experience as well as his creative faculties. Secondly, it is possible to emphasise the literary description of the selected visual images by means of drawings which will be clues, as it were, to the actual shots on the floor or on location. Here, obviously, a difficulty arises. The literary descriptions in the script are usually concerned with movement of acting material, which is difficult, if not impossible, to convey by the means of a drawing, the nature of which is static. For this reason, therefore, I suggest that the drawings should be in the nature of footnotes, clues to the actual realisation, while the necessary movements can be fully indicated by diagrammatic plans.

The scriptwriter, as we know, visualises the complete film in his imagination before it ever enters the studio to be fixed on to strips of celluloid. It is only logical that there are many aspects of the visual images that he cannot incorporate in his script in word form. It is, then, at this failure of the literary medium that the writer could turn to draughtsmanship for a clear expression of his ideas. In other words, the director should be able to work from drawings as well as from text in the realisation of the script.

It will at once be remarked that this method indicates that the scriptwriter should possess another qualification other than the many already necessary to him . . . It is obvious that he must have a specific knowledge of all the filmic methods of expression. Every property of pictorial composition, of symbolism and suggestion, of contrast and similarity in the association of ideas and shapes, of the drama of camera angles, of the rhythm achieved by editing and cutting, of the technical accomplishment of camerawork, trick devices and studio architecture, shall be in his mind to be employed in order to express the dramatic content with the greatest possible effect.

It is for the essential reason of simplifying the task of the scriptwriter that I suggest that draughtsmanship should be included in the script. It need not necessarily be the work of the writer himself. I put forward the argument that three or four persons could have the organisation of the shooting script in their control: the writer, the director, the art-director and the cameraman. Their work would proceed as follows: the selection of the theme by the writer and director and its treatment in narrative form; then, the preparation of the shooting script during which the art-director shall contribute diagrams and plans with his special knowledge of sets and their construction for emphasis of content by distortion and illusion. On these the cameraman shall suggest, in collaboration with the director, the movements and set-ups of his equipment in accordance with the lay-out of the sets. Meanwhile, the art-director shall, in collaboration again, scatter the text which is being composed with small drawings of individual shots, showing the proposed schemes of lighting, arrangement and contrast of masses, etc. In this way, there will result the nearest approach to a complete film pre-conceived and set down on paper. The script will thus be the collective work of the four most creatively-important film-makers. Both pictorially and textually the script will indicate the exact course of the events in the studio, on location and in the cutting-room.

There is, however, one danger to be avoided in this proposed method. That is the tendency it will carry to regard each visual image as a thing by itself. That is, of course, in direct opposition to the welding together of the script as a whole. It is fatal to think of a scene in terms of isolated shots. Rather, we must always visualise in a series of shots with their eventual screen realisation (as well as the symphony of sound images) uppermost in the mind. We must continually be conscious of the varying relations of the visual image lengths, for it is their rhythmic tension which ensures the increasing interest of the audience in addition to the action of the characters. The drawings in the script must be clues to the progress of the film itself; a graphic commentary on the unfolding continuity of the visual images. Although the drawings themselves are static, even as the words in the descriptive text, they are to be regarded as but the suggestion of their future filmic realisation.

Note: It will be appreciated, of course, that the above suggestions apply to the general production of studio-made films and would be antagonistic to the naturalistic methods of film-makers who aim at using only actual material. It is a plea for the closer co-operation between the script and art departments in producing concerns, in particular in England where such co-operation might bind together the loose methods of working that at present exist.

Making *Contact* 1932–33 (1973)

(From *Documentary Diary*)

After I left the EMB there followed a year's semi-employment. I rented a cheap furnished room in Manchester Street, off Baker Street, which was possible in those days. In the house was a *ménage* of theatre and film people: Miles Mander, Madeleine Carroll, Lydia Sherwood, Elizabeth Allan and the veteran actor Stewart Rome. Miles Mander, also mostly out of work, obtained an occasional script assignment for a feature film and asked me to collaborate with him. Some, like *The Mystery of the Marie Celeste* and *The Actor Manager* (from Leonard Merrick's novel) were abortive, but others, including *Fascination* (for which we wrote in a minute part for Merle Oberon—then Mierle Thompson), a remake of *The Lodger*, and *Don Quixote*, later made by Pabst with Chaliapine, reached the screen. Sometimes Miles Mander and I got paid, but often we didn't.

It was Miles Mander who introduced me to an unpleasant character, John Amery, a son of L.S. Amery, then Secretary of State for Dominion Affairs and, ironically, Chairman of the Empire Marketing Board. In some way, young John Amery had found some money, hired a cameraman, and shot thousands of feet of almost useless film of wildlife in East Africa. He now wanted a story invented to be shot in a studio in England so that his so-called 'wild animals' could be interpolated. It was to be called *Jungle Skies*. I wrote an appalling script which Amery much liked. His cheque for £50, however, did not materialise. After many broken promises, I decided to go and get the money. I needed it. His vast office was in Long Acre. On a huge desk were photographs of Mussolini and Al Capone. He at once gave me a cheque. I slipped it in my pocket and went to the door. He called me to turn round. He had a gun in his hand. He demanded the cheque. I left the room. The cheque was of course returned by my bank. With reluctance I went to see his father. He was embarrassed but not surprised by my story, but at once gave me his own cheque for the amount due. I did not mention the Empire Marketing Board. Young John Amery was hanged in 1945 for his collaboration with the Nazis during the war.

Another odd introduction by Miles Mander was to a peculiar middle-aged woman named Dinah Shurey. She had bird's nest hair. Like Harry Bruce Woolfe, she was an upstanding Empire loyalist. She had some money from an undisclosed source and a film production company called Britannia Films Ltd which had made some quite atrocious films, such as *Every Mother's Son, Carry On* and *Afraid Of Love*. I failed to grasp why Miles Mander had given me the introduction. Then she said that she had heard about a German film called *Kameradschaft*, about a mine disaster. She wanted to buy the British rights. Would I like to go to Berlin with her and while she negotiated with the producers, Nerofilm, I could make suggestions for English subtitles. It was, of course, the great film by Pabst, destined to become a classic. Why this strange woman wanted to acquire the British rights puzzled me and I never solved the puzzle. Although reluctant to be associated with Miss Shurey, I could not refuse the chance of going to Berlin again, meeting perhaps Pabst, and exploring the German film world for possible work.

In Berlin, Miss Shurey was shamefully double-crossed by the German producer, Seymour Nebenzal, who had practically sold the British rights to someone else. But poor Miss Shurey did not find this out for two weeks, during which time I wrote English subtitles for the film. Pabst himself was in North Africa preparing to make the exteriors for *Atlantis*, which was to be made in German, French and English. Nebenzal promised that I would be asked to return to Berlin and work with Pabst on the English version. It never transpired. Although I did not meet Pabst, I did meet his architect-designer, Erno Metzner, who had done the sets for *Kameradschaft* and was now designing the studio sets for *Atlantis*. Metzner and his Chinese wife were highly intelligent people; he had directed the *avant-garde* film *Überfall* which impressed many people. Later he came to England, where he was very unhappy in the studios, and went on to America.

It was the Berlin of 1931, with the depravity which repulsed Flaherty so much. I had little time to experience very much, being occupied at the laboratory with the subtitles, but I was not sorry to return to England and regretted that Miss Shurey had been defrauded out of her good intentions. On later occasions when I talked with Pabst, he told me much about Nebenzal's activities; so also did Fritz Lang, who had made *M* for Nerofilm. Such contacts as I had again in London and Berlin with the world of feature films reaffirmed my reactions at Elstree to this rat race, of which there is only one worse, the second-hand car market. I am not interested in cars, but I am in films.

I became convinced more and more that the only answer lay in the documentary method of finding film finance. Grierson had complete control over the Government's interest in documentary production. There might be the possibility of finding money in industry. I approached a big department store—Selfridges—to try and get them to sponsor a film of a day-in-the-life of a big shop, but before I had any response, I had a fortunate meeting.

If *The Film Till Now* had brought about no recognition in the film industry, it did bring contacts outside. Among these was Ralph Keene, then assistant manager at Tooth's Art Gallery in New Bond Street. As an outsider he was passionately interested in films but realised the need for economic sponsorship. A frequent visitor and occasional buyer of modern art at Tooth's Gallery, Keene told me, was J.L. Beddington, who was in charge of publicity and advertising for the giant Shell-Mex and BP oil company. Quite apart from his later interest in films, Jack Beddington used Shell money in the 1930s to sponsor many young painters and writers, some established but many unknown at that time outside a small circle. Among those who benefited from Beddington's patronage and who later gained success were, in no special order: Peter Quennell, Nicolas Bentley, John Piper, John Minchendon, E. McKnight Kauffer, Barnet Freedman, Rex Whistler, Michael Ayrton, Paul Nash, Edward Bawden, Leonard Rosarnon, Graham Sutherland, Robert Byron, Edward Ardizzone and, of course, John Betjeman who edited the admirable Shell Guides to British counties. This list of outstanding painters and writers shows Beddington's judgement in finding potential as well as established ability, and then backing it with sponsorship by a big industry. Since his death in 1959, no one so far as I know has followed in such a vital role of industrial patron.

Having heard my ideas about documentary, Ralph Keene said he would fix for us to meet Beddington, who had, Keene thought, commissioned one film to be made, *Liquid History*, which had not been a success. Keene had an idea for a short trick film to be based on the motif of seashells which he reckoned might seduce Beddington. Although far from my kind of film-making (except for the EMB Poster films), I helped Keene prepare a kind of script which was sent to Beddington. A meeting with the latter was arranged for discussion. For some reason I do not recall, Keene could not be present. Beddington in his charming but frank way had misgivings about the script, which I shared. But it was clear that he wanted to do something with the film medium. I was about to talk about the whole documentary idea, when his telephone rang.

A cryptic dialogue ensued, of which of course I heard only one end. Then Beddington put a hand over the phone mouthpiece and turned to me with a grin. 'What about making a film with Imperial Airways about their overseas air-routes? They will provide free travel and facilities if Shell will put up some hard cash.' That was exactly how I came to make my first documentary film.

Beddington commissioned me to write what could be written of a script for a modest sum. When I explained to Ralph Keene what had happened, he took up a most generous attitude. He could not, he said, leave his good job at Tooth's Gallery for such a pipe dream. He would like to contribute any ideas he might have in conceiving a script, but after that I should be on my own with the film. It was a handsome gesture that I have never forgotten.

After further discussion, talks with C.F. Snowden Gamble, the publicity manager of Imperial Airways, and visits to Croydon Airport, which was then the main London air-terminal, I submitted a kind of brief outline for the film (it could not be a script) to Beddington. He approved it at once. Shell were prepared to find a total sum of £2,500, which was to cover everything except cost of air travel. Film stock, wages, hotel accommodation abroad, laboratory charges and all the many items of film production were to be found for this figure. Then arose a problem. Shell could not contract with me as an individual to produce the film. A contract must be made with a company. I could have proposed New Era Films but because of its EMB relations decided against it. Looking around the industry, I could find only one company which had some kind of an honest reputation and which would give me services without any control over the making of the film. It was Bruce Woolfe's British Instructional Films, at Welwyn Garden City. It had been the producer of Asquith's feature films and also had its reputation for the *Secrets of Nature* series. I did not know then what I came to know about Bruce Woolfe in later days, but if I had, it would not have made any difference. I had complete control over the film on Beddington's insistence. A contract was drawn up between the Shell Company and British Instructional Films, by which they provided technical services for the production in return for 10 per cent of the contract price. My own fee was agreed at £200 for what eventually came to be a year's work of direction and editing. But it was my first film and much could result from it for the future.

For the record, because it has some importance later, Bruce Woolfe and his brother Willie, who was studio manager at Welwyn, began in the business as exhibitors in an East End cinema. Their spectacular success was when they booked a French film about the life of Christ. At the same time, *The Miracle* was being staged at the Albert Hall and being widely advertised all over London. The Woolfe Brothers toured the town very early one morning in a taxi and fixed small stickers billing their own picture and cinema's name across the huge posters for *The Miracle*. They did fantastic business. But Bruce Woolfe was a reasonably honest man in film industry terms. Among his co-directors at BIF at Welwyn were Lord Tweedsmuir (John Buchan, the novelist) and A.E. Bundy, the theatrical impresario. If Bruce Woolfe is to be remembered in cinema history as a whole, it is because he did back the amazing Percy Smith with the *Secrets of Nature* series. Percy Smith was an amateur who operated from a small house with a greenhouse attached in North London. For £10 a week he delivered a small amount of film he had made in his greenhouse or garden of plant and insect life to Bruce Woolfe, whereupon the material was 'put together' by Mary Field who, as time went by, added a banal commentary. She drew £50 a week. In its small, petty way this was typical of the exploitation methods of the industry, except that its end product was good.

No proper script could be written for *Contact* any more than Flaherty could write one for *Industrial Britain*, or Wright for *Song of Ceylon*. To write a script you must know what you are writing about. It was obvious that I knew nothing, or very little, about the countries over which the air-routes sped or the places at which planes stopped. To have researched into the backgrounds of air-routes between London and Karachi on the one hand, and Cairo to Cape Town on the other, could hardly have been possible in the time before our departure date was fixed. Even the latter did not depend on my choice. It was a matter of when Imperial Airways, already an overbooked airline, could carry our free-riding passengers. What was made very clear to me by the traffic department of Imperial Airways was that once we left London with a book of ticket reservations over three months, any variation from this schedule would mean endless delays which the film's budget would not stand. What I could not foresee was the lack of adequate co-ordination between personnel in London and personnel out on various places along the air-routes. In many places when we arrived, station staff had not heard that a film was being made and that a film unit would arrive expecting certain facilities to have been arranged.

For Beddington's sake as well as for my own, I wrote a kind of outline around which the film that I would shoot could be assembled. It spoke of Man's new Conquest of Space and Time, with emphasis laid on the closer communication between peoples being made possible by air travel, especially by airmail. In a letter to Eric Knight at the time, I set out a skeleton of headings:

Themes:
1. Poetry of the New World of the Air.
2. Prophecy for Future of Air Transport.

Sequences:
1. Conquest of Space on Land, Sea and Air (statement of fact).
2. Building of an Aircraft (the Machine) (descriptive).
3. Ground organisation at airports on three continents (descriptive commentary).
4. A big Airport (London): Airmail, People, Freight.
5. Interlude: romantic, poetic visuals of aerial impressions. A new world of being in and above the clouds.
6. The actual Air-Routes. Trans-Asia. Trans-Africa. Linking the City to the Desert, the Old to the New, and the Present to the Future.
7. Home. The return of the symbolic aircraft at dusk in England. Symphony of floodlit welcome at airport. Perhaps a fantasy of crowds as the aeroplane draws up on the tarmac having flown 14,000 miles and arriving dead on time.

Beddington, bless him, grasped my aim from this highfalutin' piece of work and his blessing was given to go ahead. He must have felt as Tallents did when Grierson started off to shoot *Drifters*, except that the risks were greater. Grierson at least knew the sea from his mine-sweeper days; I had never been in an aeroplane before. But we had one thing in common. Neither Grierson nor I knew one lens from another. He had the North Sea to dramatise; I had some 35,000 miles of unknown air-routes.

Only one thing Beddington insisted on. There must be in the film no direct reference to Shell, although they were footing the bill. If an air-stocking at some God-forsaken air-strip had on it the name SHELL, then I couldn't help but film it. But he emphasised that in no way at all was it to be considered a piece of advertisement. It was a deep gesture to be made in the early 1930s and it was to have its successors as, when the Orient Line sponsored *Shipyard*, there was to be no mention that the S.S. *Orion* was an Orient Line ship. This was public relations at its best and most imaginative.

Problems began almost at once. At the EMB Film Unit, Elton had just made his *Aero-Engine* picture with, in the last reel, some remarkable aerial photography by George Noble. Noble would be ideal for *Contact*. He agreed to take on the assignment and up till within a few days of our time for departure was keen to go. He had all inoculations done and passport ready. Then he abruptly said that he had been 'talked into staying at the EMB'. I have often, I must confess, wondered if that was sabotage. It was not George Noble's own choice; of that I am sure. The fact remained that, with less than 48 hours to go, I was without a cameraman. The flight could not be postponed. I knew of no other cameramen who were free and had to rely on one suggested by Bruce Woolfe at the studio. Horace Wheddon was a man of about 40, who came to see me wearing a bowler hat, all honey and smiles. I saw some of his exterior filming in Palestine, which was of very good quality. He could not have been a worse choice for this assignment. The bowler hat should have warned me.

Two weeks' shooting had already been done in England, at Coventry, of aircraft designing and construction, of the ground organisation at Croydon Airport, of planes arriving and departing and so forth. For this a BIF staff cameraman, Jack Parker, did admirable work, but he was too valuable to the studio for him to come with me. For my equipment, about which I knew little, the studio provided me with an old hand-turned Debrie with a tripod which was only turned by twisting handles. Subsequently, it was found that the spindle in the head was broken before we left. They also provided me with a very old Newman-Sinclair camera used by Cherry Kearton in ancient days for his animal films. This had no tripod and only one 35mm lens. Thus we had two cameras almost incapable of any camera movement, something I did not realise until too late. Some years later, when George Pocknall, who was in charge of the camera department at the studio which equipped me, came to do some filming for me, he confessed that he had had instructions from Bruce Woolfe not to 'take any kind of trouble over what equipment was supplied to Rotha'. In other words, Shell and I were given the leftovers of the camera department; it was something I did not forgive Bruce Woolfe for many years. But then, he was interested only in his company's 10 per cent cut on the contract price, not in what kind of a picture emerged. That was, and still is, the film business.

For aerial filming, no outside mounting of a camera was permitted on any aircraft. Insurance companies prohibited it. Any aerial shots would therefore have to be made through a very small sliding window in the Captain's cockpit. 30,000 ft of film stock was allocated for the journey, most of it having been sent ahead to await our arrival at stops along the route. In most cases, when we arrived, I found that it had not been cleared through customs by the local airport officials because they had had no orders from London to do so. Over and over again, it came to light that no organisation at all had been prearranged from London before our flight. We might as well have been ordinary passengers travelling as amateurs with an 8mm home-movie camera. Everything organised by the Shell people, such as local transport, worked efficiently all through. Almost everything that fell to Imperial Airways in London was a failure. Today I keep as a souvenir a bill for tea at a hotel in Khartoum which was not allowed for in our schedule; it pursued me from address to address for many years.

As film was exposed by us, it was to be sent back by air to London for laboratory processing. Bruce Woolfe was then to screen it and send me a report by cable as to its photographic quality. In my three months away from England, he sent me only one cable some half way through the 35,000-mile journey and that was to tell me that the Newman-Sinclair camera, which I had used a lot because of its portability, was giving gatetrouble which produced a jitter on the screen that could not be corrected. The camera had not been adjusted before leaving to take the kind of stock we were using. Thus most of the film taken on that camera was useless.

Somewhere along the way, however, Beddington did send me a letter in which he wrote that Bruce Woolfe had screened for him some of my material and that he had never seen such 'wonderful aerial camerawork'. This at least was some encouragement.

The unit of three (my then wife came with us and was of great help note-taking and otherwise) left London on 5 November 1932, to fly some 35,000 miles in 31 months, with no chance to break the journey except at prescribed stops as per ticket book. None of us had ever been in an aeroplane before. We flew from Croydon to Paris, by train to Brindisi because the Italians would not permit Imperial Airways to fly over their territory, by flying-boat to Lake Tiberias in Palestine, by Heracles-type biplane to Baghdad, to Sharjah on the Persian Gulf for a night-stop in the desert, and so to Karachi which was as far as the air-route went in those days. Then back the same way, but at Tiberias we missed the change-over plane to Cairo. At the time only a weekly service operated so we had an enforced wait for a week and even then we had to get to Cairo by train. Money was very short, so we travelled third class, which was an experience. From Cairo down Africa—the Sudan, Uganda, Nyasaland, Rhodesia to Cape Town. After Christmas, back up the same route but with stop-overs for filming at Kampala and Assiut of a week each, and thence to Athens. Two hundred and forty flying hours in 121 weeks.

Troubles with Horace Wheddon began early. Had I been surer of myself or had more money at my disposal, I should have changed the whole schedule, sent him back to England and waited for a substitute cameraman. But this was impossible; Imperial Airways had been adamant before I left England that in no circumstances was I to diverge from the agreed flight schedule. Near Baghdad, Wheddon point blank refused to take a shot because I wanted the camera slightly tilted. He finally agreed, but only if I gave him a letter absolving him from any responsibility, which I did with pleasure. I sat up most of that night typing out dozens of such letters for future use. Next he spent his time at nights in hotel bars telling his newly-found friends that I was a wealthy amateur and that he, Wheddon, was really making the film. This stopped when I refused to honour his bar bills. Then I found that he would not shake hands or share the same table with anyone not his own colour. Finally he fell ill with phlebitis on the return trip up Africa and I parted with him in Egypt. A substitute cameraman, Frank Goodliffe, was sent out to meet me in Athens. He proved as co-operative as Wheddon had proved difficult. Before leaving Wheddon in Assiut, I made him give me some rudimentary lessons in using the Newman-Sinclair; I was determined not to lose the opportunities of filming between Egypt and Greece. More by luck than skill, my footage was usable.

A detailed diary was kept during the three months, and many letters written. The diary entries were a day-to-day reaction to people and places, especially problems of production on a hazardous series of locations with very inadequate equipment; there were no hand-held cameras available then. My camera equipment weighed around 125 lbs. One thing does come clear from reading the diaries today and that is the dislike I formed for most of the white people with whom contact was made in Rhodesia and South Africa. A few exceptions were met: David Schrire, with whom a long friendship was begun and whose letters are quoted in this book; Volodya Meyerowitz, a Russian-born sculptor and brilliant still photographer, working in Cape Town and who committed suicide so tragically in London; and a game warden or two in Kenya and Uganda whose names I do not recall.

But some extracts between 5 November 1932 and 1 February 1933 can speak for themselves.

Over the Persian Gulf

A strange place from which to write a letter, just over 3,000 ft above the Persian Gulf and the plane batting along at 95 mph. Below are pearl-fishers, said to be slaves of the King of Muscat, with rows of nets. On the other side of the cabin is a Quetta colonel, in shorts and with a monocle. 'Way back in the 80s, my lad.' So far have only used the Newman camera from the plane. Have seen some lovely things but am scared to shoot too much from the air because the vibration is so great. Castelrosso was an enchanting small, brightly-painted harbour nestling under a mountain on the route between Athens and Galilee. The Governor tried to confiscate our camera and refused permission to film. As evidence of his authority he showed us a volume which dealt with the taking of daguerreotypes. Remarkable how this hostility has been met all the time so far. No one welcomes a film camera. Permission to shoot in Athens on the return journey is going to take almost a month to obtain.

Baghdad was disappointing—a dirty, dusty city with no magic or charm, only stench. Another disappointment was the desert fort at Rutbah Wells, quite modern and without interest. On the other hand, last night was spent under canvas in a barbed-wire compound outside Sharjah, a small town on the Musseldam Peninsula. We met the sheikh, a powerful man, who until recently was bitter against the British. Now he is more tolerant and received us with coffee and sweetmeats. On either side his falconers, some superb white horses, and a lot of white baby camels. With the aid of several interpreters, we made it clear that we wanted to shoot film next week on the return journey and he regally gave permission provided that he was photographed first.

Karachi

Arriving here had one spot of excitement. A key shot in the film is to be of an aircraft taking off from an overseas airport. But how to do this when there is only one plane and you are in it? A co-operative pilot (they all are so far) suggested that he made a landing in the usual way, dropped me and camera off (Wheddon refused to do this), then he would take off again so that it could be filmed. All went well. I lay in the grass at the perimeter of the airfield, camera on ground, no tripod. I got the shot okay and walked leisurely across the grass to the airport buildings. I was met by an excited group of officials. Hadn't I been warned that the airfield was alive with snakes? I saw no snake.

Wheddon more than difficult again. Typically British in that he dislikes any but the most conventional camerawork. Essentially of the picture postcard school. The most disheartening thing is the number of marvellous shots one sees but cannot get. Whether you haven't got permission to film, or the sun is in the wrong place, or you haven't the time. When a plane only stops at a place for ten minutes to refuel, there's no time to think of your script or your eventual editing. It's really newsreel work. The allocation of film stock is difficult. You shoot some cloud shots, say, between Galilee and Baghdad and later see something much better but you have no film stock left. It is not possible to carry much stock with us because of its weight and the customs duty to pay from country to country. Imperial Airways in London could have done so much to help in advance.

Sharjah

The guard which the Sheikh has ordered to surround the camp and the plane has been told that if anything is stolen or anything should happen to any of the passengers, then the eyes of the whole guard will be put out. Nothing happened.

Shaibah (Basra)

Have stopped for the night at a RAF aerodrome. The bar full of airforce types jokingly telling each other how they 'bombed up' a village that afternoon. I asked them why. I was told, 'Just to let them know we're here, old boy'.

One of the big difficulties of this task is that obviously during the day the aircraft is in the air and we are in it. We start at dawn and land at sunset. There is no real chance to film anything on the ground.

Basra–Baghdad

Very early 3 am start. Along rows of flares. Dawn did not break until we were near Baghdad. From the air it is clear to see the shifting course of the river and the foundations of old buildings. Wonderful luxurious banks of the Tigris. In the plane it is easy to throw oneself back into the past.

A filthy dirty hotel. Drove in a car to try and get some shots of the gaudy mosque at Khazimain. Pursued in the bazaars by mobs. Smells and dirt and heat. A knife fight in the bazaar. But typical of this city, one of the first things seen was a shoe shop wholly furnished with modern steel fittings as if in Regent Street or Fifth Avenue. On the way back shot the tomb of Haroun-el-Raschid's wife—shades of Leni's *Waxworks*. More argument with Wheddon over camera set-ups. Everything here is decaying. Deep impression of past glories but today they all look degenerate.

Spent a day out in the desert at the splendid Arch of Ctesiphon. A great span of bricks rising up out of the sand. Shot it from all angles with an inch lens. Next day went by interminable dusty road to Babylon. Donkeys looking like haystacks, camels, oxen and absurd goats. Stopped on way to take some shots of windblown sand. May find better examples later but that is one of the problems, you do not know if you will find better later on. Unlike Baghdad, Babylon was far from a disappointment. I had not expected it to be so large or in such a fine state of preservation. Wandered all over the ruins and got some good material of broken columns, animal bas-reliefs on the Ishtar Gate and the famous Lion. Had what could be a good idea when I saw some of masonry crumble and fall of its own accord. In all shots thereafter I had our guide kick dust and stones down, he himself being out of picture of course. Perhaps in this way I can get the effect of the past crumbling before the future. The present being, of course, the airplane. Shot some stuff in nearby village of Kuwairish, of palm trees and so on. Wheddon grumbling because I inevitably seem to select the local public lavatory as my favourite place to set up the camera. Nicknames the driver's boy Peter; he would make an excellent camera assistant back home. He soon got to know one lens from another. Found a two domed mosque covered with blue tiles. The sun was going rapidly and the camera jammed. Wheddon contrived to join the film with one of my wife's hairpins but I doubt if the stuff will be usable.

Still Baghdad. Discouraging and hopeless day trying to get shots in the bazaars. The material is admirable: every available type of person, stalls and produce. Rich, gorgeous coloured fruit, silks and fabrics, metal workers, and a gallery of types—Arabs, Jews, Persians, Baghdad, and a host of local tribes. But the moment we produce a camera a crowd of hundreds collects, swarming like flies around us, jeering, laughing, mocking, pushing, touching—anything to stop us filming. My God, to have a hidden camera! We tried on both sides of the Tigris but impossible. Wheddon slow and indifferent as to results. Iraqi policemen did their best to help. Then we saw a cockfight which added to my dislike of this foul place.

Saw a minute but attractive mosque. No decoration about it; plain white adobe dome and walls against a dark blue sky. So simple to contrast with all the gaudy mosques. But Wheddon, like the bloody fool he is, runs out of film after one shot! Back to the hotel to reload camera and of course I see a dozen things I want to shoot. We leave for Tiberias tomorrow morning. Glad to leave this goddamned place where no one does anything except hang around for money. The dirty foul-smelling hotel bill far too high and everyone hanging around for tips. Hell take them all! You can have Baghdad!

Baghdad–Tiberias
On a small, three-engined plane, an Avro 10, heading for Rutbah Wells. The normal Imperial Airways service could not carry us. Passed three RAF machines patrolling the desert. Watched the shadow of our plane on the sand below until my eyes ached. After Rutbah, we struck the mountainous country in Jordan. The small plane could not fly very high and thus avoid the airpockets. I was very sick and just hated flying and airplanes more than anything else in the world, not a good mood for someone making a film about the wonder of air travel. Stood in a thimble-size lavatory and was sick and sick and sick. Some compensation to find that the pilot of the little plane was being sick himself.

Learned at Simakh, the airport at the south end of the Sea of Galilee, that they had had strong storms. Saw the wreck of a Hannibal class aircraft minus wings, which had been blown to pieces on the ground. Imperial Airways had been smart enough to have its name and their name obliterated before we arrived in case we might film it. Flying-boat from Athens now 48 hours late due to weather, so no film stock for us. It will not arrive until the end of the week so we must hang around waiting to shoot. From the bedroom balcony one can see half of Tiberias. It looks clean and enchanting in the warm afternoon sunlight, the sea indigo, the houses pink and yellow. At last cleanliness and no smell. What a contrast with Baghdad!

A friendly and efficient guide called Nichole, born and bred in Tiberias. Have found much to shoot when the stock comes. And always the indigo sea in the background. Ploughing with oxen and donkeys, superb cypresses, fig trees, cacti, all green and luxuriant when compared with the barrenness of what we left in the East. The lateness of the film stock arriving will cut our schedule here, just when there is so much to shoot. Admired the craftsmanship of a man making wooden ploughs with the simplest of tools.

Everything here looks very beautiful, but now I have seen something of the cruelty that lies beneath the surface. How can they be so diabolically cruel to their animals? Chickens tied together with wire, donkeys being worked covered in sores, and while we were shooting at a mosque a small boy was playing with a decapitated sparrow. Their whole aim in life seems to be cruelty amid this lovely environment of graceful hills, whispering eucalyptus trees and white- and blue-walled houses.

Away early down to Samakh to shoot the old man making wooden ploughs. Pin broke in the Debrie camera. How Flaherty would have liked the craftsmanship of this ploughmaker. His father and grandfather made ploughs and he hopes his two sons will also make ploughs. He uses only two or three tools—a thing like a chopper, a drill worked like a violin bow and a saw.

Went to the little seaport town of Acca, of Crusades memories. Wonderful stretch of golden sand with fishermen dragging in their nets. Leave Tiberias tomorrow for Cairo. By train. No aeroplane available. Have just about got enough money for three third-class tickets. Could have done much more here if there had been time.

Cairo

At El Kantara on the Suez Canal they demanded £300 deposit on each camera. As I did not have this sort of money, they impounded the cameras, which we can claim in Cairo. To the latter, again by train. None of this need have happened if Imperial Airways had not let us down. At some places even the ground staff had not been told of our coming and this is supposed to be a film to publicise air travel! Cable here from the Cape Town Film Society welcoming me to Africa, which was nice of them.

Cairo has been a dead loss to the film. Took two days to clear the equipment through customs and then we got fined, I've forgotten how many hundred piastres, for not declaring a camelhair brush bought at Woolworths for a shilling. It is an offence to import camelhair into Egypt. Then the (English) bank refused to honour my cheque because I could not prove who I was! My passport was insufficient. Wasted a whole day trying to get a statement out of British consular official that I was me when he did not know me from Adam. By then the bank was closed. Shall just have time on Monday morning to get money needed for the flight down Africa. I did get a few dreary shots of the Sphinx and the Pyramids, the most overrated things in the world. Am depressed and despondent about the whole film.

Juba–Nairobi

Again a dawn start. Everyone getting tired of it all. One tries hard to sleep in the plane but the iron-frame chairs which some designer thought up are as hard as hell and the so-called headrest projects forward instead of back. Had breakfast at Kampala in Uganda. Should be wonderful stuff to shoot on the return. Rich foliage, giant trees, masses of brilliantly coloured flowers. The so-called *Trader Horn* country, because MGM shot their film around here. Some entertaining stories about Van Dyke (who directed the picture) from a Captain Drysdale who arranged transport for the huge MGM unit. The extravagance of it all; calling for 200 pygmies at one hour's notice. After all I wrote about *Trader Horn* in my book,[i] this is amusing. This Drysdale, a guide and a hunter, has arranged a trip for us to the Murchison Falls on our return. Here is real enthusiastic co-operation but nothing to do with Imperial Airways. Then away along the edge of the lake, low down over tropical forest with crocodiles basking in the sun. At last things look interesting. At Kisumu changed into a land machine and had a very bumpy flight to Nairobi. Seems odd being here after John Amery's *Jungle Skies*! Too late to film, but we are here for a week.

Next morning arranging transport with the Shell people and seeing the game warden of the Masai Game Reserve to get permission to film. He lives in a kind of bungalow in a grove of lemon gums and curved cactus. He was like Haggard's Allan Quatermain, in green corduroy shooting-jacket and huge padded pith helmet. A man smelling of rifles and dead animals and campfires. Very courteous and will fix anything we like, but not to carry guns, which we do not wish to do anyway. Got some good stuff in the afternoon—lovely clouded sky and beautiful foliage, Guatemala cypress, lemon gums and paw-paw.

Away in the early morning by car into the Masai Game Reserve. Over the Ngong Hills and down along a dirt road on to a seemingly huge plain on which from high up could be seen groups of game giraffe, gazelle and buck. Got some shots of vultures and carcasses of cows. Everything very dry near a Masai bomba; sheep dying of hunger. To film them the Masai demanded money, even here so far from anywhere. They demanded a shilling for each sheep. Wonderful tree forms again—candelabras and thorn bushes. Superb cloud effects on way back, but Wheddon too slow to get out camera.

On Sunday headed for the Rift Valley and the Escarpment and beyond to Lake Naivasha. Flamingoes, wildebeests, impala, Grant and Thompson's gazelle and the world's most wonderful small creature —the dikdik. Back to Nairobi in the moonlight.

Spent all Monday at the airport getting shots of aircraft being refuelled. Burnt my left arm on an outside exhaust pipe of a Shell Moth. Dislike the hotel in Nairobi with its strict colour bar. But it suits Wheddon. Next day up the Fort Hall Road. Shots of sisal growing. On to Thika for the waterfall and also to Fourteen Falls. On way back stopped at another coffee shamba owned by a Dane and saw process through. They work the native boys hard—6 am to 6 pm and no break for meals.

Raining all next day. Received first cable from Bruce Woolfe. Gate-trouble with the Newman camera. Very upsetting because so much footage has been shot on it. Impossible to repair here. All that can be done is to use the clumsy old Debrie and hope that the Newman can be repaired when we reach Cape Town. Leaving tomorrow.

Still in Nairobi. Typical Imperial Airways day. Hanging around the dreary airport (if so it can be called) because the plane won't start. Loading and then unloading all the baggage. Back to the hotel for lunch. Back to the airport. Plane still won't fly. Back to the hotel again. Why the hell didn't they send for a machine from Kisumu where we know there is a relief?

In the hotel found the following informative Japanese leaflet. 'At the rise of the hand of a policeman, stop rapidly. Do not pass him or otherwise disrespect him. When a passenger of the foot hoves into sight, tootle the horn-trumpet melodiously at first. If he still obstacles your way, tootle him with vigour and express with the word of the mouth the warning, Hi! Hi!' 'Beware of the wandering horse that he shall not take fright as you pass him. Do not exploit the exhaust-box at him. Go soothingly by.' 'Give space to the festive dog that makes sport in the roadway. Avoid entanglement of dog with your wheel-spokes.' 'Go smoothingly on the grease mud as there lies the skid demon. Press the brake of the foot as you role [sic] around the corners to save the collapse and timing.'

Mpika–Johannesburg
This has been the worst flying day of all from 3 am this morning until
touchdown at 7.45 pm at Germiston, stopping at Broken Hill, Salisbury,
Bulawayo and Pietersburg. Far too much to fly in one day in a small
aircraft like this and all for Imperial Airways' prestige, to say that the
mail arrives on time. While changing planes at Broken Hill my still-
camera was lost. Impossible to see anything of Jo'burg, far too tired.

Johannesburg–Touew's River
5 am start after usual trouble of overloading. The Big Hole of Kimberley
looks very big from the air. Engine trouble all the afternoon. Landed
here 100 miles from Cape Town, and the passengers all revolted against
going on in the dark. Too rough. Pilot gave in, so we stay the night. This
in spite of the fact that we have on board a newsreel of the Stribling–
MacQuorcadale fight and the usual mails. Notice in cabin of plane:
'SAFETY CHAINS FOR LADIES TRAVELLING ALONE.'

(Note: Of the week in Cape Town little need be recorded. My diary's
main entries reveal my disgust at the European behaviour to the African.
We had Christmas there and more drunkenness among white people I
have never seen. My wife was warned not to sit in the sun in case she got
sunburnt and might be mistaken for a native. She said 'That would be
nice.' Tried to film in the notorious District Six area but the police
stopped it. The city and surrounding country are beautiful, but it is a keg
of dynamite waiting for the match. The Shell people gave a party and
were upset that I hadn't got a dinner-jacket with me. Hell, flying some
35,000 miles with one suitcase!)

Cape Town–Johannesburg
By train; Imperial Airways could not carry us. It is more comfortable at
least. Rolling veldt until the first white slagheaps of the Rand Valley. A
35-year-old city built on gold. Pretentious and lacking in any kind of
good taste. A gimcrack city. Gold runs through the whole place and yet
all talk is of the crisis whether to come off the gold standard or not! Next
day at the Crown mine, filming. They work the Africans hard. We
watched them coming up in cages after an 8½ hour shift. Each with a
brass bangle bearing his number. They live in a compound (which we
were not allowed to visit) and are shown old Hollywood westerns once a
week as a treat. Many of the miners were bleeding and bruised as they
came up blinking into the sunlight. They looked utterly exhausted. The
Manager was with us the whole time and very strict as to what we

filmed. Shall not be sorry to leave this hell-hole behind tomorrow. From my hotel window all I can see are the signs flashing out FORD, SHELL, DODGE, CASTLE BEERS, HAIG. The whole place is shoddy.

(Note: the journey north was uninteresting until after leaving Dodoma we had a crash landing)

Kigwe

It would seem that this is the first time the pilot has flown over this part of the route, so he lost his way and ran out of petrol. Made a beautiful landing in the thorn trees near a small railway station with a single-track line that goes God knows where. One train goes once a week and that was yesterday. But at least there is a telephone and a very excited African in charge. This is obviously the great moment in his life, a crashed aeroplane. Against all orders from Imperial Airways before leaving England, I filmed the landing in the thorn bushes from the cockpit window. Both wings and engines were ripped off, leaving the fuselage suspended in the trees. It was a very skilful landing. No one hurt, no fire, just a long wait in the sun until a relief train can be sent in heaven knows how many hours' time. The only food and drink are what was on the plane. A fat American woman has a box of peaches she had brought with her. She does not offer to share them out. I persuade Wheddon to take some shots I wanted, but he is reluctant, so 'shaken by the crash'. Eventually, in the early evening the train shows up, an engine and one carriage. Someone had thoughtfully stocked it with food and bottles of beer. Made Dodoma just after nightfall. New Year's Eve. We shack up in a dreary little 'hotel' run by a Greek. Some Englishmen, locals I assume, in their moth-eaten dinner-jackets, are trying to start a party. Charles Nichols, a young American who is a passenger on the plane, and I do our best to break up the party without success. The Englishmen just look at us fish-like. So Nichols and I end up the evening driving the train up and down the line with its searchlight full on. Kid stuff but it breaks the monotony.

Dodoma–Nairobi

A relief plane sent down from Nairobi, but with no seats in it because it was assumed that the ones in the crashed plane could be transferred. They were wrong. So they put into the relief plane some dining-room chairs which obviously slide all over the place. Sitting on the floor of the plane is preferable. Flew very low over bush country. The relief Captain has a hangover. After all it was New Year's Eve last night. A memorable crossing of the Escarpment down into Moshi. Kilimanjaro covered in cloud. Almost thought we would hit the hills. Then over the Athie Plains, flying very low over scattering game—zebra, giraffe and buck —should be good film if Wheddon has done his job well. The sun casting long shadows over the plain. Nairobi again and its usual crowd of bar-loafers. They will make Wheddon happy. Now he *has* a story to tell. The crash in the bush!

Nairobi–Kampala

The plane heavily overloaded so we must take a Wilson Airways Moth as far as Kisumu. More like real flying in a small aircraft. Then into the flying-boat and over the lake to Kampala. We are a day late owing to the forced landing. Drysdale, as promised, has everything laid on. We go straight to the Murchison Falls. Hurried loading of the cameras in hotel and then a 168-mile car ride through the night to Buiaba. Several leopards in the car headlights. Transferred on board the S.S. *Livingstone*, like a small tug, and away up the choppy lake.

Kampala–Murchison Falls

After a restless night because of the rolling boat, woke to see the banks of the Nile with papyrus, and the tug steaming slowly up the middle of the Nile. All morning we sat on deck with cameras ready and got what I hope will be good shots of crocodiles and hippos. Many wonderful strange birds and buck on the river banks. The place is teaming with game, but then it is rightly a game reserve. After the many almost unbelievable stories of the *Trader Horn* unit, with all its expensive equipment and big-time team of technicians, I hope to do better with my two unreliable cameras and a reluctant cameraman. Spotted fine bull elephant meandering around the shore. We put off in a small whale boat to stalk it. The river banks here are made up of ribs of hilly bush and shallow but thickly wooded valleys. So long as we stick to the ribs we shall be out of the elephant's way but can get close to him. Drysdale, Wheddon (with Newman camera), two native boys and myself, in single file climb one of the ribs of hill. The thorn bushes are alive with spikes and one must go carefully. We are very near the elephant now. He is peacefully eating leaves off a tree. Suddenly, from just in front of us, there is a roar which I shall never forget.

We saw a magnificent lion about ten yards away. Drysdale shouted, 'Run like hell!' We did. Wheddon promptly dropped the camera. Lion or no lion, I picked it up. Down that hill, which had taken so long to climb, we pelted irrespective of the thorn bushes. The lion did not follow us. It was Drysdale's theory that it was guarding its cubs. We reached the whale boat and were on board the tug in a matter of minutes. Drysdale insisted we were washed down with iodine, which was more painful than the thorn scratches. Poor Wheddon was so scared, I almost felt sorry for him, and then remembered how he threw away the camera. Later we continued on our way towards the foot of the Falls. That night I slept with a lion's roar in my ears; it must have been MGM's, which Van Dyke had left behind. Crocodiles and hippos bump against the side of the tug all night.

Early next morning, after a breakfast of fried bacon and pineapple, we put off in the whale boat for the foot of the Falls. The tropical vegetation and clouds are magnificent. We put ashore in a little bay since known as the *Trader Horn* crocodile pool. Drysdale remembers that the MGM unit were very cruel to the animals in order to 'get a performance' out of them. Here Wheddon made an announcement. He was not going to land without adequate armed protection. Drysdale, who had by now summed up the situation, quietly said, 'All right, Mr Wheddon, you sit in the sun all day. It will be very hot, I will leave one boy with you to guard you.' There were, of course, no firearms with the party. So I had Wheddon set the exposure on the Newman camera for me, and Drysdale, my wife and I, with two boys, set off up the narrow path that led up to the top of the Falls. It was rather like being on Hampstead Heath, except for the foliage. At the head of the Falls the drama was fantastic. The Nile tears and twists itself through a gorge about 20 ft wide to cascade down into the main river. Deafening and awe-inspiring. I shot a 200 ft magazine of film, all I had with me. Then we retraced our way down the path.

About three hundred yards from the shore where the whale boat was moored, in the middle of the track, was a big elephant spoor. It had not been there when we climbed the track a few hours before. Then we saw him, the same bull as the previous day, again peacefully eating at a tree. Drysdale said, 'We'd better wait for a while. He'll make off soon'. The boys lit a fire so that the smoke would drift in the elephant's direction. We sat under a tree. My wife said, 'It's rather like waiting for a No. 53 bus.' She then looked up into the tree and above us was coiled a big snake. It was not moving. By then the elephant had ambled away and we made the whale boat safely. Wheddon was sitting in his shirt sleeves, a bottle of whisky in one hand. I gave him the camera. He calmly told me that the exposure was wrong and that I must have altered it. So all that possibly magnificent material of the Falls is wasted. I would swear for ever that the lens stop had been deliberately set wrong.

Exquisite quietness as the boat sailed along the Nile in the half-light, forest fires burning on the banks. Drysdale talked about his dream project of making a film about the River Nile, tracing it from its source in the Mountains of the Moon to the moment when it meets the Mediterranean. I suggest that it is called *The River of Life*.

(Note: Back in England later, I tried for several years to get this project set-up. I drew up an outline, with maps and detailed notes, and a costing based on Drysdale's estimates. No British company would hear of it.)

Kampala

Wheddon in local bar tonight, I am told, trying to get a letter stating that he has been in dangerous territory without proper protection. Regret leaving Uganda, a country I should like to come back to, with a proper cameraman and more time. The colour is superb.

(Note: The air journey North was without event, until Assouan. The Governor at Wadi-Halfa had laid on a small party for us but when he heard that I had no dinner-jacket, the party was called off.)

Assouan

Several wasted days here in thick mist. The Shell man a very intelligent Egyptian, most interested in cinema. Wheddon goes sick, acting theatrically as if drunk. Then some sun so we go, minus Wheddon, out into the desert on camels. If my exposure and focus are right, it could be good stuff. Wish now that I had had some elementary training in using a camera before leaving England, but never foresaw a cameraman like Horace Wheddon. Called a doctor for him. He must stay in bed for several weeks. I cable Bruce Woolfe to send me another cameraman but the earliest he can meet up with us is at Athens. That means that between here and there if there is any shooting to do, I must do it. Had a try at the great Assouan Dam today. Fine material if only my work is okay. At the airfield the incoming plane brought mail from England. An invitation to Eric Knight's wedding in Philadelphia.

Athens

Little of any event took place on the way back to England. Frank Goodliffe, a good and co-operative cameraman, met us in Athens. Much time lost in getting permits to film on the Acropolis, permits that

Imperial Airways had been asked to obtain two months ago. When we did get them, in a method reminiscent of René Clair, we were dogged by bad weather. Snow in Athens! The last thing I expected. In one week only two hours of sun.

Piraeus–Brindisi
So, 30,000 ft of film stock. 24,000 miles. 240 flying hours. 3 months' journey. Wish it had taken twice as long, had three times the amount of film stock, had an intelligent co-operative cameraman and that the whole journey had been far better planned in advance by Imperial Airways in the London head-office.

To all intents and purposes, my diaries and letters end there. If the above extracts are overlong, they are used to show some of the problems of the early documentary film-makers. But the difficulties helped in one way. When in 1936 Alexander Shaw, Ralph Keene, John Taylor and George Noble set off from England to Australia to make several films for Imperial Airways, I made it my business to see that their organisation was far more fully prepared and that they got proper producership from London while they were away. Their negative came back to England quickly, I screened a print in London at once and sent detailed cables the same day as to its quality, and actual frame-clips from the shots the next day. They were hardly out of touch with me for more than two weeks at a time even when in the Dutch East Indies and Australia. It was rather different from the service provided by Bruce Woolfe and his British Instructional Films in 1932–33.

On returning to England, a screening of all the footage was the first step. It revealed that about one quarter of what I had shot was unusable as a result of the camera fault, for which the staff at the studio was wholly responsible. But it must be said that the actual photographic quality of Horace Wheddon's work was excellent. That is only fair to say. Now there was to come the editing of what film was usable down to the agreed final length of 4 reels, about 45 minutes of screen time. Here I quote from my letters to Eric Knight, in America.

Welwyn Studios, 8 Feb. 1933
This studio is like a morgue; no films of any size have been made here since Asquith's *Tell England* three years ago. But one good thing; as it is not British Instructional's film, I am left wholly to myself. No interference, but no assistance either. I am doing every foot of my own cutting, joining and all that. It brings me down to the guts of things. It is

only by editing material that you have shot yourself that you realise your mistakes. All the same, I know that if I had had proper equipment overseas, I would have shot it differently. There would have been, for one thing, a great deal more camera movement. I know that I shan't produce a masterpiece but hope to make a workmanlike picture that may lead to more films to make.

I can already see that the film will suffer by being too static for two reasons. First, my training at the Slade as a painter did not influence me to appreciate the importance of movement. Second, the single tripod I had with me allowed for no kind of real camera movement; every shot had to be conceived statically. No amount of skilful editing can achieve movement on the screen if the movement is not there already in the shot.

I've a camp-bed installed in the cutting-room so that I can live with the film.

10 April 1933
Contact grows apace. But very slowly. Sometimes I take what must seem like a ridiculous length of time about a sequence of shots when most technicians would see the way to cut it at once. But I have to sit and think it out for myself. You must remember that, apart from the little Poster films at the EMB, this is the first film I have edited and it's got to run four reels. People at the studio constantly ask, 'When will your picture be ready?', to which I can only reply, 'There are sixteen frames to a foot of film, and my film will be 4,000 ft long. Every foot of film is worth thinking about for ten minutes. Work it out for yourself'. And they walk away thinking I am mad. Happily, Beddington at Shell is content to be patient and tells me to take my time. But as I am being paid a single fee for the whole job, it makes living difficult.

19 April 1933
Have just finished a rough-cut of the first three reels of the picture. I wonder if I have cut it too fast? It's all very well to cut fast for your friends who know film, but will the ordinary public follow it? I've just edited an impression of an Eastern town—the muck and filth and cruelty contrasted with the gilded mosques and lovely foliage of the trees. Just any mid-Eastern town unnamed. Then later will come a similar kind of town in Africa. Over each flies the airliner, disturbing man and beast as they watch it travel overhead. But the machine itself is

not shown; we hear only the increasing and then decreasing sound of its engines.

Editing was finished by the end of April. Now came the sound-track. I decided to have no spoken commentary but where absolutely necessary a minimum of subtitles, very short ones. Clarence Raybould, a conductor working at the BBC but also a composer, was brought in to write an original music score, but in the time available (Bruce Woolfe was urging me to get finished) he only wrote music for the first reel. For the other 3 reels he adapted music from other sources, Mozart, Rossini and Tchaikovsky. For reasons of economy, the whole 45 minutes of music had to be recorded in one day. It was put on TobisKlangfilm, a German system.

10 May 1933

To all intents the film is finished. The negative is now being cut. There is little I can do but wait. Now I realise that the film should have been shot in colour but where would the extra cost have come from? There is talk that the film may be given a première at a so-called gala performance which our patriotic Film Trade is giving to the delegates from God-knows-how-many countries soon about to meet in London for the World Economic Conference. Before sending the picture for negative cutting, I showed it to Beddington and with his agreement asked Grierson too. They were both kind about it, especially Beddington. What the hell! I've done a job in rough conditions and I haven't the slightest idea of what I shall do next.

That was the first time that Beddington met Grierson and like so many others came under his spell of persuasive talk. (Only one man in the film industry could talk more persuasively than Grierson—Alexander Korda, but then he was a Hungarian.) From that meeting over *Contact* there later came a request to Grierson to write a report for the Shell Company as to how it could use films in the widest sense, and eventually from the report came the setting-up of the Shell Film Unit. I had the impression that Grierson came rather to deprecate Beddington for his concern with aesthetics, for at that time the mere mention of the word was anathema to Grierson.

July 1933

The film still has not had its first showing. The gala performance I wrote about earlier is now fixed for one night next week, after a slap-up dinner at the Dorchester Hotel. The audience, we are told, will include the

Prince of Wales, all the overseas delegates at the Conference who want to attend, and the foreign and British Press. Aw, hell take them all, say I.

16 July 1933

The picture has had its stuffed-shirt showing to an audience of ministers and their wives, economists and their wives, and a herd of newspapermen, the lot filled up with liquor and food. In name the performance was put on by the Film Industry as a whole, but in fact Gaumont-British muscled in for themselves. The Ostrer Brothers saw a fine opportunity for publicity. The bloody Prime Minister and sundry members of the Cabinet were also there. At the dinner, one of the Ostrer Brothers rose and welcomed the guests in the name not of the British Film Industry as was expected but of Gaumont-British. Their rival studio company, British International Pictures, looked pretty sick. After the stuffing and drinking, everyone adjourned to the New Victoria Cinema, London's newest and most garish theatre, where the stage was set with the flags of all the nations except Germany and the USSR.

The programme began with the usual newsreel (Gaumont-British), went on to a poor travelogue of Windsor Castle (produced by C.A. Lejeune's husband, now at G-B, in charge of the Gainsborough Miniatures series of shorts) and then to an extract from a Movietone reel of the Derby and Trooping the Colour. By now the well-fed, cigar-smoking audience was ripe for a musical or some such entertainment. Instead they got *Contact*.

They watched in silence. At the end of the first reel, after we have seen the building of the aircraft accompanied by Raybould's fugue, they gave it a hand. Half a reel later, they gave it a bigger hand. About 300 ft from the end, when the airliner comes in to land in the dusk, they began applauding again and kept it up until the end.

After the interval, Gaumont-British presented their feature, a comedy. It was a complete flop. As it showed, the audience dribbled up to the foyer to drink G-B's champagne. Everyone said what a wonderful evening it was and how the British film industry was doing so well. I went to a pub I know in those parts and puked in the toilet.

23 July 1933

Complications have now arisen over the film's release. While I was editing the film, British International bought out British Instructional. They (British International) are very angry that my film was shown at all as the performance turned out to be a bonanza staged by Gaumont-British. Bruce Woolfe tells me that they were annoyed that the Selection Committee chose *Contact*. It would seem that Wardour Films, who are the BIP distribution company, are doubtful if they want to release the film at all. There is, however, a contract guaranteeing release signed between Shell and Wardour.

30 July 1933
It is now clear that Wardour dislike the film and all it stands for because it is a new kind of film-making which they are incompetent to market. They fear for its success, says Bruce Woolfe, and are doing all in their power to shelve it. The matter came to a head last week at a meeting of salesmen when the managing-director of Wardour Films, Arthur Dent, said, I am told, that, 'Me and the boys have seen this lousy tripe called *Contact*. It's about 90 per cent stock-library material, dull and dreary, with no real story. It might make a small return if cut down to one reel with a running commentary added.' This in spite of the film's undisputed success at the gala performance and in face of the Prime Minister of Canada sending a letter saying that it was one of the best films he had ever seen (Imperial Airways were delighted by this) and the *Evening Standard* writing a 'remarkable achievement in film-craft'. After Dent had made his statement, Bruce Woolfe handed in his resignation. It was about the only decent thing he did during the whole picture.

Now it seems the problem is to get the film away from Wardour. The bastards won't give it up to another distributor. They are holding a Trade Show for exhibitors at the lousiest and smallest projection theatre in Wardour Street and are issuing no Press invitations. Both Shell and Imperial Airways are angry at the whole situation. They even talk of suing Wardour for breach of contract.

30 November 1933
The film has now been running for a week at the big Regal Cinema at Marble Arch as a second feature to a shocking George Arliss picture, *The Working Man*. The manager of the theatre tells me that *Contact* gets a hand at every performance and that he will play it for another three weeks. I also hear that despite Wardour's attitude, it is being booked well all over the country. At the Regal it is being shown on a newly-installed wide screen which means that the top and bottom of the picture frame are cut off. Thus all the carefully composed close-ups, especially of faces,

are castrated. On complaining to the manager, a Mr Pepper, he told me to mind my own business; it was his affair to know how a film should be projected. He's very proud of his wide screen.

Later I was able to write to Knight that *Contact* had been booked for a further five weeks at another West End cinema, after which it played at three other cinemas in central London.

5 February 1934

In spite of Wardour's vulgar advertising, *Contact* has now been booked to more than 1,500 cinemas in the United Kingdom. This should mean a gross revenue of more than £12,000. Allowing for cost of prints, advertising and other what are called 'exploitation' costs, this should mean some return to Shell for their £2,500 investment, although it was not their intention to make money out of the film. All they wanted were showings.

The arguments, horse-trading, double-dealing and crooked box-office returns arising from the distribution of *Contact* revealed to me the corruption of the Film Trade, perhaps not so much today as in the 1930s. All I found out confirmed what I once wrote, that the film business ranks only second to the second-hand car market for crookedness.

Beddington told me later that Shell never saw a shilling from Wardour for the cinema takings. They would have sued but for the dignity of a big corporation. But they were more than satisfied by the prestige gained. On 15 November, Beddington wrote to me from Shell-Mex House, 'I can't help writing to tell you that I have heard this week from two completely independent sources what a very good film *Contact* is; in both cases friends of mine have been to the Rialto Cinema and said that the film had an extraordinarily good reception.'

In general, the film had mixed reviews in the Trade Press but very enthusiastic ones in the general lay Press. Here, only one is given because it was revealing:

> This description of Imperial Airways is Rotha's first film, and shows him more mature in criticism than in production. The film is never quite permitted to get off the ground. Always the critical mind of Rotha seems to be jabbing and hedging and taking care lest the mistakes he has recognised in others' work appear to damn his own. The photography is too careful, the editing too studied, and sequences of the film too altogether cerebral. A careless rapture or

two would have made his airplanes fly higher and faster, would have supplied a necessary breeze to his photography, and made the contacts between continents warmer and more exciting. These criticisms are noted only because Rotha is coming into the first line of documentary and calls for all the heavy weather we can make for him. Even if the photography were not as beautiful as it is, the size and scope of *Contact* would make it important in this year's documentary account. The trouble with Rotha is that he doesn't think about cinema (like Eisenstein), nor does he patently enjoy making it (like Elton): he worries about it. If, in his next, he forgets half of what he knows, doesn't care so much about the other half, and sets out to enjoy his material as well as shoot it, he will do something very exciting indeed.[ii]

In fairness to Grierson, he did see the film a second time at the Tatler Cinema and in the columns of *New Britain* wholly retracted his criticism. He wrote that the film 'marched'.

Unknown to me, Bruce Woolfe entered the film for the Venice Film Festival in 1934. To Richard Griffith I wrote:

4 August 1934
I've just had a clipping from an Italian newspaper saying that *Contact* evoked cheers from the Venice Festival audience. What the hell, who would ask that when the great mass of Italian people are suffering under the Mussolini lash? I am ashamed that the film was shown there and want no part of it. Bruce Woolfe, who was there, was given some kind of phoney gilt medal which he now hangs on his office wall.

There had, of course, been many examples of publicity and advertising films being previously made for industrial firms in Britain but these were far from the documentary conception. *Contact*, however, was not the first British documentary film to find its economics for production in sponsorship. *Drifters* must have been the first but that sponsorship was by a government using public money. Elton's *Voice of the World* was probably the first documentary to use industrial backing for prestige for the Gramophone Company. *Contact* for Shell was the second. They took no credit on the titles of the film, but it soon became widely known who had backed it. With Elton's film, it was to set the road for many such financed films in the 1930s and subsequent years. If the facts about *Contact's* release have been set out at some length, it is because it is important even today for a film-maker to know how much his work is at the mercy of the often ill-equipped distributor and exhibitor. There are of course, exceptions but the wholesale and retail sides of the industry are in my long experience gravely lacking in all but a kind of very vulgar and often inefficient showmanship.

Notes

ⁱ *Celluloid: The Film Today*, pp. 196–211.
ⁱⁱ *Cinema Quarterly*, autumn 1933, review by John Grierson.

Presenting the World to the World (1956)

(From *Films and Filming*, April 1956; reprinted in *Rotha on the Film*)

People often ask what sparked the idea that has lain behind 'The World' series of films and television programmes with which I have been associated on and off over the past fifteen years. They began way back in 1942 when the then Ministry of Information commissioned what it intended to be a short film for non-commercial audiences about how the British were benefiting from American food under Lease-Lend. What finally evolved was *World of Plenty*, the first film about the world-to-be after the war had been won, and which had ultimately as wide a distribution in many countries as possibly any other documentary of the war years. That was fourteen years ago.

Today, the theme is being continued in the BBC television series *The World Is Ours*, initiated by me there in April, 1954, and ably produced by Norman Swallow. Eight have so far been shown and four more are in preparation.

Now there is a new film which I hope to make for the United Nations this year from a script that I have written on the peaceful uses of atomic energy in relation to world energy resources as a whole.

In between there have been *The World is Rich*, made in 1946–47, which stirred up so much fuss in spite of its being officially sponsored by the Government, and *World Without End*, made for UNESCO in 1959–53 by Basil Wright and myself, which has had probably the biggest world distribution of any documentary made since the war. Other units, too, have taken other aspects of 'The World' story and made such excellent films as *Today and Tomorrow* by Robin Carruthers and Arthur Calder-Marshall, *The Teeth of the Wind* by James Carr and the recent brilliant *The Rival World* made by Bert Haanstra for the Shell Film Unit, while the United Nations Films Division itself has made numerous less ambitious films over the past ten years.

To my own 'World' films many people have contributed and deserve great credit, but the real credit for the theme of the original *World of Plenty* lay with the late Eric Knight, best known oddly enough as the author of *Lassie*, on sequels to which so many other and lesser pens have worked. Those who read the extracts from Knight's letters (written between 1932 and 1943) published three years ago under the title of *Portrait of a Flying Yorkshireman*, will recall that that tough fighter for goodwill among men was deeply perturbed way back in the 'thirties by the inequality of food distribution throughout the world. He was then farming himself, as well as writing, and came up against the crazy stupidity of farmers being compelled to restrict their output while at the same time people were dying of hunger.

In the winter of 1942 Knight was in England and offered to write a script for the Ministry of Information without fee. Together we saw the scope of *World of Plenty*. Actually, Knight was unable to complete here because, immediately after Pearl Harbor, he returned to the United States to take up service there. We continued to collaborate by air-mail and cable and he spoke one of the main voices of the film before being killed in an air-crash in January, 1943. At a later stage that noted actor and playwright, Miles Malleson, contributed some final dialogue.

The opening words of *World of Plenty*—wonderfully spoken by the American radio reporter and writer Robert St John—were: 'This is a film about Food—the World Strategy of Food. How it is grown—how it is harvested—how it is marketed—how it is eaten. In peace or war, Food is Man's Security Number One.' The film went on to show the problems of world food 'as it was', 'as it is', and 'as it might be'. We had the inspiration of Sir John (now Lord) Boyd-Orr, the great nutrition expert, of Ritchie Calder (the science-writer who has done so much in his own medium for the 'World' theme and collaborated later on several films), of the novelist Arthur Calder-Marshall (at that time script-editor at the Ministry of Information) and the late Carl Mayer (the script-writer of the early German films such as *The Cabinet of Dr Caligari* and *The Last Laugh*, who was working with my unit at the time). So we proceeded to turn what was meant to be a little picture about Lease-Lend food into a film that challenged the world and astonished the three hundred delegates and Pressmen from forty-four allied and neutral countries who had assembled for the first World Food Conference at Hot Springs, Virginia, in May, 1943, by anticipating many of their conclusions.

World of Plenty was not made without many difficulties, official and otherwise, being put in our way; but with our immense faith in the basic rightness and common sense of our 'message' it finally reached a world public. Of the many, many letters and comments that reached me about the film, perhaps the one that moved me most was a postcard from a girl sergeant in the ATS on 48-hour leave in London who simply wrote. 'Your film more than anything else has shown me why I am fighting in this war.'

In 1946, a direct request came from the Prime Minister's Office to the British documentary people for three major films on international subjects, the first to be again on world food in the light of the post-war situation and the setting-up of the United Nations and its Specialised Agencies. As it was in direct continuity to *World of Plenty*, the film came to me to make and I invited Calder-Marshall to script, with Ritchie Calder again as adviser. It was finished the next year and again encountered many obstacles to its showing, both official and trade. At last, after good friends in Fleet Street and in Parliament had thrown their weight behind it, a British release was obtained and it also was shown widely overseas, with stimulating results.

It is often said that *World of Plenty* began a new technique of film argument, derived from the American stage *Living Newspapers*. This is only partially correct. The first film in which I tried this technique of using every trick and device of the movie medium—stock library footage, diagrams, cut-in interviews, an argumentative voice track, trick optical effects and so on—was in *New Worlds for Old*, written and made in 1938 on my return from New York. It was a curious combination of *Hellzapoppin*, and the *Living Newspaper* that suggested to me that in film one could take this 'argument' approach even further than on the stage.

The technique of *World of Plenty* was also a matter of expediency. At the same time as making it, I had seven or eight other films to produce at my unit. As a result of Lease-Lend, it was possible to obtain a great deal of stock footage from American sources at cost or for free. Thus, compilation in the cutting-room with little fresh shooting became the only way out if it was to be a 'personal' film. The method was subsequently developed in my film about Housing—*Land of Promise*, in 1945 (assistant Francis Gysin) and *The World is Rich* (assistant Michael Orrom). The latter film, however, largely dropped the use of direct speech because of the need for a wide number of foreign versions; but it retained the 'argument-between-voices' which I have again used in my script about world energy and what atomic power can do for mankind if used for peaceful purposes.

The odd-man-out of the group was *World Without End* but only in its style, necessitated by two directors collaborating to make a single unified film from footage shot by them separately in two countries 10,000 miles apart—Siam and Mexico. This Unesco film, now seen by many, many millions in eight different language versions, carried the same basic theme of there being one world in which we are all neighbours, a theme beautifully interpreted by Rex Warner's writing of the narration from a draft by Basil Wright and myself. Perhaps because Wright, my co-director, is one of my oldest friends, this was the happiest and most harmonious picture on which I have worked in the twenty-eight years of my film career. It has been said by a shrewd critic in New York that this happiness pervades the film itself and hence audiences respond to its warmth.

In naming the many contributors to these films I must mention the big part played by music, always specially written. William Alwyn, Clifton Parker and Elizabeth Lutyens each in turn wrote magnificently and tried out many musical experiments. Credit, too, must be given to the team at the Isotype Institute for their diagram designs which helped to explain some of the complex 'economic' aspects of the two food films. Their long experience in developing an international picture language with symbols without doubt helped to secure the world audiences for these films.

None of these films has been easy to get made and, when made, to be found a release. They have carried a message of goodwill and the need for a more equal sharing out of the world's riches, neither likely to be popular subjects with the film trade. But once the films had been lifted over the hurdles to the public, that public responded fourfold. To make a film in which you believe something important to mankind is said with sincerity and passion has always been a fight, and never more so than today. From the great D.W. Griffith to De Sica—by way of Flaherty, Vigo, Stroheim and many others—the path has been grim and difficult, but it is the only path that a film-maker who believes in the basic goodness of human beings can take if he is true to his medium and to himself.

Select Filmography[1]

1. Films as Director

This section lists those productions on which Rotha was the main creative force. In addition to being director, Rotha also wrote, edited and produced these films, except for those instances where someone else is credited.

1933
Contact
Production company: British Instructional Films, for Imperial Airways and Shell Mex & BP/Wardour Films. Photography by Horace Wheddon, Jack Parker, Frank Goodliffe, George Pocknall. Music by Clarence Raybould. 42 minutes. (First full-length British documentary film to have a wide commercial release in Great Britain. Premiered at the World Economic Conference, London, in 1933 and awarded gold medal at Venice Film Festival.)

Roadworks
Production Company: British Independent Productions, for BSA and Daimler. Photography by Jack Parker. 25 minutes.

1934
Rising Tide
Production company Gaumont Instructional, for Southern Railways/Gaumont-British Distributors. Produced by Bruce Woolfe. Photography by Jimmy Rogers, George Pocknall, Frank Goodliffe. Music by Clarence Raybould. 25 minutes. (In 1935 Gaumont-British released a slightly shortened theatrical version of this film as *Great Cargoes*, unauthorised by Rotha.)

1935
Shipyard
Production company: Gaumont-British Instructional, for Vickers Armstrong

and the Orient Shipping Company/Gaumont-British Distributors. Photography by George Pocknall, Frank Bundy, Harry Rignold, Frank Goodliffe. 24 minutes.

The Face of Britain
Production company: Gaumont-British Instructional, for the Central Electricity Board/Gaumont-British Distributors. Photography by George Pocknall, Frank Bundy. Commentary by A.J. Cummings. 19 minutes. (Gold medal winner, Brussels Film Festival.)

1936
Death On The Road
Production company: Gaumont-British Equipments for *News of the World*. 17 Minutes.

Peace of Britain (a.k.a. *The Peace Film*)
Production company: Freenat Films Ltd/Dofil. Written by Ritchie Calder and Paul Rotha. Music by Benjamin Britten. 3 minutes.

1938
New Worlds for Old
Production company: Realist, for the British Gas Council. Photography by Harry Rignold, S. Onions, A.E. Jeakins. Commentary by Alistair Cooke. Music by William Alwyn. 26 minutes.

1940
The Fourth Estate
Production company: Realist, for Times Publishing Company. Photography by Jimmy Rogers, Harry Rignold, A.E. Jeakins. Script consultant: Carl Mayer. Commentary by Geoffrey Dell, Nicholas Hannen, Denis Arundell. Music by Walter Leigh. 60 minutes.

Mr Borland Thinks Again
Production company: British Films, for the Ministry of Information. Photography by James Rogers. Story by C. Day Lewis. With Herbert Lomas, Emlyn Williams, Beatrix Lehmann, Bush Bailey, Robert Wilton, Richard Lee, Armand Coeffer. 5 minutes.

1943
World of Plenty
Production company: Paul Rotha Productions for the Ministry of Information. Written by Eric Knight and Paul Rotha. Additional dialogue by Miles Malleson. Photography by Peter Hennessy, Wolfgang Suschitzky. Music by William Alwyn. Narration by Eric Knight, E.V.H. Emmett, Robert St John,

Thomas Chalmers, Henry Hallatt. With Marjorie Rhodes, John Boyd Orr, Lord Woolton, Lord Horder, Sir John Russell, L.F. Easterbrook. 46 Minutes.

1945

Total War in Britain
Production company: Films of Fact, for the Ministry of Information. Written by Ritchie Calder and Miles Tomalin, Commentary by John Mills. Music by William Alwyn. 21 minutes.

Land of Promise
Production company: Films of Fact, for the British Gas Council/Film Traders Ltd. Written by Ara Calder-Marshall, Wolfgang Wilhelm, Miles Malleson, Miles Tomalin and Paul Rotha. Photography by Harold Young, Peter Hennessy, Reg Wyer, Cyril Arapoff. Music by William Alwyn. With John Mills, Miles Malleson, Marjorie Rhodes, Frederick Allen, Herbert Lomas, Elizabeth Cowell, Henry Hallatt. 68 minutes.

1946

A City Speaks
Production company: Films of Fact, for Manchester City Corporation. Written by Walter Greenwood, Ara Calder-Marshall and Paul Rotha. Photography by Harold Young, Cyril Arapoff. Music by William Alwyn. Voices by Valentine Dyall, Derryck Guyler, Alexander Grandison. 68 minutes.

1947

The World Is Rich
Production company: Films of Fact, for the Central Office of Information. Written by Arthur Calder-Marshall. Photography by James Ritchie. Music by Clifton Parker. Voices: James McKechnie, Valentine Dyall, Allan Michey, Robert Adams, Elizabeth Cowell, Leonard Sachs, Roy Plomley. 47 minutes.

1951

No Resting Place
Produced by Colin Lesslie. Production company: Colin Lesslie Production/ Associated British Film Distributors. Written by Paul Rotha, Colin Lesslie and Michael Orrom, from the novel by Ian Niall. Photography by Wolfgang Suschitzky. Edited by Michael Orrom, Betty Orgar. Music by William Alwyn. Art Direction by Tony Inglis. With Michael Gough, Noel Purcell, Jack McGowran, Eithne Dunne, Brian O'Higgins, Diane Campbell, Christy Lawrence, Maureen O'Sullivan, May Craig, Fred Johnson, Robert Hennessy. 77 minutes. (Feature production.)

1953

World Without End

Co-directed and produced by Basil Wright. Production company: International Realist, for UNESCO. Written by Rex Warner. Photography by José Carlos and Adrian Jeakin. Music by Elizabeth Lutyens. Commentary by Michael Gough. 60 minutes. (Won British Film Academy Award.)

1958

Cat and Mouse

Produced and written by Paul Rotha from a novel by Michael Halliday. Production company: Anvil Films/Eros. Photography by Wolfgang Suschitzky. Edited by William Freeman. Art Direction by Tony Inglis. With Lee Patterson, Ann Sears, Hilton Edwards, Victor Madden, George Rose, Roddy McMillan. 79 minutes. (Feature production.)

1959

Cradle of Genius

Production company: Plough Productions. Photography by Wolfgang Suschitzky. Edited by William Freeman. Art direction by Tony Inglis. Music by Gerard Victory. With Sean O'Casey, Barry Fitzgerald, Cyril Cusack, Siobahn McKenna, Maureen Delaney, Denis O'Dea, Eithne Dunne, Padraic Colum, Ria Mooney, Shelah Richards, May Craig, Gabriel Fallon, Harry Brogan, Eileen Crowe, Eric Gorman, Seaghan Barlow. 25 minutes.

1961

The Life of Adolf Hitler

Produced by Walther Koppel. Production company: Real Films, Studio Hamburg/British Lion. Written by Paul Rotha, Robert Neumann and Helga Koppel. Associate editor: Robert Kruger, Music by Siegfried Franz. Voices for English version Leo Genn and Marius Goring. 102 minutes. (Released in German and English versions.)

1962

De Overval (English version *The Silent Raid*)

Produced by Rudolf Meyer. Production company: Sapphire Films, Amsterdam/Rank. Written by Paul Rotha and Dr L. de Jong. Photography by Prosper De Keukeleire, Edited by Robert Kruger. Art direction by Wim Bijmoer. Music by Else van Epen-de Groot. With Kees Brusse, Rob de Vries, Yoka Berretty, Hans Culeman, Piet Romer, Hans Boswinkel, Bernhard Droog, André van den Heuvel, Sacco van der Made. 80 minutes. (Feature Production.)

2. Select Films as Producer

Rotha oversaw numerous documentary productions for various companies throughout his career. This included periods in charge of production for Strand Films between 1935 and 1937, Realist films between 1939 and 1941 and for his own companies Paul Rotha Productions (1941–1944) and Films of Fact (1944–1948).

1936
Cover to Cover
Directed by Alexander Shaw and Donald Alexander. Production company: Strand Films for the National Book Council. 21 minutes.

1937
The Future's in the Air
Directed by Alexander Shaw. Production company: Strand Films for Imperial Airways. 37 minutes.

Today We Live
Directed by Ralph Bond and Ruby Grierson. Production company: Strand Films for the National Council of Social Service. 24 minutes.

1941
Our School
Directed by Donald Alexander. Production company: Realist Films for the Ministry of Information. 17 minutes.

1941
Five and Under
Directed by Donald Alexander. Production company: Paul Rotha Productions for the MOI. 16 minutes.

Blood Transfusion
Directed by Hans Nieter. Production company: Paul Rotha Productions for the MOI and the Ministry of Health. 21 minutes.

1942
Life Begins Again
Directed by Donald Alexander. Paul Rotha Productions for the MOI and the Ministry of Health. 20 minutes.

Night Shift
Directed by Jack Chambers. Paul Rotha Productions for the MOI and the Ministry of Supply.

1943

Highland Doctor
Directed by Kay Mander. Paul Rotha Productions for the MOI and the
Department of Health for Scotland. 21 minutes.

Power for the Highlands
Directed by Jack Chambers. Paul Rotha Productions for the MOI and the
Scottish Office. 31 Minutes.

1944

Children in the City
Directed by Budge Cooper. Paul Rotha Productions for the MOI, the Scottish
Education Department, and the Scottish Home Department. 32 minutes.

New Builders
Directed by Kay Mander. Paul Rotha Productions for the MOI. 20 minutes.

1948

The Story of Printing
Directed by Peter Bradford. Films of Fact for the COI and the Ministry of
Education. 44 minutes.

The History of Handwriting
Directed by John Martin Jones and Bill Symonds. Films of Fact for the COI
and the Ministry of Education. 44 minutes.

*Between 1953 and 1955 Rotha was Head of the BBC-TV documentary film
department. At the BBC he was executive producer of more than 75 films. This
included the series The World is Ours which he initiated. Among the issues he
made a specific writing contribution to are:*

No. 1, 'World Health'. Txd: 6 April 1954. 60 minutes.
No. 10, 'World Bank'. Txd: 23 May 1956. 45 minutes.
No. 12, 'The Forgotten Indians'. Txd: 28 November 1956. 43 minutes.

Other major films for the BBC include:

1956

The Challenge of Television
Written and Produced by Paul Rotha. Txd: 3 September 1956. 45 minutes.

Note

1. A more extensive filmography can be found in Paul Morris (ed.) *Paul
   Rotha: BFI Dossier 16* (London: BFI 1982).

Select Bibliography

1. Books Written by Rotha

The Film Till Now (London: Jonathan Cape, 1930).

Second Edition, Revised with additional section 'The Film Since Then' by Richard Griffiths (London: Vision Press, 1949).

Third Edition, with 'Epilogue 1948–1958' by Rotha (London: Vision Press, 1960).

Fourth Edition, with 'Postscript' by Rotha (London: Spring Books, 1967).

Celluloid: The Film Today (London: Longman's Green, 1931).

Documentary Film (London, Faber & Faber, 1935).

Second Edition, with additional 'Foreword' and chapter 'Whither Documentary?' by Rotha (London: Faber & Faber, 1939).

Third Edition, with a further 'Foreword' by Rotha and a 'Preface' by John Grierson, plus an additional section 'Documentary Film Since 1939' by Sinclair Road and an Appendix 'The Use of Films by the U.S. Armed Services' by Richard Griffiths (London: Faber & Faber, 1952).

Movie Parade: A Pictorial Survey of the Cinema (London: Studio Publications, 1936).

Enlarged Edition, with Roger Manvell (London: Studio Publications, 1950).

World of Plenty: Book of the Film, with Eric Knight (London: Nicholson and Watson, 1945).

Rotha on the Film, Edited and Introduced by Rotha (London: Faber & Faber, 1958).

Documentary Diary: An Informal History of the British Documentary Film, 1928–1939 (London: Secker & Warburg, 1973).

Robert J. Flaterty: A Biography (Philadelphia: University of Pennsylvania Press, 1983), edited by J. Ruby.

2. Books edited by Rotha

Portrait of a Flying Yorkshireman (London: Chapman and Hall, 1952).
Television in the Making, (London: Focal Press, 1956).
Richard Winnington, *Film Criticism and Caricatures 1943–1953* (London: Elek Books, 1975).
Shots in the Dark (London: Allen Wingate, 1951), co-edited by Edgar Anstey, Roger Manvell and Ernest Lindgren.

3. Contributions to books by Rotha

'Preface' to Rudolf Arnheim, *Film* (London: Faber & Faber, 1933).
'The Development of the Cinema' in R.S. Lambert (ed.) *For Filmgoers Only: The Intelligent Filmgoer's Guide to Film* (London: Faber & Faber, 1934).
'Documentary is Neither Too Short or Too Long', in *Informational Film Yearbook, 1947* (Edinburgh: Albyn Press, 1946).
'Is Stroheim a Genius?' in Peter Noble (ed.) *Hollywood Scapegoat: The Biography of Erich von Stroheim* (London: Fortune Press, 1950).
'The Small Budget Film' in William Whitebait (ed.) *International Film Annual No. 3* (London: John Calder, 1959).
Contribution, with Basil Wright, to Arthur Calder-Marshall, *The Innocent Eye: The Life of Robert J. Flaherty* (London: W.H. Allen, 1963).
'Some Principles of Documentary' (from *Documentary Film*) in Daniel Talbot (ed.) *Film: an Anthology* (Berkeley: University of California Press, 1966).
'Afterthought (1972)' and 'Films and the Labour Party' (1936) in Ian Aitken (ed.) *The Documentary Film Movement: an Anthology* (Edinburgh: Edinburgh University Press, 1998).

4. Contributions to Journals

Rotha contributed articles and reviews to numerous publications over his lifetime. Listed below are some of the publications with approximate dates of Rotha's involvement with them.

The Connoisseur, 1927–28.
Film Weekly, 1928–1930.
Film Pictorial, 1929.
Close-Up, 1931–33.
Cinema Quarterly, 1932–35.
Sight and Sound, 1932–35.
Twentieth Century, 1932–33.
Philadelphia Public Ledger, 1933–34 (articles in this also syndicated in the *New York Post*).

World Film News, 1938.
New York Times, 1937–38.
Documentary News Letter, 1940–47.
Documentary Film News, 1948–49.
Today's Cinema and *Kinematograph Weekly*, 1945–48.
National Film Association Journal 1948–50.
Film Today, 1948.
Public Opinion, 1949–51.
British Film Academy Journal, 1950s.
Films and Filming, 1956–59, 1966–67.

Rotha also made more sporadic contributions to many other journals, magazines and newspapers including *Tribune, Radio Times, The Listener, New Statesman and nation, The Times, Manchester Guardian, News Chronicle*.

5. Works on Rotha

The only major critical works (Books and Articles) on Rotha are:

Herbert G. Luft, 'Rotha and the World', in *Quarterly of Film, Radio and TV*, vol. x, no. 1, Fall 1955.
V.F. Perkins, *Film as Film* (Harmonsworth: Penguin, 1972), Chapter 1: 'The Sins of the Pioneers'.
Paul Marris (ed.) *Paul Rotha: BFI Dossier 16* (London: BFI, 1982).
Oxford Film-Maker's Workshop Ltd., *Rotha as Film Socialist*, Pamphlet in connection with an exhibition and film programme of Rotha's work, December 1982.
Edgar Anstey, 'Paul Rotha and Thorold Dickinson', *Sight and Sound* vol. 53, no. 3, Summer 1984.
Michael Orrom, 'A Great Man', in *A Fragment of Memory*, unpublished autobiography. Transcript held in BFI Special Collections.

Interviews with Rotha appear in
Elizabeth Sussex, *The Rise and fall of British Documentary* (Berkeley: University of California Press, 1975).
Eva Orbanz, *Journey to a Legend and Back: The British Realistic Film* (West Berlin: Volker Apeiss, 1977).

While the following books contain considerations of Rotha and his work

Jan Leyda, *Films Beget Films: a Study of the Compilation Film* (New York: Hill and Wang, 1964).

Rachael Low, *Documentary and Educational Films of the 1930s* (London: Allen and Unwin, 1979).

Rachael Low, *Films of Comment and Persuasion of the 1930s* (London: Allen and Unwin, 1979).

Brian Winston, *Claiming the Real: The Documentary Film Revisited* (London: BFI, 1995).

Index

Absolute Films, Opera 2, 3, and 4 (1923–1925), 48
adaptations to film, 94
Aëlita (1924), 99
Air-City (*Aerograd*) (1935), 154
Aldo, G.R., 175
Alexandrov, Grigori, 49, 61
All Quiet on the Western Front (1930), 145
American cinema, 49–50, 55, 69, 77
Anstey, Edgar, 165
Antonioni, Michelangelo, 72
Arnheim, Rudolph, 46, 53, 60, 61–2, 78
Arsenal (1929), 138
art cinema *see* intellectual film culture
art-direction in film, 233, 239–40, 242–3
Asquith, Anthony, 46, 47, 50, 75, 196, 199–200
Associated Realist Film Producers (ARFP), 28
Atlantic (1930), 201–2
Autant-Lara, Claude, 237

Balázs, Béla, 53
Balcon, Michael, 46, 47
Bamberger, Rudolph, 237
Barbary Sheep (1917), 11
Basse, Wilfried, 151–2
Battleship Potemkin (1925), 50, 59, 61, 63, 96, 154, 162–3, 164, 199
Bazin, André, 46, 60, 62, 71, 73–4

BBC: The Voice of Britain (1934), 155
Beddington, J.L. (Jack), 25, 246–7, 249, 251, 267
Benjamin, Walter, 68–70
Berlin: Symphony of a Great City (1927), 66, 114, 151–2
Bicycle Thieves (*Ladri di Biciclette*) (1948), 74, 89, 169–72, 173, 175
Birth of a Nation, The (1915), 163
Blackmail (1929), 201
Body and Soul (1931), 142
British cinema, 49–50, 73, 75, 195–202, 208–25; bookings and rentals, 214; distribution policy, 217–20, 224; documentary film *see* documentary film; experimental films, 228–9; export markets, 213–14; government funding and support, 181, 208–20, 221–5; import of American films, 208–9, 212–13; independent film-making, 209–12; influence of dialogue film, 197–8; intellectual film culture, 45, 46–50, 183–6, 187–90, 191–4; realist cinema, 73, 75; short films, 181, 226–9; showing of continental films, 179, 183–6; use of foreign talent, 180, 198
British Film Institute, 180
British Instructional Films, 202, 247–8, 265, 268
British International Pictures, 14, 51, 197, 201, 268–9

British Transport Film Unit, 25, 40
Brunel, Adrian, 48

Cabinet of Dr Caligari, The (1919), 11,
   56, 87, 96–9, 180, 274
Cagney, James, 167–8
camera technique: panning, 114;
   travelling shot, 114
Canudo, Riccioto, 52
Cat and Mouse (1958), 36
Catherine the Great (1934), 203, 205
Cavalcanti, Alberto, 46, 51, 66, 166
Celluloid: The Film Today (1931), 63–4
Champion Charlie (1916), 48
Chapayev (1934), 154, 164
Chaplin, Charles, 48, 88, 102, 120–31
Childhood of Maxim Gorky (1938), 164
cinégraphie, 54
Circus, The (1928), 121
Citizen Kane (1941), 147
City Lights (1931), 88, 120–31
Clair, René, 48, 51, 102, 131
Close Up (film journal), 49–50, 51–2, 55,
   61, 75
Coalface (1935), 157, 166
colour film, 61–2
Comédie Française, La, 94
Contact (1933), 19, 25, 88, 165, 233,
   244–72; at Venice Film Festival, 271;
   camera work by Horace Wheddon,
   250, 252, 254–6, 261–4, 265;
   commissioning, 246–50; distribution
   by Wardour Films, 269–70; editing of,
   265–7; London release, 269–70; music
   for, 267; national release, 270; outline
   for, 249; premiere of, 268; reviewed by
   Grierson, 270–1
contrast in film, 106, 113
costume design, 237–8
Cottage on Dartmoor, A (1930), 196, 200
Counterplan (1932), 155
Country Comes to Town, The (1931), 165
Criminal Code, The (1930), 142
Crisis (1928), 113
Cross, Pearl, 193
cross-cutting *see* film editing and cutting
Crossfire (1947), 223

cubism in film, 99
cutting of film *see* film editing and cutting
Czinner, Paul, 101

dance in film, 18, 113
Davis, Stuart, 183–5
Day, Will, 192–3
De Sica, Vittorio, 73, 74, 89, 169–76
Delluc, Louis, 53, 54
Deserter, The (1933), 154
Deutschland von Gestern und Heute, 152
Dinamov, Sergei, 154, 163
Doctor Mabuse the Gambler (1922), 100
documentary film: American cinema,
   161, 167; British cinema, 164–6;
   German cinema, 151–2; government
   support, 181, 215–17; influence of
   1920s and 1930s, 67–9; principles of,
   148–60; Soviet cinema, 154–5, 162–4;
   sponsorship, 63, 69, 164, 215–17, 227;
   use of propaganda, 66–9, 157
Documentary Film (1935), 62–70, 74
Dog's Life, A (1918), 128
Dolce Vita, La (1960), 73
Dovzhenko, Alexander, 48, 59, 88,
   132–43, 154, 186
Dracula (1922), 193
Dreyer, Carl, 48, 57, 102, 140, 240
Drifters (1929), 20, 59, 157, 165, 197,
   199, 249
Dupont, E.A., 51, 180, 198, 201–2, 237

Earth (1930), 88, 132–43, 186
editing of film *see* film editing and cutting
8 ½ (1963), 73
Eisenstein, Sergei, 46, 48, 49, 51, 53,
   54–5, 59, 61, 63, 66, 67, 76–7, 78, 95,
   104, 106–7, 141, 142, 154, 162–3,
   196, 199, 240
Elton, Arthur, 153, 165
Elvey, Maurice, 196
Empire Marketing Board (EMB) Film
   Unit, 20–4, 65, 155; production of
   Poster films, 24, 42–3, 266
End of St Petersburg, The (1927), 50, 104,
   105
Epstein, Jean, 51, 53, 78, 197, 199, 240

experimental films, 228–9
expressionism in film, 56, 74, 91–109

Face of Britain, The (1935), 28
Fairbanks, Douglas Snr., 10, 11, 13, 17, 77, 117–19
Fanck, Arnold, 63
Feet First (1930), 129–30
Fellini, Federico, 72
Ferguson, Elsie, 11
film as art, 53–5, 71, 192, 239
film editing and cutting, 17, 54, 58, 62, 74, 76–7, 87–8, 111–12, 113–16, 241; cross-cutting and intercutting, 105, 106; rhythm in, 54, 56, 113–16, 153, 163, 243; *see also* flash-back technique; montage
Film Finance Corporation, 221–5
Film Group, The, 185–6, 188
film institute and museum, proposals for, 179–80, 187–90, 191–4
film music, 17–18
film publicity, 110–11
film societies, 187–8
Film Society, The, 47–9, 59
Film Till Now, The (1930), 51–62, 71, 73, 74, 246
Films and Filming (journal), 75
Films of Fact, 35
Finis Terrae (1928), 197, 199
Firstborn, The (1928), 199–200
Flaherty, Robert, 19–20, 66, 73, 74, 102, 149–51, 156, 158, 159, 165, 167, 240
flash-back technique, 114–15
Flying Scotsman, The (1929), 197
Ford, John, 199
formalist film theory, 46, 52–3, 70, 74
formative film theory, 47, 52–3, 61–2, 71, 75–6, 77
Fourth Estate, The (1940), 30
French cinema, 53–4, 73, 94, 101–2, 185
Future's in the Air, The (1937), 165

Galeen, Henrik, 51, 198, 238
Garbo, Greta, 146
General Line, The (1929), 141, 154

German cinema, 57, 71, 74, 96–101, 184, 228, 239
Germany Year Zero (1947), 73
Godard, Jean-Luc, 72, 73
GPO Film Unit, 65, 155
Great Train Robbery, The (1903), 93
Greed (1924), 49, 74, 163, 175
Grierson, John, 16, 20–4, 35–6, 40, 41, 46, 47, 57, 59, 63, 65–7, 69, 71, 88, 89, 153, 154, 165, 197, 199, 249, 267, 271–2
Griffith, D.W., 163
Group 3, 35–6, 229
Grune, Karl, 100, 101
Gunning, Tom, 77

He Comes Up Smiling (1918), 10
High Treason (1930), 196
Hitchcock, Alfred, 46, 47, 50, 75, 201
Housing Problems (1935), 157, 165
How Broncho Billy Left Bear Country (1912), 48

Industrial Britain (1933), 19–20, 150–1, 165, 166, 167
intellectual film culture, 45, 46–50, 183–6, 187–90, 192
intercutting *see* film editing and cutting
Intolerance (1916), 163
Iron Horse (1924), 199
isotypes, 276
Italian cinema, 73–4, 89, 169–76
Ivens, Joris, 73, 167

James, Norah C., 51
Johannsen, Ernst, 145
Joyless Street, The (1925), 64, 146
Jünge, Alfred, 233, 237–8

Kameradschaft (1931), 88, 144–6, 168, 245
Kaufman, Boris, 151
Keaton, Buster, 129–30
Knight, Castleton, 197
Knight, Eric, 274
Korda, Alexander, 180, 203–5
Kracauer, Siegfried, 46, 71–3, 78
Kubrick, Stanley, 146

Lacombe, Georges, 51
Lambert, Gavin, 175
Land of Promise (1945), 31, 32–3, 275
Lang, Fritz, 57, 100
Last Command, The (1928), 114–15
Last Laugh, The (1924), 56, 87, 99–100, 180, 274
Leni, Paul, 48, 237, 240
Life of Adolf Hitler, The (1961), 27, 34, 37–9, 228, 234
Life of Emile Zola, The (1937), 167–8
Lindsay, Vachel, 52
Lloyd, Harold, 129–30
Lodger, The (1926), 201
London Film Society, 179, 183, 188, 193, 194
Look at Life (Rank short films), 226, 227
Lorentz, Pare, 167
Loves of Jeanne Ney, The (1927), 112, 146, 184, 238
Lubitsch, Ernst, 102
Lupu-Pick, 100, 101

Macpherson, Kenneth, 49–50, 52
Man of Aran (1934), 149, 150, 167
Man From Painted Post, The (1917), 10
Mander, Miles, 199–200
Manvell, Roger, 70
March of Time (newsreel), 161–2, 166
Marriage Circle, The (1924), 102
Mayer, Carl, 11, 99, 180, 274
melodrama in film, 94–5
Men and Jobs (1932), 155
Metropolis (1926), 111
Metzner, Erno, 245
Milestone, Lewis, 145
Ministry of Information (MOI), 31–2, 40
Miracle in Milan (1951), 173
Mr Fix-It (1918), 11
Moana (1926), 66, 102, 197
modernism in film, 72, 76
montage, 54–5, 57–8, 59, 61, 70, 74, 76, 106–7, 115–16, 163, 240, 275
Montagu, Ivor, 51, 202
Mother (1926), 154, 162
Moussinac, Léon, 54
Muni, Paul, 167–8

Munsterberg, Hugo, 53, 60
Murnau, F.W., 56, 75, 99, 193

Nanook of the North (1922), 66, 102, 149, 157
National Coal Board Film Unit, 25, 40
National Film Finance Corporation, 181
National Film Theatre, 180
neo-realism, 70–5, 89, 169–76
New Era film company, 202
New Worlds for Old (1938), 18, 30, 33, 275
newsreel film, 161–2
Night Mail (1936), 165, 166
No Resting Place (1951), 36–7, 89
Notte, La (1961), 73
nouvelle vague, 73

October (*Ten Days that Shook the World*) (1927), 50, 61, 63, 77, 95, 104
O'er Hill and Dale (1932), 165
Orr, John Boyd, 39, 274
Ossessione (1942), 173
Overval, De (The Silent Raid) (1962), 37

Pabst, Georg Wilhelm, 48, 63–4, 88, 100, 113, 144–7, 168, 184, 238, 239, 245
Paisa (1946), 73
Palache Report (1944), 180–1, 208
Parlor, Bedroom and Bath (1931), 129–30
Passion de Jeanne d'Arc, La (1928), 57, 102, 140, 240
Pathé Pictorial (ABC short films), 226, 227
Paths of Glory (1957), 146
Patriot, The (1928), 114
photogénie, 53–4
Piccadilly (1929), 114, 198, 201, 237
Plow that Broke the Plains, The (1936), 167
Pommer, Erich, 51, 101
Powell, Michael, 75
Pressburger, Emeric, 75
Private Life of Henry VIII, The (1933), 180, 205–7
production values, 110–12
propaganda in film, 66–9, 157

Protazanov, Yakov, 99
psychoanalysis and film, 49, 100–1
Public Enemy, The (1931), 168
Pudovkin, Vsevolod, 48, 49, 53, 54,
   58–9, 61, 64, 65, 66, 104, 115, 142,
   154, 162–3, 197, 202, 240

Rank Organisation, 180, 203
Raskolnikov (1923), 98
realism in film, 46, 56, 62–75, 91–5,
   151–3, 162, 167–8; locations, 63–4
Renoir, Jean, 48
rhythm in film *see* film editing and cutting
Richter, Hans, 48, 56
Rien que les heures (1926), 66
River, The (1937), 167
Robin Hood (1921), 11, 13
Robison, Arthur, 190, 198
Röhrig, Walther, 237
Rome—Open City (1945), 73, 173
Rossellini, Roberto, 73–4, 89, 173
Rotha on Film (1958), 71
Rotha, Paul (1907–1984)
   childhood and family: childhood, 4–8,
   10–12; early interest in cinema, 10–11;
   influence of father, 5–7, 12; influence
   of mother, 7; parentage, 4
   education: schooldays, 6, 11–12;
   student at Slade School of Art, 12–13,
   50
   career as film-maker and critic:
   attitude to propaganda, 66–9; BBC
   Television, 35, 273; Empire
   Marketing Board Film Unit, 20–4,
   233; experiences in 1940 Blitz, 8–10;
   as film-editor, 17; finances, 7–8; and
   formative film theory, 47, 55–7, 61–2;
   influence of 1920s and 1930s, 46, 63,
   67–9, 74; influence of John Grierson,
   20–4, 65–7, 88; influence of Soviet
   cinema, 51, 58–60, 76, 87–9; and
   intellectual film culture, 45–52, 180–1;
   interest in neo-realism, 70–5;
   involvement in The Film Society, 47,
   50–1; marriages, 4; name change, 4–5;
   opposition to dialogue film, 60; Paul
   Rotha Productions Ltd (PRP) &

Films of Fact, 31–5; and realism in
   film, 62–6; set-dresser at British
   International Pictures, 14, 51, 233; as
   social democrat, 27; Strand Films,
   29–30; theory of documentary, 64–9;
   writing style, 8–10
   films: *Contact* (1933), 19, 25, 88, 165,
   233, 244–72; *The Face of Britain*
   (1935), 28; *Shipyard* (1935), 27–8, 40,
   165, 250; *New Worlds for Old* (1938),
   18, 30, 33, 275; *The Fourth Estate*
   (1940), 30; *World of Plenty* (1943), 31,
   32–3, 234, 273–6; *Land of Promise*
   (1945), 31, 32–3, 275; *The World is
   Rich* (1948), 31, 33–4, 234, 273, 275;
   No Resting Place (1951), 36–7, 89;
   World Without End (1953), 35, 234,
   276; *The World is Ours* (1954–1956
   BBC TV series), 234, 273; *Cat and
   Mouse* (1958), 36; *The Life of Adolf
   Hitler* (1961), 27, 34, 37–9, 228, 234;
   De Overval (The Silent Raid) (1962), 37
   publications: *The Connoisseur* (journal),
   51; *Film Weekly* (journal), 51; *The Film
   Till Now* (1930–1967), 50–62, 71, 73,
   74, 246; *Celluloid: The Film Today*
   (1931), 63–4; *Close Up* (journal), 51;
   Sight and Sound (journal), 51;
   Documentary Film (1935), 21–2,
   62–70; *Films and Filming* (journal), 75;
   Rotha on Film (1958), 71; *Documentary
   Diary* (1973), 27

Rupert of Hentzau (1914), 10
Russian cinema *see* Soviet cinema
Ruttmann, Walther, 48, 56, 66, 114,
   151, 152, 155

Saving of Bill Blewitt, The (1936), 166
Say Young Fellow (1918), 10
Scandal Sheet (1931), 142
scriptwriting, 233, 240–3
Shipyard (1935), 27–8, 40, 165, 250
shooting script *see* scriptwriting
short films, 181, 226–9
Shoulder Arms (1918), 128
Sight and Sound (film journal), 51, 180

Simple Case, A (1930), 154
slapstick comedy, 77, 94–5
Song of Ceylon, The (1934), 13, 165
sound in film: 60–2, 107; multi-voice
 technique, 234, 275–6; use as
 montage, 61
Sous les Toits de Paris (1930), 131
Soviet cinema, 49, 50, 54–5, 57, 58–9,
 63, 66, 69, 74, 76, 87–9, 113, 132–43,
 162–4, 185–6, 192
Spanish Earth, The (1937), 167
spectacle in film, 77–8
Stage Society, The, 48
stereoscopic film, 61–2
Sternberg, Josef von, 147
Storm over Asia (1928), 164, 197, 202
Strand Films, 29–30
Strike (1924), 104
Stroheim, Erich Von, 49, 74, 75, 111,
 163, 175

Tallents, Stephen, 21, 24, 249
Terra Trema, La (1948), 175
The Film Till Now (1930), 283
Three Musketeers, The (1921), 11
time in film, 58–9
titling in silent films, 56, 115
Today We Live (1932), 166–7
Truffaut, François, 73
Turin, Victor, 66
Turksib (1928), 66
Typical Budget (1925), 48

Umberto D (1952), 74, 89, 173–6
Underground (1930), 197, 200
unity of film, 57–8, 243

Vertov, Dziga, 48, 66, 154, 174, 240
Vigo, Jean, 48
Visconti, Luchino, 73, 175
Voice of the World (1932), 153
Vuillermoz, Emile, 53

Wave, The (1935), 167
Waxworks (1924), 48, 237
Way Down East (1920), 13
We Live in Two Worlds (1937), 166
Wedding March, The (1928), 111, 115
Welles, Orson, 62, 146
Westfront 1918 (1930), 88, 144–6
Wheddon, Horace (cameraman), 250,
 252, 254–6, 261–4, 265
White Hell of Pitz Palu, The (1929) 63
Wiene, Robert, 56, 96–9
Winnington, Richard, 70
Winston, Brian, 65–6, 69
Woman of Paris, A (1923), 102
Woolfe, Bruce, 202, 247–8, 250, 251, 259
Workers and Jobs (1935), 165
World is Ours, The (1954–1955 BBC TV
 series), 234, 273
World is Rich, The (1948), 31, 33–4, 234,
 273, 275
World of Plenty (1943), 31, 32–3, 234,
 273–6
World Without End (1953), 35, 234, 276
Wright, Basil, 13, 35, 47, 273, 276
Wyler, William, 62

Zavattini, Cesare, 74, 89, 173–6
Zola, Emile, 64
Zukor, Adolph, 56
Zvenigora (1928), 138–9, 141